"Sally Richards has done something amazing. Her book is a totally fascinating read—in it we meet real people, telling real tales of *really* strange phenomena. It's not a scholarly text or dry accounting or a namby-pamby hit-or-miss retelling of what *might've been* a ghostly encounter—these stories resound with gritty authenticity and amazing first-person reports of real encounters with the paranormal. I recommend it to skeptics and believers alike."

— *Melissa Martin-Ellis, author of* The Everything Ghost
Hunting Book *and* 101 Ways to Find a Ghost

"There are voices out there if you listen. This book could show you how."

— *Frank Sumption, creator of the Frank's Box ITC device*

"The history introduced into the storyline adds intrigue to each chapter. I find it compelling to witness in words what the individuals did in real time. Loved it!"

— *Robbie Thomas, psychic profiler and bestselling author*
(robbiethomas.net)

"Sally Richards takes the reader on a historically haunted tour de force with this utterly engaging paranormal travelogue. She brings us up close and personal to the spookiest places Southern California has to offer in a book that will fascinate, inform, and entertain."

— *Marie D. Jones, author of* PSIence: How New
Discoveries in Quantum Physics and New Science
May Explain the Existence of Paranormal Phenomena

(Continued on next page)

GHOSTHUNTING SOUTHERN CALIFORNIA

AMERICA'S
HAUNTED ROAD TRIP

Titles in the *America's Haunted Road Trip* Series:

GHOSTHUNTING SOUTHERN CALIFORNIA

SALLY RICHARDS

CLERISY PRESS

Ghosthunting Southern California

For further information, contact the publisher:

CLERISY PRESS
306 Greenup Street
Covington, KY 41011
clerisypress.com

Cataloging-in-Publication Data is available from the Library of Congress.

ISBN-13: 978-1-57860-515-6

Distributed by Publishers Group West
Printed in the United States of America
First edition, second printing 2016

Editor: Donna Poehner
Cover design: Scott McGrew
Cover and interior photos provided by the author unless otherwise noted

A special thanks to my husband, who held down the fort, took care of the children, and kept the hounds of Baskerville and the cats of the Serengeti at bay on my many nights away on investigations, radio and TV shows, and conferences. Jeff, have I told you lately how much I love you? Thank you for your support in everything I do.

You make my heart soar and sing to my soul.

Sydney and Zildjian—thank you for your inspiration and love, and for forgiving me for missing our Summerland time together to get this book in. I missed you a great deal!

You are the best kids ever!

Please read before you visit any of the locations in this book.

As this book goes to press, all the locations in it have public access through private tours or during open hours. Policies change, so please call and inquire before you visit them. Website addresses have been provided so that you can find access to information and policies. Not all locations in this book are open at night, nor is it suggested that you visit them after-hours. I do not advocate trespassing at any of these locations, as it is unlawful and I'm not paying your bail.

Many of these locales have uneven paths, so please watch your footing. Not all locations are handicap-accessible; please contact the venue for more information.

As with any venture, it's highly advisable that you go to the location during the day to check things out. During the day, as well as at night, you run the risk of being seriously injured, and I strongly recommend that you take extra care in locations new to you. Some of the areas require a little hiking, so make sure you are physically fit, and be aware that wildlife such as rattlesnakes, coyotes, cougars—and man's worst predator . . . man—may be at any of these locations. Security and crime in these areas fluctuate—so do your research! Lock up your equipment when not using it, be aware of your surroundings, and do bring a charged cell phone in case you need to call for emergency assistance. Also, you should let someone know where you are going and at what time you might return.

Please use discretion when investigating in public places such as restaurants, historic locations, cemeteries, and memorial locations. Allow those around you to conduct themselves without interruption and in privacy. Use common sense when investigating areas on or near roads—go during the day so you'll be seen.

One last thing: please do not disturb any of the locations, and carry out your investigations without the use of flammables (candles, etc.)—Southern California is one big tinderbox. Many of these locations have survived a hundred years; all it takes is one investigator scratching up antiques or a wooden floor with his or her equipment to ruin it for the rest of us, so please tread lightly upon history. Above all, please listen to your intuition.

Enjoy your investigation, but please be responsible!

Thank you,
Sally Richards

TABLE OF CONTENTS

NORTHERN AND EASTERN SAN DIEGO 89

THE ANZA-BORREGO DESERT AND SURROUNDING AREA 127

COASTAL SOUTHERN CALIFORNIA 167

ORANGE AND LOS ANGELES COUNTIES 219

SANTA BARBARA, VENTURA, AND SAN LUIS OBISPO COUNTIES 275

Acknowledgments

A GREAT DEAL OF THANKS goes out to Marie D. Jones, who didn't have time to write this book and suggested that *America's Haunted Road Trip* series editor John B. Kachuba contact me to write it. The rest is history. And a special thank-you to Molly Merkle, chief operating officer at Keen Communications, for straightening out the details. Thanks, John and Molly, for bringing me into the Clerisy stable of writers. Also BIG thank-yous go out to editor Donna Poehner, graphic designer Scott McGrew, and cartographer Steve Jones. This has been a fabulous book to write—filled with adventures, meeting new people, and getting to know the people I already knew so much better. Thanks to the members of Roadside Paranormal and Ghosts Happen: Jennifer Donohue, Anne Marie, Eugenia Swingle, Leo Aréchiga, Megan Meadows, Michelle Myers, Kim, and all of the others who took part in these investigations—and to those who didn't make it into the book. Alex Boese—your healthy skepticism is always greatly appreciated. Thank you to the hundreds of people who participated in the investigations in this book. And thanks to Jodi Carmichael—the one person I have in mind every time I write one of these stories and hear my inner writer saying, "Would Jodi want me to leave this in or out?"

Thanks to my parents, who taught me that communication with anyone or *anything* is a good thing.

Here's to all of the spirits who bothered to answer my calls in the dark to them—especially the ones who had meaningful conversations . . . even if many of those conversations were in languages I do not know.

Last but not least—a HUGE bouquet of appreciation to all of you readers. I hope you enjoy the book!

Welcome to America's Haunted Road Trip

Do you believe in ghosts?

If you are like 52 percent of Americans (according to a recent Harris Poll), you *do* believe that ghosts walk among us. Perhaps you have heard your name called in a dark and empty house. It could be that you have awakened to the sound of footsteps outside your bedroom door, only to find no one there. It is possible that you saw your grandmother sitting in her favorite rocker chair, the same grandmother who had passed away several years before. Maybe you took a photo of a crumbling, deserted farmhouse and discovered strange mists and orbs in the photo, anomalies that were not visible to your naked eye.

If you have experienced similar paranormal events, then you know that ghosts exist. Even if you have not yet experienced these things, you are curious about the paranormal world, the spirit realm. If you weren't, you would not now be reading this preface to the latest book in the *America's Haunted Road Trip* series from Clerisy Press.

Over the last several years, I have investigated haunted locations across the country and with each new site, I found myself becoming more fascinated with ghosts. What are they? How do they manifest themselves? Why are they here? These are just a few of the questions I have been asking. No doubt you have been asking the same questions.

The books in the *America's Haunted Road Trip* series can help you find the answers to your questions about ghosts. We've gathered together some of America's top ghost writers (no pun intended) and researchers and asked them to write about their states' favorite haunts. Each location that they write about is open to the public so that you can visit it for yourself and try out your ghosthunting skills. In addition to telling you about their often hair-raising adventures, the writers have included maps and travel directions so that you can take your own haunted road trip.

People may think that Southern California is nothing more than desert, blue skies, and sandy beaches populated by starlets, surfers, and sun-worshippers, but Sally Richards's *Ghosthunting Southern California* proves that the deserts are home to shadowy entities that are seen only for an instant before disappearing in the haze, as well as spirits that frequent old, weathered buildings in real "ghost towns." The book is a spine-tingling trip through the southern counties of the Golden State, with stops at resorts and hotels, Wild West jails and stagecoach stations, old ships, historic Spanish and Native American sites and cemeteries—all of them haunted.

Ride shotgun with Sally as she seeks out the ghosts of dearly departed sailors aboard the *Queen Mary* in Long Beach and the *Star of India* in San Diego. Travel with her to Coronado, where the sorrowful ghost of Kate Morgan can be seen walking the grounds of the Hotel del Coronado, the place in which she was found mysteriously shot, or sit for a spell in the old jail at Julian and listen for the laments of long-gone cowboy inmates. And who is that ghostly man in boots and a large hat seen on the stairs of the Whaley House in Old Town, San Diego? Hang on tight: *Ghosthunting Southern California* is a scary ride.

But once you've finished reading this book, don't unbuckle your seatbelt. There are still forty-nine states left for your haunted road trip! See you on the road!

John Kachuba
Editor, America's Haunted Road Trip

Introduction
What Came Before,
What Comes After

I WAS BORN INTO A REALM that many cannot see.
My earliest memories were before I was a toddler, seeing my
parents reach down in the playpen for me, halos of brightly col-
ored light swirling around them and my grandmothers holding
me closely in their arms. And always, the silent women behind
them whom I didn't know but whose warm smiles comforted
me. I would see them from time to time when my grandmothers weren't visiting; as I became older, they became more scarce.
I didn't know those women's names, and no one ever seemed
to know whom I was speaking about when I referenced them.
Soon they became only outlines of beings filled with less bright
lights—my mother says I called them falling stars. I would most
often see the *starlights,* as I later began to call them, walking
with people, guiding them on their way and away from harm.
Everyone had at least one of these beings, though older people's
were more of an opaque shade and barely visible.

For some reason, when I was five, I became curious about
our young newspaper boy, interacting with him at every opportunity. He was ten and as reliable as jeweled clockwork when he
dropped off the weekly paper. He always rolled his bike up to
the porch to toss me the paper to catch. He'd kill a few minutes
of time telling me some silly joke that would leave me roaring
with laughter and running off to tell it to someone else. He was
kind. One day I asked him where his *being* was, and he gave me
a puzzled look. I tried to explain that all things had a starlight

looking over them. Even the dogs and cats had a little sparkle that followed—even my turtle and the horned toads in my reptile zoo. I told him of the dark shade that floated along behind his bike. He shrugged and gave me an odd look that older kids do when younger ones babble incoherently. He waved goodbye with a quirky smile and a nod, and that was the last time I saw him . . . alive.

The next week he didn't come, and that Saturday a funeral cortege drove slowly by, the long line of cars blazing with headlights against the foggy coastal sky. The black car in the lead held my curiosity. I'd never seen a car with curtains before; it seemed to me the perfect mobile dollhouse. I looked hard to see who was inside, a mystery that clearly needed explaining. I asked my father what it all meant. He hesitated and told me a car had hit our newspaper boy and killed him, and he took the opportunity to impress upon me some rules about bike safety, as I'd just gotten my training wheels off. Having been so young and having never known death, I asked him what *killed* meant. He looked at me, his face twisted in puzzlement, trying to put together the right words that would leave me unscathed until I really needed to know. He told me our paperboy would be sleeping for a very, *very* long time. Nothing like this had ever occurred. I was really confused.

Over the days that followed, I pestered him to take me to find the paperboy so I could wake him from his enchanted sleep of *killed*. My father told me he was at the cemetery. In Monterey, California, there is a cemetery next to Dennis the Menace Park. One day he took me to the park to play and I sounded out the words on the sign nearby—San Carlos Cemetery. I begged him to take me inside. He hesitated, but I began to tear up and got a very disappointed look on my face, then crossed my arms in defiance. He knew he would have a fight on his hands, so he took the high road and said, "Okay." Off we went, me skipping speedily away from him in a pastel dress, my Keds leaping and my pigtails flying behind me. I now imagine my father trying to think of a way to explain the whole sleeping thing as we traveled toward Death's gates.

I'm sure my father thought he had an out, as we hadn't known the newspaper boy's name and in the huge cemetery it would have been like finding a needle in a haystack. So that might have been the end of the story, except it wasn't. It was just the start. I looked down the rows of old tombstones, overwhelmed by the possibilities of which one could be his marker over the subterranean place he lay in his slumber of *killed*. I wondered how he was breathing since there was no air underground; we had no time to lose. We had to get him out quickly! I remembered the frantic state in which I began looking for some kind of clue for his location. I suddenly looked up and saw a brief glimpse of a boy in a familiar baseball cap dodge behind a tree. It was *him*, and he wasn't sleeping at all, or underground. As we hadn't even brought shovels, I was flooded with relief.

I broke into a run, stumbling over the uneven ground. I skinned my knees, each time I fell catching myself just in time to keep from landing flat on my face on the old earthquake-damaged cement curbs. After what seemed like a million close calls and ignoring my father's shouts to slow down, I arrived at the tree. Looking down, I touched the etched words in a ground marker warm with sunshine. I traced what I felt was surely his name. My father, out of breath, caught up with me and looked at the marker. He was pale as the words came slowly from his mouth, "How did you find it?"

"He was here, at the tree. He's playing hide-and-seek," I explained, "This *killed* sleep is wrong, Daddy. He was here; he's not sleeping at all." I looked around, trying to offer my father some proof the boy was still among us—as I thought someone should tell his mother—but found nothing.

My life got stranger and stranger. As happens with most children, I stopped seeing auras when everyone else said they didn't exist. But I continued to see other things, things that became harder and harder to explain. We moved to Hawaii, and I became well versed in the local lore and the spirits of the islands that are always present and acknowledged by the locals. I was surrounded by people who saw what I saw and kids who wouldn't go down jungle paths because of an ancestral war that happened there hundreds of years before. Kids who respected the dead because the dead weren't so dead after all.

When I was eight, I cut school and drowned while surfing. After I was done fighting the undertow, I surrendered to having the most amazing, peaceful experience, which I would later liken to what Einstein said about what death must feel like—all of the body's atoms exploding into the universe and becoming part of everything else. More recently the experience was described by Steve Jobs's last words on his deathbed: "Oh, wow! Oh, wow! Oh, wow!" *Oh, wow!* indeed.

I was dead when a sailor dragged me out of the surf, pumped the salt water out of my lungs, and brought me back, bringing forth a trail of expletives even *he* couldn't fathom coming from the small girl whom he had awakened from what I now call *The Perfect Sleep.*

My father was in special ops, and after his seven tours in Vietnam, my family moved back to the mainland (the Silicon Valley, in this case). I learned to wear shoes and jeans; one experience wearing a traditional *mu'umu'u* to school with trendy Silicon Valley kids was all it took for me to learn new dress codes and to take the flowers out of my hair. The new kids I met didn't have mythology, or a common background. I'd gone from the happiest place on earth to some pretty harsh realities—not only were these kids kind of mean, but they knew nothing of the spirit world except fear.

Life changed as my parents became engineers, and I found new friends—and they were nothing like my old friends. My best friend, Deedee Gates, was a trippy chick the same age as I was, who knew all about life *after* death, could light candles in her house without getting into trouble, and turned me on to her mom's metaphysical library, which I voraciously devoured over a summer. She disappeared just as quickly as she'd appeared in my life and moved away to points unknown, but not before leaving a major impact and introducing me to the great mystic Sybil Leek. I was soon leading ghost tours through the abandoned Victorian houses surrounded by tract-housing developments that seemed to spring up overnight in the rich soil of old Santa Clara Valley fruit orchards. The grand old homes were earmarked for demolition to make way for more tract housing.

I told the groups of kids on the tours about the people who once lived in the houses and the current spirits that inhabited them, often conducting séances that would bring about unexplained rappings from the walls and ceilings. Kids were frightened and ready to jump at any unexplained sound—including the police we'd often have to outrun for trespassing, which only added to the infamy and popularity of the tours. Charging for the tours over many summers, I saved enough to purchase a 1969 Ford Mustang on my sixteenth birthday.

Off to college, where I had little time for anything else but work and school, and then off to life and career. Although I was happy in my positions as investigative journalist, author, managing editor, technologist, and startup consultant (and many other career experiences), I still found myself wanting more. I took a job to do a company turnaround in Vegas and one lonely evening lit a candle that the candle-maker had wrapped with a label reading LOVE. A week later, my old high school sweetheart living in another state came to find me. It was then

I surrendered my heart, moved back to California, and connected with my haunted roots.

The next year, I drove to BookExpo America in New York City. On the way, I ran into pre-Katrina weather from Florida to Texas, where I was hit by lightning. This, only a few days before I was expected home and then to get back on a plane to cover the story of Lily Dale, New York, the city inhabited by mediums who talk with the dead. The lightning strike has left me with health concerns. I had to remove all the metal from my teeth because the strike had made any food on a metal utensil taste like aluminum foil, and it also did a job on my optic nerves—but, in the end, I'm okay. Exhausted and fragile, I flew out on schedule, reached Lily Dale, and began receiving messages from my old dead friend, Paul, who was contacting everyone around me with his name and detailed descriptions of himself, his job, and our friendship. He gave them all messages to tell me he was still a physicist on the Other Side and was still working hard. Working hard on what? I still don't know.

Sure, I was a believer when I left Lily Dale. A believer in what I'd already known since the not-so-dead newspaper boy led me to his grave.

Months later, my husband and I created our miracle baby—the baby whom no less than five doctors told my husband and me would be impossible to conceive. Sometimes lightning, and whatever else that doesn't kill you, does make you stronger . . . and sometimes may even help to get you pregnant. Now we have a wonderful child who fills our hearts and who feels the presence of her long-dead great-grandmothers and her grandfather around her and is quite reassured by their guidance.

After the baby came, I began taking classes in Spiritualism (a belief system that asserts ghosts are among the living 24/7 and that anyone has the means to contact them) for mediumship annually at Lily Dale and at Harmony Grove, a Spiritualist camp community in San Diego; both more than a century old. I finally learned how to decipher all that had come before. I started a paranormal-investigation group on Meetup called Ghosts Happen (**meetup.com/ghostshappen**). I chose the cream of the crop from the members and created Roadside Paranormal, a group dedicated to investigating locations where disturbing events have taken place and victims still do not rest in peace (such as home and workplace homicides, suicides, and accident scenes). We pass on information from spirits to friends and family that may give entities, and ultimately their friends and family, closure. My group uses state-of-the-art science to document the data we find. We also test new types of equipment to determine whether they're valid and to help make them standards in the industry if they are.

Having investigated in many other states and around the world, I've documented proof of energy beyond the death of the body in places such as the assassination site of John Lennon, Civil War battlefields, and European World War II battle locations, the ancient graveyards of Southeast Asia, and even the underground catacombs of Paris. I've concluded that no matter where you go, spirit energy and paranormal activity fall into the same categories—active, imprint, and intelligent. And I bet if you're reading this book that you've had an experience with at least one of these forms of energy—why else would you be so drawn to the topic?

When we feel the energy in a place that's reportedly haunted, it's often something we can't put a finger on, but it's like a sign planted into the ground that states, *Something happened here, and it's not going away anytime soon.* It's the kind of energy that makes the hair on the back of your neck stand up and take notice, and causes what I call chicken skin to crawl up your spine and down your arms. You know the feeling—when someone *walks over your grave.* The mind, body, and our innate senses—our *intuition*—know when we've come across it. Don't discount intuition: sometimes it's the only thing keeping you from becoming part of the spirit world.

Normally, people will drive an extra mile to avoid the haunted, abandoned house that's been for sale since a family was murdered there. The living can just feel someone—*or something*—watching them through the crack in the dusty curtains if they have to drive by. Not everyone avoids these kinds of energy-pit locations. Some seek them out looking for proof of a life beyond death, whether that be ghosts, demons, inert energy (the soul), or parallel universes in the form of vortexes. My team seeks it out—we feel it, we explore it, we document it, and we compile proof to convince others that energy beyond death exists. A point comes when no further proof is needed to convince ourselves, but rather we are ready present the proof to others and start them on their own journeys.

So, why are people compelled to search for existence of The Beyond? I suppose it's because we all have one thing in common—one day we will all find the truth. Is it more comforting to find out beforehand? Will it convince us to live in the here and now? Is it fear? Or, are we just curious by nature with our mortality staring us in the face from the moment we learn to reason. Whatever your reason, you're here now. My job from this moment on is to give you the straight-up accounts of some of the truth I have encountered, narratives that may set you on your own paranormal trek to look for your own truths about what happens in The End. Not the end of this book, but rather the mother of all The Ends—the end of you, of me, of life as we know it. We are creatures of habit. We don't even like the thought of our daily routine being canceled by inconvenience, let alone death. There's one question you have to ask yourself before reading this book: *Do you really want to know?* If your answer is *Yes*, then this book will end the world as you know it.

So after all that, if you're still compelled to find out what lies beyond the veil, I can only guess it's because of a personal experience you've had; something you've seen or heard but cannot explain even after rolling it over in your mind a couple thousand times. Maybe you're even losing sleep over it. This book has more than thirty locations where you may be able to find the kind of energy you can work with to pursue your ongoing paranormal learning experiences.

As you read this, a couple of your own places probably come to mind. For many people, their own homes have become rife with the kind of energy prime for investigation, but not necessarily because their homes are truly haunted, but rather because they themselves have begun drawing this type of energy to themselves. Believe me, people can be more haunted than any castle. If you're looking for locations but can't get to the ones listed in this book, the case studies contained here can be used as a primer for investigation skills, as they are filled with practical advice on technique, tools, and advice—it's all here. The rest will come intuitively.

Ghosthunting Southern California was created from the most compelling investigations of publicly accessible locations (some infamous for being haunted, others making their first appearance) I've found in Southern California. I've gone to these locations with my team and others to find out the history, the characters involved (both past and present), and why on earth someone would leave that wonderful Perfect Sleep that I found when I drowned only to hang out to contact—and sometimes terrify—those left behind. I discuss the equipment used, the evidence found, and the best times to seek places out (it's not very often in the dead of night)—and provide a detailed description of the investigation with interviews of those involved. Though the firsthand accounts in this book may prompt you to sleep with the night-light on, I hope you instead choose to flip the light switches off and endeavor to find out what lies in the murky darkness beyond.

Take my hand, and free-fall into a place you've never wanted to go to but can't stop thinking about as soon as you hear the tree branches scratching on the window on a still night, when the floorboards bend under weight in a house where only you reside . . . or so you thought. Push yourself to analyze each chapter and its relevance to your own path, as there are connections all around us. You just need to continue searching for the truth and the dots will begin to connect. Be cautious, be open-minded but skeptical, and above all go into this as a learning experience, and you won't be disappointed. I wish you luck on your journey to touch the Other Side, and I trust that you'll find what you're looking for.

I won't leave the porch light on for you . . . it's for your own good.

Enjoy the journey,
Sally Richards
Los Angeles, July 2012

Old Town San Diego

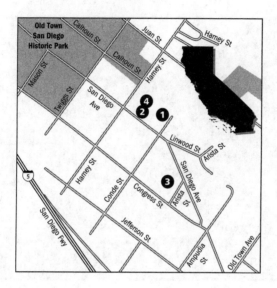

Old Town San Diego
Creole Café **(2)**
El Campo Santo Cemetery **(4)**
Four Winds Trading Company **(1)**
The Whaley House **(3)**

CHAPTER 1

Four Winds Trading Company
OLD TOWN SAN DIEGO

Four Winds is visible from San Diego Avenue.

I HAD MY FIRST MAJOR San Diego paranormal experience in 2003 when I'd first moved to the city. I'd not yet gotten acclimated to the area and had to do some holiday shopping—I wasn't clear where to go, but I knew I didn't want to end up at a mall. My husband called and let me know he needed to work a little later than usual, and I asked him where I should do some shopping. He suggested I might like the atmosphere better in Old Town rather than the malls. I put Old Town, San Diego, into the GPS, followed the directions, and ended up on a street filled with quaint shops and holiday revelers drinking and spreading good cheer. My GPS said, *You have arrived at your destination.* I pulled my Miata off into a tiny space in front of a cemetery on San Diego Avenue. As I got out of my car, my heel hitched on a curious, round brass marker in the street. I took my keychain penlight and shined it on the ground. The round marker read GRAVESITE. *Spooky girl is off to a good start,* I thought and smiled to myself, but not even I could imagine what my next encounter would be.

Walking down the street, I noticed the irritating smell of cigar smoke as I headed toward what seemed to be the center of town, and then the smell was gone. I looked into a shop and was intrigued by the amazing Native American artifacts that seemed to fill every space of the high-ceilinged store; I realized I should have brought the bigger car. The sign read FOUR WINDS TRADING.

I walked in and immediately saw potentially ten gifts; I was definitely in the right place. There were a few people perusing the store, and the woman at the counter was cheerfully helping them out. She said hello as I passed by, and I smiled and nodded. I already loved the store. A few more people came in behind me, and I walked the length of the store with Katsina carvings, fetishes of all sizes, jewelry from tribes across the country, antique weavings, and intricately beaded bags and dolls. The place was amazing. As I continued walking to the rear of the store, I suddenly walked into a wall of cigar smoke and could barely breathe. I started coughing and gave an angry look at the gentleman in a canvaslike duster jacket sitting like he owned the place in a large chair, one boot-clad leg crossed over his thigh. He puffed away on his cigar, blowing smoke in my direction. Intense eyes betrayed his smiling bearded face as he put his hand on his hat and tipped it to me.

My eyes shot daggers at him as I prepared to storm out of the store. By that time, the store had cleared out, and I couldn't help but think the cigar smoke had something to do with it. I stopped to speak to the woman at the counter, "I was going to buy some things here tonight, but I can't support a store that allows people to smoke cigars and smell up all these beautiful things!" I said indignantly. I hadn't expected her response.

"You *saw* him?" she asked.

"You mean the jerk smoking the cigar? Kinda hard to miss. Yeah, he's right over—" I swung around to point him out, but he was gone and, oddly enough, so was the smoke. I couldn't smell or see even a trace of it. "What just happened?"

"You just saw Mr. Whaley," the helpful woman behind the counter informed me. She went on to tell me who Mr. Whaley was (see Whaley House chapter) and that although they'd been smelling his cigar smoke for a good long while, I was the only one who'd ever seen him in the store. Feeling like I'd just walked into the Twilight Zone, I purchased a few things just to bring some normalcy back to my life, thanked her, and drove straight home.

Since that time, I'd walked into the store at least two dozen times hoping to find the woman I'd met that night to apologize for my behavior, but I always missed the times she was working, and it wasn't for another eight years that I'd finally see her again. I walked in and introduced myself.

I refreshed her memory about that night and asked her if she remembered me. "Yes, I totally remember—it's been a while," said "Cathy," smiling and remembering the incident clearly.

I also had my five-year-old with me, who found everything (breakable) in the store fascinating. Luckily, Cathy is a retired elementary school teacher who has the patience of a saint. I asked to interview her for the book, and the rest of the story unfolded. The store used to have an auxiliary store that just happened to be where the Creole Café's indoor seating is now (see Creole Café chapter).

"The Whaley House is legendary, but I used to be the biggest skeptic before I started working over there," Cathy said. "I used to feel a presence in the room with me when I worked over there. I also used to hear what sounded like children running around, and I'd get my hair tugged at and I'd hear children laughing. I also heard 'Momma' whispered to me a few times. I used to smell jasmine perfume that Mrs. Whaley is known for. One time I felt something lick my foot and I gave a little scream and a docent came over and said, 'Oh, that's just Dolly—the Whaley's dog.'

"We used to have a bunch of wind chimes, and one day they all went crazy and people came over to see if there were children playing with them, or what was going on. Then all but one stopped, and that one just kept dancing on its own. We had quite a crowd—there seemed to be a lot of energy around—and all it once it smelled like roses."

"Although the little store was not known for being haunted, the store would get visitors declaring there was a presence there, and requests to investigate further. A husband and wife who were regulars used to come in when we were located by the Whaley House. They were there once, and there was pounding on the wall—at first I just thought it was the Creole Café, but then I remembered that our walls didn't touch. He was taking pictures—and there was the face of Anna Whaley! It was quite an experience. When we were getting ready to close that store, there was this image coming through the mirror on the back wall (see Creole Café chapter) that looked like it was developing—into a picture of Thomas Whaley."

Several years later when it was the Creole Café, in a series of photos I took in the mirror, I captured an image *developing* as it became a girl. Her translucent skirt spilled out onto the floor in front of the mirror before she disappeared when someone else took a picture of the mirror with a flash.

During the years Cathy has worked at the store on San Diego Avenue, many people have come in to tell her about the paranormal experiences they've had in and around the Old Town area. For years she'd been aware that the ghost of Thomas Whaley had been seen, and although she had many experiences at the other store involving her senses of touch, feel, smell and hearing, other than the chimes, she'd not witnessed any paranormal occurrences.

"Then one day," explained Cathy, "they were doing some work on the road, so I had to leave my car in the state-park parking lot. It was about a quarter to ten in the morning when I passed by a gentleman in period clothing sitting on the bricks in front of the Whaley House—of course, there's nothing odd about that because there are tons of people dressed in period clothing around here. But, there was something about his penetrating eyes and the way he looked at me and said, 'Good morning.' So I looked back just a second later and he was gone.

"The man I saw was much younger than Whaley was when he died. I searched and searched for a picture of Mr. Whaley when he was younger. I couldn't find anything, but one day I was watching PBS and they had a special on Old Town—and there *it* was, a picture of young Mr. Whaley. I'd been taping it and I rewound it and took a picture." Cathy pulled out her cell phone and she showed me the young Mr. Whaley. "It was him— that's who I saw out in front of the Whaley House."

It was at that point I realized I hadn't tried to identify the spirit I'd seen. Although it had been a while, I had taken down some notes that night in my journal. I went back and looked at the notes and dug around on the Internet to find pictures of Thomas Whaley. In the end, I decided the man I saw might not have been Thomas Whaley. My apparition was a tall guy, his boots were on *long* legs. He was also dressed more in the style of Doc Holliday, with a duster, boots, button-up shirt, and one of those old riverboat-gambler kind of hats popular in the mid-1800s. His face was also broader, with a full salt-and-pepper beard, and he had stunning blue eyes.

Julie Kitterman, a sales associate at Four Winds, has also experienced a number of things at the store. "We had an antique chief's rug," says Kitterman. "The rug seemed angry about being here, and people would come up and make comments to us about it not having good energy. There was also this bin of things in that room, and to get the container out the door you'd have to hold it way up—and we would have seen someone do that. But, one day it was just gone."

Kitterman is used to smelling the cigar and the sweet perfume wafting through the store, but she also remembers a mobile, but centralized, foul-smelling odor that came and hung out in the store for a while. The store has a lot of sage in case a room needs to be "cleansed" of negative energy that comes to visit every once in a great while; the spirit energy attached to the smell finally left after they burned enough sage, and the spirit probably realized the losing battle it was waging against the store's usual good cheer and positive environment. There is a lot of spirit activity in this store as many of the store's more precious artifacts are vintage Native American art; one can literally pick up a piece of vintage art and feel the decades it has lived and the artisan's energy first put into it.

"There used to be a stand out front, and the woman's daughter used to run it—she was a teenager," says Kitterman. "One day she came in and told us a little boy had come out of the store who was about seven. He was dressed in period clothing, and he talked to her for a little bit and told her his name was Sebastian, and then he just disappeared. Sometimes when I lock up at night, the light in the bathroom will go on and I'll have to go back in and turn it off. One night that happened, and I went to open the door to turn off the light, and all of a sudden it felt like someone was keeping it from opening from the other side. Then the pressure from the other side let up, and I turned off the light and locked up."

Carol DiBene, owner of Four Winds, began collecting Native American art in preparation for opening the store in 1992 with her husband, who had reconnected with his heritage at the Round Valley Reservation (Wailaki tribe), where his mother lived. DiBene's love and knowledge of Native American arts continued to grow, and she knew she could do better than the shows she'd been doing—it was time to open a store. Her store has become one of the most stable and well-known stores in the Old Town community; you'll often see people from all over the country shopping there and arranging to ship their items home.

"In the other building I would close up and hear someone come up, and I'd go to open the door—and there would be no one there," says DiBene. "We'd also get a lot of cigar and sweet-smelling violet-like smells. There was a man who came in and filmed, and he captured seventeen different entities on his computer—and all of these different voices. People come in and sometimes I'll mention Mr. Whaley to them, and then all of a sudden it will begin smelling like cigars, or sometimes lavender. They come and go as they want, but we're not frightened of the spirits. It feels like we're being watched over and protected by Mr. Whaley because we're women; we're good with having him—*them*—here. They're not harming anyone—and this was their home first."

CHAPTER 2

Creole Café
OLD TOWN SAN DIEGO

The dining room for the Creole Café (the main office and kitchen is in the next building to the right) is one of the oldest buildings in San Diego—and apparently has become some kind of vortex for paranormal activity.

WHEN ANNA AND CHARLES WHALEY decided to put down roots in what would become the heart of Old Town San Diego, it seems there was a plan to bring a bit of Louisiana to Southern California. Anna Whaley, of French descent, planted the majestic pepper trees outside her house in 1856. Her trees, and other New Orleans touches, were recognized by Mark Bihm more than 150 years later, drawing him to the next stage in his career. He was intrigued by the blind real estate ad that read "Deli in a parklike setting," describing the historic building that shares the Whaley House courtyard.

"I wanted to open a restaurant, and I didn't want to see concrete or cars," Bihm says. He immediately came out to look at the property and fell in love with it; the place reminded him of his homeland—his family has been in Louisiana since 1750. "The New Orleans style of the Whaley House [see Whaley House chapter], the gas lamps, the pepper trees—it was *kismet*." And the rest is history.

Bihm's San Diego Creole Café is part of the historic courtyard that Save Our Heritage Organization (SOHO) created from the buildings saved from demolition and painstakingly restored to preserve San Diego's early history. The adopted buildings are now part of the family surrounding the historic Whaley House. What Bihm didn't realize, but now knows very well, is that he was moving into one of America's most haunted locations.

"I was raised a hard-shell Southern Baptist; my family wanted me to have *the calling*," says Bihm, a Southern gentleman to the core. Instead of the ministry, Bihm went into corporate restaurant management, which eventually led him west to Baghdad by the Bay's classic San Franciscan venue on Fisherman's Wharf— and finally to San Diego, where he had fond memories of family vacations and the city's Wild West history.

So what does Bihm say about ghosts? "I know the Bible, and it's a good archetype for living, sure, but I've always wondered what the nuts and bolts of the afterlife are. Certainly using the scientific methods we have today we can perhaps find out more than we thought was possible about the afterlife. I think it would be good for our society to know . . . to be able to integrate this

Mark Bihm *(left)* and Humberto Villegas in front of the Creole Café, sitting at their Día de los Muertos altar

into our culture for a better outcome. Maybe knowing would give us hope."

Bihm and his life and business partner, Humberto Villegas, have both experienced many paranormal events in the buildings that house the Creole Café, moved from what was one of the oldest areas of San Diego called New Town, which is now part of San Diego's downtown area. The two wooden structures with false facades definitely have a *feeling* about them, and many customers comment about their own experiences there.

Villegas has experienced the feeling of being watched. When they first moved into the building, he would sense someone walking up the path and into the building, but when he'd turn around there would be no one there.

"We've been here for eight years," says Villegas. "Once, I was wiping down a table for the next guests when a woman here with another woman and a child said, 'Is this building haunted? I definitely get the feeling there is someone else sitting here at our table.' And that's how it is for many people who come here. We get comments like that from tourists who don't know the history of the Whaley House."

One morning Bihm found himself in a not-so-typical paranormal event for Old Town. As we sat on the porch, he said, "I was coming to work and came in early because there's a lot of stuff I have to do to get ready to open. I stopped at the gate [on Harney Street], and as I'm going though the gate I felt a gentle pushing on me and I got this feeling—no voices or anything, but just the feeling to stop and hold off from going in. It really affected me and I didn't want to go in.

"One of the Whaley House docents, Casey, was following behind me, and I said, 'Don't go to the house.' And she said, 'Well, I have to—we open in ten minutes. Let's go up to the Hacienda [The Hacienda Hotel in Old Town, just up the street from the Whaley House] and ask them if there's anything going on.' And we did. But they said nothing was going on that they were aware of—just a normal day. Casey said, 'If you don't want to go to the restaurant, come with me to the house—you can come open the house with me and we'll be safe together.'

"Well, as soon as we started walking up, all of a sudden out of nowhere there's a police helicopter, police dogs, and police cars," Bihm continued about the incident. "Come to find out there was a guy under the restaurant's porch with a gun that they'd been looking for all night. They pulled up a board," he said, showing me the board, "and they pulled him up—he was a skinny little thing—totally pierced up, in black leather. He had little horns coming out of his head—he had his hair done up like that! I just thought, 'Oh, look, it's the devil!' That was back in '05 or so."

Bihm feels that the spirits at the restaurant don't mind his presence there, and after that incident have actually tried to take care of the partners in the face of danger. He once slipped and would have had a worse fall had something not intervened and actually kept him afloat and cleared him of the porch. I've heard of four other people having similar experiences in and around the surrounding buildings.

"There was one time I was out in the bathroom putting soap out there and I heard a banging on the door," Bihm said. "It made me angry because they were banging way too hard. I said, 'Stop that!' And I came out and there was this couple outside, and they looked frightened and said, 'We heard that banging, too!'"

The bathroom is approximately in the area where the outhouse for the Whaley household used to be. That's where Violet Whaley, Charles and Anna's daughter, killed herself with a revolver and bled to death inside the home.

"Maybe the pounding is that of her father reliving the moments he heard the gun and was trying to get in to help her," Bihm said, trying to make sense of the pounding. Bihm has empathy for what the Whaleys went through in their time at the house and respects the area where they lived, which is perhaps why they seem to keep an eye out for him.

The Creole Café spirits are also known to play tricks on Bihm and Villegas. "We have a special knife we cut the shrimp with, and Humberto said, 'I wish I could find that knife; I've been looking everywhere for it.' So I'm looking around for it everywhere. Humberto is sitting at the counter and cutting the shrimp with a big knife, and all at once we look over—and there it was on the cutting board. That would have been pretty hard for both of us to miss when we'd looked so hard. Things will disappear, but they turn right back up again."

Customers and visitors comment constantly regarding the spirits and paranormal activity in the buildings.

"One day, I was sitting in the restaurant, and a man says, 'I'm a psychic. Can we go into this building for a minute to talk?'" The mysterious man pointed to the indoor seating area (the building to the left of the kitchen building) where many have had paranormal experiences. "He was telling me there's a woman here and her name is Amelia—she's telling him the building used to be her brothel, and she's showing him how it used to look, and she was very proud of her business. Then he suddenly stopped and said, 'Your parents are here and they want you to know how pleased they are with what you're doing—and they know things are slow here, but things will pick up in March and it'll be really busy—you're new here and give yourself a chance. Your grandmother is also here, and she wants you to know how much she loved doing dishes with you when you were a baby.' Well, this is an old family joke; I'm kind of known for this—more like supervising washing the dishes with Grandma. It gave credence to his whole message. Then he added, 'They want me to tell you that when you die, they're going to embrace you,' Of course, I asked, 'Is that anytime *soon*?' He assured me it wasn't."

The spirits in this group of buildings let people know about their presence by means of touch, smell, movement of objects, and speaking.

"I had a friend visiting and she was just kind of making fun of Amelia," said Bihm. "It was the dead of winter and she stepped down off the steps, and I just saw her jump. She'd hit a wall of the scent of sweet-smelling flowers in front of her. She didn't make fun of Amelia again. I've also smelled baking in the Whaley House with docents, when there was no baking going on anywhere else. I guess if you like to bake, it continues no matter where you go." Bihm smiles, at ease with the idea of living among ghosts.

"We have this kitchen hood fan that sucks up an enormous amount of air. All of a sudden I smelled this cigar smoke, like someone next to me just blew it in my face to get my attention. I also felt this warmth—like a body standing next to me. I felt like I knew how tall this ghost was, so I went over to the Whaley House to ask a docent how tall Mr. Whaley was—they know everything there. I went to the back door and I leaned over the chain to get someone's attention. All of a sudden the chandelier in the dining room started swinging violently—and just when it slowed down it would speed up again. It was summer and the house was packed—fifty people saw it."

The Creole Café buildings are known by local paranormal groups as hopping with activity. Several groups, including my own Meetup group, Ghosts Happen, have used the dining space after the restaurant has closed to carry out investigations. One evening my group was having a séance with two Spiritualist mediums, Fran and Pete Monroe, discussing how mediumship works in regard to contacting spirits, and several messages came through. There was activity on all of the meters. We also had Frank's Box #55 out and were listening for responses to questions at the end of the evening. Many people had already left, and we were getting ready to pack up when someone asked the box, "How many people are still here?" The box answered, "Fifteen." We did a quick head count to find that there were, in fact, fifteen people remaining.

One evening we were seated for a dinner investigation sponsored by the San Diego Ghost and Paranormal Group. I sat taking pictures with my cell phone when a woman in the group began describing a young woman—more like a child—with long blond hair and a Victorian-era pastel blue dress coming through. As she described this spirit, I began shooting my camera, sans flash, at the mirror in the room—in my mind's eye, and in the camera's frame, I saw a huge multicolored light shoot through and then a girl in a dress began appearing from the mirror and came right out of the mirror, her dress spilling out onto the floor. I captured the emerging image in a series of five frames. I said, "I have the pictures of what you're describing," and the group examined the pictures. The woman in the SDGAP Group affirmed that the images paralleled what she'd been psychically receiving.

This photo was taken into a mirror that seems to serve as a portal for paranormal activity. I photographed a girl coming in through the mirror until her hooped dress spilled onto the floor. When the woman reflected in the mirror (holding camera) acknowledged the apparition, it disappeared.

I believe the spirits in Old Town have the confidence to walk among the living and be noticed day or night. The paranormal stories surrounding the Whaley House and Creole Café abound—and the time of the incidents is rarely confined to the darkness of night, or to the person involved being alone.

"I've been witnessing phenomena—and I have all my life," says Bihm. "It just seems here it's more accentuated. We all want to believe in them, and I know without a doubt that if we can figure out how they move chandeliers—goodbye energy crises, hello world prosperity. How do they do that? As far as the spirits here—too many people have come here and had the same things happen for generations—people who don't even know each other. How else can they come up with the same phenomena? I do believe in them—absolutely. I'm not afraid. I mean, sure, there's bad stuff out there, but not here."

CHAPTER 3

El Campo Santo Cemetery
OLD TOWN SAN DIEGO

El Campo Santo Cemetery in Old Town is one of the oldest pioneer cemeteries in the state and an amazing mix of cultures. This is where the Day of the Dead festivities end, when hundreds of people with skeleton makeup fill the cemetery and spill out into the street to write notes and light candles for their loved ones who've passed on. It's an amazing place to capture EVPs.

ONE OF THE SMALLEST EXISTING CEMETERIES in San Diego is the El Campo Santo Cemetery, on San Diego Avenue in Old Town. Unlike other cemeteries within the city limits, El Campo Santo seems to have visitors at all hours of the day and night, every day of the year. The energy fluctuates in an ebb-and-flow manner inside the small plot of land—energy that allows the dead to rise anytime they wish to interact with the living.

The graveyard is especially active with souls and the living on October 30, when Old Town (and most of the missions in California) as well as Old Town San Diego State Historic Park celebrate Día de los Muertos (Day of the Dead). On this day and the day after, All Saints' Day, all of Old Town is awash in bright orange marigolds, the color of remembrance.

The celebration begins with the community coming into El Campo Santo to clean the graves and decorate them for the celebration, hanging huge, colorful crepe flowers in the trees and ladening the graves with offerings to let the dead know they are not forgotten. In the streets of Old Town, you'll see face painting on many corners. The adornment of skulls and the making of crepe paper flowers—as well as live music in the Whaley House courtyard—are all part of the nearly round-the-clock activities. All of Old Town's stores have elaborate altars with photos of family members who have passed and their favorite things to honor them. In the evening, people dressed in skeleton or period costumes walk in a candlelit procession from the Whaley House altar to El Campo Santo Cemetery, where speeches are made in remembrance of the pioneers of Old Town. People walk from grave to grave to leave orange flowers and notes to their relatives.

The cemetery was established in 1849 as a Roman Catholic burial lot. It took thirty-one years to somehow squeeze 477 bodies into an area that became even smaller in 1889, when a streetcar line was built through part of the cemetery. In 1942, the streetcar route was paved over and became San Diego Avenue. What you may not notice is that there are graves under the streets and sidewalks and lots surrounding the cemetery.

The sacred grounds have been under siege by the city government ever since it stopped making money, but thanks to the outcry from the community, it was saved and didn't go completely under like Calvary and Buena Vista cemeteries. You'll notice brass medallion markers in the street that read GRAVE-SITE, marking the location of twenty or so graves that were paved over and discovered again in the 1930s by scientists from the Geophysics Group of Escondido. Nearly all of the original markers in the cemetery have now been removed by vandals, fallen apart, or gone missing at some point. Most of those standing today are modern replacements.

Although the cemetery is hardly in a low-traffic area—business owners and homeowners are within earshot night and day—it seems somehow isolated. Last time I was there, I counted four wireless night cameras trained on the area, so you are never truly alone there, at least not on video playback. But during the night, you see many people carrying digital recorders as they question the dead. Sometimes, on a good night, the living interact with the dead. On a bad night, the living interact with the living—which can be much scarier than any ghosts I've ever encountered.

Maritza Skandunas, medium and founder of San Diego Ghost Hunters, was with her team at El Campo Santo one night doing EVP work when an odd incident took place around 2 a.m. They were in the rear of the cemetery when they heard noises out front.

"All of a sudden we turned around and this guy—he had to be on drugs—he'd been walking with his head down and was out in front on the other side of the wall. He hadn't realized we were there. I don't think he was really even aware of his surroundings. He was probably nineteen. He reached over the wall and we saw his hands come over and grab the cross on a grave right out in front and just pull it out of the ground. We said to each other, 'Someone is stealing a cross!' and went running over—that's when he took off running down the street. We chased after him. There were two guys closer to where he was that saw what was going on and ran after him," says Skandunas. "He dropped the cross and we grabbed it and took it back. It just seemed like he didn't even know what he was doing when he did it."

Vandals are always visiting the cemetery; it seems like there is always someone doing something to desecrate the area. Late one night I visited the cemetery with Jennifer Donohue, Roadside Paranormal lead investigator and medium, to find two mason jars filled with "charms" and what looked like animal intestines floating in some kind of liquid buried in one of the children's graves. We could see the lids and began unearthing them by hand.

We had our digital recorders on and lying on the ground while we were digging them out. The full moon would be over the next day, and the Satanists would probably be back for their "spell jars." So we set them on the wall as a sign to let them know their plan had been foiled and they were not welcome in the graveyard, and to let the community know that something was afoot.

We'd set our recorders down when we first started the digging, and with the task at hand we'd forgotten to pick them up again. We went down the street to a late-night bar to get some coffee to go for our drives home. When we realized what we'd done, we went back for them—both recorders had been physically turned off. You'd think if someone was going to take the trouble to turn them off, they might have also taken the recorders (worth a few hundred dollars each).

Later, when we played them back, we found that each recorder had picked up different sounds. Jennifer's recording began with unusual sounds as we approached the grave. What sounded like a child having a coughing fit was barely audible in between the cars going by. Had the noise been in our own ambient surrounding, we would have noticed. A few minutes later, Jennifer was speaking with the spirit of the girl who was buried there, consoling her and apologizing to her as she pulled out one of the jars. On the tape, just as Jennifer acknowledged that she'd pulled out the jar and that we were taking them away, the coughing (it was all fairly faint) stopped all together. In the twenty minutes it took us to get coffee and realize we'd forgotten the recorders, we heard ourselves leave and then heard what sounded like someone walking heavily around in the leaves (there was no wind that night) and a grunt. Then Jennifer's recorder shut off.

When we were digging up the jars, a man's voice could be heard on my recorder, but none of the coughing came through. The voice sounded like it was saying "yup" or "up" sporadically. We also heard what sounded like earth being dug up with a shovel, occasionally hitting rocks. It took us no more than five minutes to dig up the jars. Even after we left, the sounds of digging and the male voice continued for about fifteen minutes— five more minutes after Jennifer's recorder had stopped. Why had the recordings stopped? Why had they stopped at separate times? They had to have been physically turned off. The batteries were still fine, and the recorders were in good repair. They were in the same position as we'd remembered leaving them. It's a mystery. My recording actually sounded like a grave being dug, or shoveled over. Was it the old gravedigger, Rafael Mamudes? Of all those interred in El Campo Santo—the criminals executed by gunfire as they stood directly over their graves, the murderers and murdered, the famous and infamous, and just ordinary people trying to make their way in lawless Old Town—I'd say that Rafael Mamudes is probably one of the most memorable (see **tinyurl.com/mamudes**).

According to a sign staked on Mamudes's grave, he was born in Hermosillo in the Mexican state of Sonora. He was a baker, a miner, a traveler . . . and a murderer. He owned the land where the old jail once stood. He murdered his wife, but the priests saw fit to give him only the task of ringing the church bells at the appropriate times to pay for his crime. I'm assuming this was done in the days when the mission priests were in charge of administering local justice. Other than the bell ringing, life for Mamudes (sans wife) seemed to go on as usual. Although his birth and death dates remain unknown, the gravedigger was believed to be more than one hundred years old when he had to face his wife again. He'd been known as a handyman with a shovel, who dug everything from wells to graves. I hadn't really given much thought to him, or even connected him to the sounds of the digging, until I spoke recently with Skandunas and heard her Mamudes story.

Skandunas and her team were in El Campo Santo one evening in 2000 doing EVP sessions, when they got an interesting response from him. "We were sitting at the bench near his grave, and he answered us with his name," Skandunas says. "When we first started talking with him and were near his grave, I felt like he had his hands around my throat. Even on EVPs we'd talk to him and at first we'd hear a lot of yelling, so we gave him a wide berth. As more people started talking with him, he started to lighten up a bit."

There is a spirit of a child at El Campo Santo that likes tugging on clothes. Janine Haynes, cofounder and paranormal investigator of S.P.I.R.I.T. SoCal, had quite an experience that manifested itself in a photograph. "I hadn't been out to Old Town in years and was walking through the graveyard, and this one grave in particular kept drawing me to it. I was standing there and felt a tug on my sleeve, and I turned around to tell my sister not to be tugging on me in the cemetery. She wasn't there—I went running off to the front of the cemetery where she was. She told me to go back and take a picture, and I did. I only had my cell phone with me, but there between the wrought-iron bars was a little kid peeking though!"

I've seen the eerie picture and brought it up in some evaluation software—it wasn't Photoshopped. I would have included it in this book, but it would have lost its nuances in the printing. Over the decades since the cemetery has been closed to burials, many specters have made appearances, and there is never a shortage of paranormal investigators who've felt challenged to meet them face to face.

"I spent the better part of a night there hoping to confirm the reports of ghosts and supernatural sounds," says author and paranormal investigator Richard Senate (see **ghost-stalker .com** for his classes, lectures, and tours in Ventura County). "I didn't really expect to find much and if I did, I was targeting perhaps the most famous resident—Yankee Jim Robinson, who was hanged for the crime of stealing a rowboat while drunk. Crime and punishment were harsh in those Gold Rush years, and his death was seen, even then, as beyond the usual standards of the day. I was stationed next to Yankee Jim's grave with all of my many tools hoping to capture a fleeting glimpse of the hanged man. It was dark there, and I recall the place seemed to get colder as the hours passed after midnight.

"I tried to capture an EVP, and all I was able to record was my own sneezing and the tires of passing cars," says Senate, author of the upcoming *Phantomology: the Art of Ghost Hunting*, about his thirty-three years as a ghosthunter. "It was close to two when I saw the figure. I turned back toward the rear of the cemetery and saw a movement, first out of the corner of my eye. I glanced back at the spot where I had detected the movement. I guess it was maybe fifteen minutes later that I looked back to that spot, only this time a sudden chill raced down my back—there was something there! It wasn't a shadow, but a fully formed woman in a long nineteenth-century-style dress. It was all black in Victorian mourning style, with long sleeves and ruffles around the skirt. Her head was bent low, and she wore a sort of bonnet with a low brim, also black. She was moving silently across the ground. I felt a terrible sadness about the specter; it was silent and visible for about ten or twelve seconds and then was gone. I felt she was still there in some form, perhaps visiting the graves of lost children or a beloved husband. I never got an image or anything related to poor Yankee Jim, but I did see the form of a woman—confirming that old Campo Santo is indeed haunted."

The phantom woman is a ghost that's been sighted over the decades since the cemetery closed; this affirmation was nice to hear from such a trusted source in the paranormal community. El Campo Santo is one of the most active locations in San Diego, but also one of the most watched over, considering the amount of traffic it gets from the paranormal community, which checks in on a regular basis.

"Treat them with respect," says Skandunas, with advice for anyone going to the Old Town cemetery. "El Campo Santo is their burial place. Honor what they were in life—bring positive energy with you. Be respectful. Walk in letting them know you're only there to communicate with positive spirits; surround yourself with positive light. And when you leave, say that they are not allowed to follow you home."

CHAPTER 4

The Whaley House
OLD TOWN SAN DIEGO

The Whaley House is incredibly loved by the community and honored for the pioneering family that once lived there—and it's one of America's most haunted buildings.

ANYONE INTERESTED IN THE PARANORMAL has heard of the infamous Whaley House, one of the most visited of California's historic houses. It's also a home occupied by spirits—the entire Whaley family and their pets—seem to have made an appearance at one time or another. Built in 1857 for the sum of $10,000 in materials and labor, the wood-and-brick structure was extravagant for Thomas Whaley, a man with big dreams and modest means.

The Whaley family became pioneers in the San Diego area. Born in New York City in 1823, the enterprising Thomas Whaley came to San Diego via San Francisco, where he had a storefront on Montgomery Street during the forty-niner Gold Rush days. His store was successful, perhaps too much so, as it burned down in what was suspected arson. This incident became typical of the Whaley family's luck. Thomas Whaley was never a wealthy man for any period of time; his luck seemed to ebb and flow in between mysterious fires and family tragedies. His wife, Anna Eloise DeLaunay, bore him six children, none of whom carried the family name forward as Whaley probably envisioned they might when he made the harrowing sea journey to San Francisco.

When Thomas and Anna arrived in Old Town, they found little societal infrastructure. The area was rough-and-tumble—actually, downright lawless—and so unlike San Francisco or New York City. Life on State Street was difficult at best, but they made a life worth living; existing journals and letters show their love for one another.

The land where the Whaley House now stands, purchased for $1.50, was once where a gallows stood, its rope bringing swift justice to those criminals whose bodies were then buried on the same street just a few blocks away (see El Campo Santo chapter). Despite the hardships, the family seemed to thrive for years. Just as Whaley was gaining traction, his store was destroyed in a fire—again. Some say the work of an arsonist. In 1867, he moved the family back to San Francisco while he worked a lucrative job in Alaska and was able to support them in the lifestyle to which they'd grown accustomed.

In 1869, Thomas Whaley leased several of the rooms of Whaley House and turned the unused space into revenue; the largest room of the home was converted into a county courtroom—it had also been a dairy, a Sunday school, a morgue, and a store. The rooms upstairs were converted into a theater. Later, the family was once again reunited in San Diego, and everything was going well for the family, but not for the town.

There was much political upheaval in Old Town as its role as the county seat was ripped away. Soon it became just another colorful neighborhood in the weave of the county's tapestry. Whaley became a shadow of the man who'd arrived in California to fulfill his destiny and take his place in history. Once known informally as the "Mayor of San Diego" and appointed president of the San Diego City Board of Trustees, he saw his life begin its downward spiral. In 1871, the county clerk rode to the Whaley home courthouse and forcibly took the city records that had been stored there.

On January 5, 1882, Whaley's daughters Violet and Anna Amelia had a wonderful double wedding; Anna Amelia married her first cousin, John T. Whaley, and Violet wedded George T. Bertolacci, whom she divorced a little more than a year later. Violet suffered a great deal of clinical depression before she took her own life in 1885 (see Creole Café chapter). With the death of their dear Violet and their son Thomas Jr., Thomas and Anna wanted to leave the home's memories behind, so they moved to what is now downtown. Whaley became an employee of city government and retired in 1888 and passed away in his downtown home in 1890 at the age of sixty-seven. Anna Amelia Whaley passed away in Modesto in 1905.

Thomas Whaley had rented out their home on San Diego Avenue, and it had fallen into great disrepair. In 1909, tourism took hold of San Diego as everyone readied for the Panama-Pacific International Exposition, and Helen Hunt Jackson's novel *Ramona* had planted a wildly romantic view of Southern California in the rest of the world's imagination (see Rancho Camulos chapter). So people continued to come to Southern California and vacation up and down the coast. Thomas Whaley's son Francis undertook making the home a tourist attraction; he posted signs outside promoting its history and entertained visitors with his guitar on the porch of his childhood home and charged a small fee for a tour. The Whaley matriarch, Anna, along with Corinne Lillian, Francis, and George, one again took up residence in the old Whaley House in 1912. In 1913, the family suffered the loss of Anna at age eighty. A year later, Francis Whaley passed away, followed by George Whaley in 1928. Corinne Lillian Whaley continued living in what must have been a house of spirits by then until her death in 1953.

There's not much about the Whaley family in today's history books; even the family burial plot is not especially ornate or conspicuous (see Mount Hope chapter). If it were not for Save Our Heritage Organization (SOHO) and the vision they had to preserve the home Whaley left behind, the family name might not be known at all today.

New to the area in 2002, I took a tour of the Whaley House because of my own love for historic architecture. I was taking pictures with my cell phone from all angles, but stopped dead in my tracks as I looked at the digital photo I'd taken while shooting up the stairs. There, midway up the stairs, was the figure of a little boy in period clothing staring down at me. I looked at the picture, at the stairs, and back at the camera. I immediately went upstairs to search the rooms for the child who seemed to have disappeared the moment I took his picture. I found no one. I went downstairs and showed people the photo and asked them if they'd seen the child come down. There was quite a stir, and in all the excitement I'd forgotten to save the photo. During the time my phone was being passing around, the photo was deleted, but the memory of the child dressed in Victorian clothing sitting halfway up the stairs and looking quite forlorn was not.

As I formed my Meetup group, Ghosts Happen, and brought them to the location (see Creole Café chapter), I began a rapport

The Whaley family altar outside their home on the annual celebration of the Day of the Dead. The streets of Old Town are lined with altars, covered with candles and marigolds, that honor the dead. This is where the procession to El Campo Santo Cemetery begins.

with the people responsible for raising the money to pay the bills every month. Each of them has their own stories of the home, not because they're gullible people or because they're prone to hallucinations, but because, I believe, the Whaleys have adopted them as family. The stories I hear are not scary or bloodcurdling; instead, they are rather caring.

What you find with the staff of the Whaley House isn't indicative of the history museums you see all over the country—filled with senior volunteers who are desperately trying to save history for the next generation. Instead, you find young people—people who started caring about preserving history in their teens—who were somehow born into the love of history and filled with enthusiasm and innovative ideas to preserve the property and reach out to the community. And when they talk about the ghosts that reside in the Whaley manse, they're respectful and protective—apparently to give the entities the room they need to coexist on the property.

Victor Santana, director of interpretive services for SOHO, shares that dedication to history and came to the Whaley House through the junior docent program when he was sixteen. You can tell Santana is proud of what SOHO has done for the Whaley home, and that he takes a great deal of care in the way he presents the home to the public. All of the employees are quite protective of the Whaley family and the buildings in the square.

"I think we can all have different assumptions about what ghosts are, and why they're still here, and what to call them, but unless you hear it directly from them you're not going to have a definitive answer," says Santana. "You go with the obvious answer; it's probably the Whaleys—it is their home. There's no reason why it wouldn't be them—they had their good times and they had their tragedies here, but it's still their home."

Santana has experienced quite a bit of paranormal activity over the years. His first experience happened on his first night locking up alone. "I was locking up one night after a private tour with a newlywed couple. It was about eleven. I was nearly done when I heard footsteps upstairs, and I thought, 'This isn't good—it's my first night—someone must have snuck in.' So I went upstairs to see what was going on, and there was no one up there. I came back and the footsteps starting sounding so *real* and so *loud* that I actually called my boss at the time and I told her, 'I think the house is *really* haunted.' She asked, 'What are you still doing there?' And I told her that I was locking up and still hearing noises like someone is still here. She told me to just set the alarm and lock up. As I'm setting the alarm, I heard a woman's voice whisper, 'Why are you still here?'

"For all the years I've been here, I've not *heard* anything else . . . ." Santana shrugs. "But I've heard recordings of the voices in the house. The San Diego Ghost Hunters do EVP sessions here [see El Campo Santo chapter]. I'm not a ghosthunter, but I do believe in ghosts. I think it's really cool what they [ghost-hunters] do. I listened to a recording where the San Diego Ghost Hunters ask, 'Thomas Whaley, are you here?' 'Anna Whaley, are you here?' And then they say, 'Maybe it's the little girl who lives here?' When you listen back you can clearly hear a little girl answering *Yes* or *No* questions so close to the microphone, it's like she's in the same room."

As is everyone connected to the Whaley House, Santana is very respectful of the property and the spirits residing there. "Don't base what you're going to do on what you see on television," says Santana to visitors of the Whaley House. "A lot of people come in here and try to offend the ghosts and yell out at them. You don't go to someone's house and cuss or call them out."

Dean Glass, administrative manager of SOHO, had an experience that brought him face-to-face with the master of the house. One thing about all the people working with the Whaley House is that they're credible witnesses that don't seem to be the type who see spirits everywhere. I've seen many who lie their way through a story, and this is not what they're about. Each has only a handful of stories for the length of time they've been working at the house, and all of them preface their stories with a type of story that explains how they wouldn't believe their own stories had they not lived through them themselves.

"It's been about six years now," said Glass of the morning that gave him a story that still gave him goose bumps (I noticed) when he told it. "I was opening up the house one morning and walking up the stairs, and I noticed out of the corner of my eye something that looked like pants legs in between the rails. I cocked my head and looked up—and there was a man standing there. His hands were outstretched on the railing at the top, and he was staring straight at me. He had really distinctive eyes—if you look at the portrait of Thomas Whaley in the parlor, they were the same eyes . . . really piercing. Lillian Whaley used to call them the 'Intelligent Whaley eyes' [see **whaleyhouse.org** to find out more; Lillian's papers are now available there]. He was just staring right at me. He startled me because no one was supposed to be there. He wore a wide-brimmed hat, but I couldn't see the style of the hat because I just saw from underneath. He was shades of gray; I don't remember if I could see through him or not. He had a look on his face like he was wondering about who I was and why I was there. And the next moment he was gone. Another thing I remember is that he was in his mid-twenties; not an older man like Thomas Whaley was when he died, but I always got the feeling it was Thomas Whaley.

"I always say hello to anyone who may be seeing or hearing me," said Glass. "And every time I go up the stairs—*every time*—I always look to see if he's there. All these years later, and I still look for him."

Facility Manager Robert Daniel Wilson has worked at the house for three years and is a favorite of tourists because he seems to know everything about the property and the Whaley family.

"I always say that my experiences are very limited because I'm not very sensitive to the paranormal aspect of the house. I just get the basic things that someone would get if you're in the right place at the right time," says Wilson. "They're [the ghosts] not evil, believe me—if people were getting hurt here, I wouldn't be working here. The spirits here are intelligent, and I believe they know what's going on here. For instance, Thomas Whaley knows that the money spent on tickets here helps keep the house in its present condition. He understands this because he used to do the same thing by renting out the rooms in his home.

"I was working here one Friday morning when a woman poked her head in and asked what the house was all about. I gave her a brief history. She spoke with a very thick French accent and was difficult to understand, but she told me she'd be back. She brought back eight foreign-exchange students, and in about thirty minutes her group was in the courtroom and they seemed to be having a good time touring the home. On her way out, she thanked me and told me she'd be back on Sunday with more students. I told her we'd look forward to seeing them.

"She was back on Sunday with more students, and they were in the courtroom and she kept asking the same question over and over again, but I couldn't understand her. One of the other docents came in and we figured out she was asking if we could 'do it again' over and over. Well, we didn't know what she was talking about. Then she looked back in the courtroom and smiled and nodded at us. Apparently, the last time she'd come in, the chandelier was swinging, and she thought we'd rigged something to do that. And when she looked back in the court-room, the chandelier was swinging again—she thought we'd done it! She willed it to happen on her own. I like to think people have different levels of spiritual attractiveness; just like we're attracted to people with similar interests, so are spirits. I think that would explain a lot."

Carrie Higginson, former gift-shop manager, worked on the property for four years and recalled an incident similar to one described in the Creole Café chapter. "I was running in between the gift shop and the Whaley House porch, and on the far left side in between the first two pillars—when you're facing the street—I slipped and my arms went up in the air and my feet went flying out from under me facing the avenue. I thought I was going to break my head on the bricks—I *should* have broken my head on the bricks because of the way I was landing. Instead, I brushed myself off and hoped that no one had seen me. The next day, my coworker pointed out I had a bruise on my arm that looked like a handprint—it was a right-hand imprint on my right arm, so I had a thumb-bruise outline going diagonally and four finger outlines on the outside of my arm. I thought the bruise was dirt; I poked it in a few places, but there was no pain whatsoever. It freaked me out, and I still don't presume to know what happened.

"A lot of my coworkers will give personalities to the ghosts. I'm not quite ready to do that . . . well, except for the ones in the gift shop. I notice if I don't say goodnight to Mrs. Verna, who was the previous occupant of the home [saved from the wrecking ball and moved to the Whaley Complex Community Park], I have problems with the lock. I mean, it's the same lock—I use it every day, it's the same rotation, and sometimes when I don't say goodnight, it just clicks funny, and I'll remember that I didn't say good night. When I remember this and say, 'Good night, Mrs. Verna,' the lock is fine again."

Corinne Lillian Whaley, the youngest child of Thomas and Anna Whaley, wrote about her memories of Old Town, and they were compiled into a book titled *California's Oldest Town* (available at the Whaley House gift shop). She used Old Town's plummet from the up-and-coming to the dilapidated place it became as a metaphor of her own mortality. The book is a wonderful collection of her memories growing up in the Whaley home, a definite must-read for anyone interested in what life once was in Old Town. Corinne Lillian was the last full-time resident of the home, living there alone with her memories that still echo through its hallways and stairwell.

The two old palm trees at the entrance of town stand like old and trusted sentinels, the only living witnesses of my own growth and fall. Never again shall the same happy-hearted people walk my streets and share the primitive pleasures of the olden time. I stand today a dilapidated monument of the past. I am, indeed, deserted.

—Corinne Lillian Whaley, Nov. 26, 1882

Spotlight On:
What Are Ghosts?

Ghosts have always played a part in the world's gestalt—cultures from all over the world have stories of spirits appearing throughout their mythologies, histories, and belief systems. From man's earliest cave drawings, spiritlike entities have been illustrated giving messages or appearing from the sky. Why do ghosts appear at their own tragic accident scenes for an eternity to give warnings from beyond the grave? Why, when people least expect it, do spirits materialize and pass by unaware of their surroundings as though conducting everyday business . . . and then fade into a wall? Are they all here to finish off unfinished business? Or are we seeing something else?

What are ghosts? What if we've been trying to apply a single word—*ghost*—to time travelers, *doppelgängers*, people popping in and out of parallel universes, and even remote viewers? What if people die and just move on to another universe where they have the opportunity to touch our lives every once in a while? Brilliant minds such as Carl Jung and Thomas Edison believed that if we could just find the right way to think, dream, or build an amazing communication device we'd be able to touch the Other Side with ease. Jung kept a chair in his study for the spirit of his dead wife to sit in when she visited, had a weakness for séances, and claimed to have seen UFOs. He also believed in a dream tapestry where we all go at night and meet in our sleep—threads of our own dreams interwoven with others—group dreaming. Edison's parents were Spiritualists and conducted séances in his boyhood home; he believed he could build a machine to contact the dead.

These men were the thinkers of their day—they allowed themselves to think out of the box and accept what they'd perhaps seen to influence the projects they chose to develop. They, like us, were seeking the truth and scientific verification. It wasn't such a big deal back in the day for scientists to believe in life after death, or at least it wasn't the taboo it is now. So, knowing what we know today and looking at things with an open, scientific mind, can "earthbound spirits" be explained away with science? And what if *we* are some other parallel universe's ghosts? What then?

"The theories of parallel universes, alternate dimensions, the multiverse, and the holographic-universe model all point to the possibility that somewhere, out there, copies of you exist and that somehow you get an occasional glimpse of them—perhaps even in a doppelgänger experience," says Marie D. Jones, author of *PSIence: How New Discoveries in Quantum Physics and New Science May Explain the Existence of Paranormal Phenomena*. "You cannot in one reality be two places at once, but on another level of reality, your mirror image may reside, doing exactly the same thing at the same time you are doing it in your reality. The multiverse theory opens the possibility for an infinite number of yous to exist out there, each with its own conscious awareness of the reality it exists in, yet also possibly able, at times, to breach the barriers between realities and show up as your eerie double, or even as a déjà vu event.

"Maybe time travel is possible, then, if we believe in these theories, because although we are met with numerous paradoxes and limitations in our own reality for going back to the past or forward into the future," Jones continues, "those paradoxes may not exist in the multiverse, or in another dimension, where the laws of physics may look to us like *magic*."

One instance that illustrates Jones's theories beautifully is that told by Debbie Senate, paranormal investigator and medium—who for a few moments had an experience that allowed her to see through the window in time . . . literally.

"We [she and her husband, author Richard Senate] had been investigating a place for almost a month. The husband had said there had been a moon shining through a window that woke him up. He'd walk over to shut the window—there was no window there. Richard was downstairs, and I was upstairs with two other people. And there it was—*the window!* I put my head through it—everything looked very two-dimensional; I was nauseous and moving around like I was in quicksand. It really took effort to move. Outside it was like I could see back in time; there was a sawmill—where there really wasn't a mill—and girls jumping rope. The girl looked up at me, and her mouth opened and she said, *Oh!* Like she'd seen a ghost—*like I was her ghost!* She was frightened. But I didn't hear her; there was no sound on the other side of the window. The two people who were with me had a hold of me from each arm—they saw me going through the wall. I was getting really sick, and it was all I could do to nudge them—and they pulled me back in! Just as they did, the window disappeared, which led me to ask, what if I'd still had my head through it when it disappeared? I wonder now if that little girl grew up thinking she'd seen a ghost?

"Richard did some research and found that there had been a window in that spot, and it had been built over in the '40s," says Debbie of the affirmation of the time-traveling experience. "He also found a sawmill right where the one I'd seen had been—it had burned down in 1939!"

Downtown San Diego and Surrounding Area

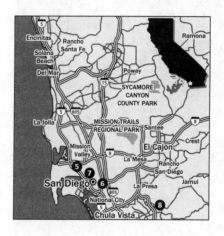

Chula Vista
Proctor Valley Road **(8)**

San Diego
Cabrillo Bridge **(7)**
Calvary Cemetery/Pioneer Park **(5)**
Mount Hope Cemetery **(6)**

CHAPTER 5

Calvary Cemetery/Pioneer Park
San Diego

Medium and Roadside Paranormal member Jennifer Donohue takes readings at the active area around the handful of tombstones that remain from the four thousand bodies still buried in the park.

WHEN YOU VISIT THE BEAUTIFUL tree-filled park at 1501 Washington Place in San Diego, your first impression will probably be how peaceful the park looks and what a caring city dedicated this space for its children. That is, until you realize there are roughly four thousand decomposed bodies under the lovely green grass that many use as a soccer field and dog park. This certainly accounts for the overwhelming paranormal activity that abounds in this location. One thing is certain: It doesn't need to be dark for this park's residents to reach out beyond the grave.

The Mission Hills neighborhood used this property as a burial ground named Calvary Cemetery from 1875 into the next century, when the last body was buried in 1960. A decade later, the city decided to sweep the surface clean of the unsightly markers for the dead, plant grass, and turn the former cemetery into a park.

The exact boundaries of the cemetery were uncertain, and many neighbors have reported finding pieces of headstones—and, occasionally, human bones—when digging in their yards to bury water pipes, cable, and electricity lines.

A cluster of gravestones, mostly of priests who were buried in the cemetery when it was used as a Catholic cemetery from 1875 to 1919, still remains in the farthest corner from the parking lot. The rest of the headstones were collected and disappeared. There are also plaques placed in the cemetery with the names of the dead, although the list seems to be incomplete; the Internet is full of posts from people asking for information about how to get their loved ones' names placed on the plaques. Others post asking where they can get a complete map, as they can no longer find where their loved ones are buried. It breaks my heart to read these comments.

In an odd move by the city, many of the seven hundred headstones were taken to the Mount Hope Cemetery (see Mount Hope Cemetery chapter), another of the city's properties. Eighteen years later, after much public outcry about how the whole situation was handled, a handful of monuments were unearthed and cemented into the ground in Mount Hope's gulley, where the city trolley slides (an area pretty much hidden if you're just visiting) next to the monuments (and through the middle of the cemetery).

There was a long history of the city desiring to reclaim the cemetery property for other uses, including an action in 1942 that allowed the U.S. Navy to use it as a temporary observation point. In 1948, the city went about trying to prove that the property was abandoned by letting go of the caretaker and pressuring the Roman Catholic bishop to sign the papers of quitclaim, releasing itself from any responsibility or liability for the grounds. The city worked with Democratic Assemblyman Michael Wornum, a man who was "in the doghouse" with his constituents after a story broke in the press in 1988 criticizing him and his wife for building a $15,000 four-bedroom doghouse complete with a tiled bathtub and TV for their ten Salukis. He was clearly a man who cared for his dogs and would have liked to make dog runs of all the state's property; he was infamous for his dog-friendly legislation. That's a great thing (I have spoiled dogs; I get it)—unless your family burial plot with interred members going back more than a hundred years gets in the way of city "improvements."

Wornum introduced legislation that allowed California city governments to take over any cemetery property and do anything they wished regarding the bodies buried on the property once it was declared abandoned. From there, it was a slippery slope. Literally. Much of the debris that used to be the cemetery was bulldozed down the hill that slopes down to Washington Street. People today are still finding pieces of broken tombstones there.

Wornum was unavailable for comment regarding the legislation that cleared many of San Diego's historic cemeteries and hundreds of other cemeteries throughout the state, making them available for developers to build upon (see Hunter Steakhouse chapter). He passed away in 1995 of stomach cancer and, from what I can tell, was cremated, as I didn't find any burial records. Imagine that—perhaps he'd seen the eventual future of all cemeteries once they were full and decided to opt out of the burial system altogether.

With all of this action disturbing the final resting spot of some of California's early residents, I imagine the paranormal activity found in this park is a reaction to the massive and deliberate desecration of the graves still located in the heavily trafficked area.

"I vaguely remember the first time I heard about Pioneer Park," says Leo Aréchiga, a lead investigator and case manager for Roadside Paranormal. "I believe it was a local KPBS show on interesting places in San Diego. I wasn't paying too much attention to the TV until I heard, 'Bodies still underground.' My reaction was one of shock and amazement. It didn't make sense. Endless questions swirled in my mind. *Why would the city of San Diego build a park over a historic cemetery and leave the bodies? Who were the people buried there?* My main question was *Why?* Cold hard cash, that's why. Mission Hills, where the cemetery once stood, needed a park. Land isn't cheap, especially if it has houses sitting on it. An old, decrepit cemetery is the next best thing. But the cost of removing and reburying the bodies and all the legal aspects that could arise from descendants were truly limitless. So the decision was made to leave all of the bodies there and simply build the park above it. Evil Genius. When I think about all those headstones—some the only record of birth and death, especially since deaths did not need to be officially recorded until 1905, I shake my head at the people behind this.

"Our team has investigated this site many times, and there's no doubt that it feels like you're being watched," says Leo. "On one occasion, as I was doing an EVP session I told the spirits that I too speak Spanish, and if they chose, they could join me in a prayer. It's a fact that many Spanish-speaking Catholics were buried here and thus not unreasonable to think one *could* answer. I slowly recited the Lord's Prayer, and when I finished, I reviewed the file. In the dead space that followed my words I heard a low, faint answer, *Gracias*. It was a male disembodied voice that came from beyond to thank me. A cold chill ran through my body when I heard that one single word that told me so much about who or what remained at Pioneer Park.

"K-II and EMF meters signal the presence of random energy throughout the park," Leo continues. "It's as if the spirits of the deceased are wandering the old cemetery searching for the headstones that their loved ones, in their agonizing sorrow, placed as tribute to them. In every tragic case our team investigates, I ask myself, *How would I feel about that? What would my reaction be?* In the case of Pioneer Park, I'd be turning over in my grave."

I've held a few Ghosts Happen meetings at the park that began with the group meeting—usually a talk about equipment or detection skills—and ending with an investigation in the park for several hours. This place has a *lot* of activity. I've seen many shadow people scurrying throughout the park and disappearing behind trees—even during the day. I've seen those I thought were among the living walk through the park who simply disappeared. I've noted odd low-light orbs bounce around slowly in the trees, photographed green lights shimmering in the park, and heard many audible disembodied voices that other people heard as well; some we recorded.

Sometimes the real activity comes from the humans inhabiting the park after nightfall. One particular evening around 10 p.m., my Meetup group had broken up into smaller groups. We were investigating an area with our equipment when a middle-aged woman walking through stopped to speak with us. She asked if we were looking for ghosts. We said we were. She told us about the beautiful cemetery that used to be there, and how she used to cut through it on her way home from school. She pointed to the grass and trees and explained what used to be here and there, including angel statues, and where the main path used to be. It was amazing to have the cemetery verbally re-created for us by someone who used such vivid description; it was clear that the neighbors once loved the cemetery. She asked the group to come to her mother's house, as it was, she told us, *quite haunted.*

Although I was speaking to an adult, I asked if she wanted to call her mother first and ask if it was okay. I felt like I was back in junior high. But she assured us it would be all right, as she took care of her mother and was in charge of the household. She advised us that her mother was sleeping; we'd just have to be quiet. I felt a bit uncomfortable about going but thought the woman seemed quite in charge of things, and activity had slowed down at the park and it had gotten cold outside. At the very least it would be a good learning experience for those wondering how to handle such an investigation. I thought we'd just go with it.

We walked to the lovely home a few blocks away only to find the porch and home stacked floor-to-ceiling with antique furniture—chairs and bookcases stacked precariously on top of tables. A treasure picker's dream, but not really practical for a large group to walk around in without nudging over something that would start a domino effect. A few of the group began sweeping the area with instruments. I was feeling more uncomfortable about being there and was about to get everyone out and say goodnight, when the woman's mother, looking a bit like a specter in a white nightgown opened what I assume was a bedroom door and poked her head out with wide eyes. I smiled, waved, and got everyone out, leaving her daughter to explain the appearance of a dozen-odd people with strange equipment in her house.

"With a constant flow of skateboarders, screaming kids, and large periodic drum circles [even at night], the environment at Pioneer Park isn't always cooperative to paranormal investigation," says Jennifer Donohue, medium and investigator for Roadside Paranormal. "My most interesting experience there fell on a cool, overcast day when the park was nearly empty. We were taking readings by the line of headstones, and the K-II, Mel Meter, and Frank's Box were quiet. I thought Sara [another team member] passed to my right and I turned to say something, but she wasn't there. When I looked around, she was toward the end of the row of headstones, nowhere close to me. Out of the corner of my eye I caught movement again, but saw nothing when I looked. This continued the rest of the afternoon. Pretty typical of shadow people.

"No sooner had I turned one direction when another would pass by me in another direction. I used the K-II, and the lights were going on and off as I pointed in the direction of movement in my peripheral vision. As soon as it would capture a signal, it was gone, and then it would find another source of energy to track, and then it was gone. After I reviewed my quick-burst EVP sessions, I found a response. It was actually a question to Sara, as she'd just walked up. 'Is it time to go?' I asked, the answer to that question was clearly stated by what sounded like an older man answering, 'Yes.' This was my first clear EVP I'd ever gotten in response to a question with a recorded device. There was no one else around and it was clear as day. Since then, I've gotten quite a few. This place is awesome for investigations."

This location was first brought to my attention by David Hanson, leader of San Diego Ghost and Paranormal (SDGAP), who heard about it from one of his members. The group often holds its monthly meetings at the park because it's the perfect Meetup location. "It's free and it's haunted," says Hanson, "and it's centrally located. The areas near the northern trees, and many areas just north of the back corner with the grave markers, seem to have the most activity."

Despite the friendly neighborhood, the park does get quite a few homeless and seemingly shady characters in the evening. "There's no real problems, per se," says Hanson, "though we don't recommend that the women go there alone after dark. We did hear one story where two of our members were doing EVP recording back by the gravestones, and when they asked the question 'Do you have a message for us?,' they both heard a faint voice saying 'Help me!' When they investigated the source, it turned out that it was one of the homeless guys nearby who was just messing with them.

"K-II meters and audio recorders seem to get the best results," advises Hanson. "If you know where to look, there are a handful of spots around the park where you can consistently get interactions on a K-II meter. You ask the ghost to flash the lights, and they will . . . almost on command. Others prefer to go for the EVPs, with some results being very interesting. Recently several of our members were doing recordings in the park and picked up the same message on both an incoming cell phone call from an unknown source and on a camcorder that was being used a few minutes later. Those in the group who are psychic or sensitive have sensed ghosts near our meetings, some of which are said to come right up to certain members to interact with them."

Why does Hanson feel the park has so much paranormal activity? "The disrespect that was shown to those interred there is obviously a prime candidate in why this cemetery seems more active than most," says Hanson. "I do have to wonder—how haunted was the cemetery when the markers were still in place? How many ghosts remained attached to their gravesite now that they'd been dishonored? Are there perhaps one or more portals at the park? I would guess that there is at least one portal there, as I've had different psychics tell me that they believe a portal is present, near one of the trees. I would be more likely to ask the question from a pseudoscientific rather than from a moral or psychic nature—is it possible that there is an underlying geographic feature, like a high quartz content in the bedrock, or a source of flowing water underneath the park that provides more natural energy and enables the spirits to manifest better than most places? In the end, I would guess that it is a mixture of factors, some of which we aren't even aware of, that makes the park as active as it is."

CHAPTER 6

Mount Hope Cemetery
SAN DIEGO

Mount Hope Cemetery's reminder of what happened to Calvary Cemetery

THERE'S AN HISTORICAL JEWEL existing between two realms in San Diego—that of the living and that of the dead. Mount Hope Cemetery is 115 acres of rolling hills, green grass, and tall palms swaying in the gentle breeze. The City of San Diego does a beautiful job maintaining the 142-year-old property.

The city's landmark is serious about schedule and security; I've even been locked in with my car—earlier than the posted closing signs—as have several members of my team. I've also heard of people getting locked into the mausoleum, and they would have stayed there all night had they not been able to use their cell phones.

The cemetery is filled with old surnames prominent in San Diego's history—early settlers such as Charles Whaley and his family (see Whaley House chapter) and "The Beautiful Stranger," Kate Morgan, whose mysterious death at the Hotel del Coronado was never questioned by her grandfather (see the Hotel del Coronado chapter). Instead, he discreetly wired funds to bury her. Noir writer and La Jolla resident Raymond Chandler calls this place his eternal home. Even suicides are welcome. It wasn't always that way; for centuries they were strictly *persona non grata* on holy ground. As long as you have the funds, there's a place for everyone here—as long as there are still plots available, that is.

Buried near Thomas Whaley is Alonzo E. Horton, another local household name (the Horton Plaza mall is named for him). He's the person who first proposed to the settlement of San Diego that groundbreaking begin on a new public cemetery. Before then, and even after, small cemeteries were popping up all over the area—at least one hundred of them accounting for thousands of bodies, many with no records of death or birth. One of the only ways we even find out about these old cemeteries now is when someone is putting in a sprinkler system and hits a femur or skull with their shovel. Only a few dozen of the originals remain today. Horton made the proposal in 1869, and a year later the first interment took place. Mount Hope Cemetery was established outside the growing city for health reasons—bodies had a way of leaching into the water supply because embalming hadn't quite yet caught on, coffins didn't have the permanent seals they have today, and cement vaults were not required. The founders believed it would take a while for the population to grow around the large cemetery property.

The Beautiful Stranger's gravesite. Note the focus anomaly: the engraving on the stone is blurry, as if there was something over it that caused it to be out of focus. The hole below the stone, however, is perfectly in focus.

The cemetery has grown to 169 acres, with no room left to expand. It sits side-by-side with Greenwood Cemetery, a private cemetery and mortuary (they share a fence line) founded in 1907. Mount Hope plots that originally sold for $5–$20—nothing to shake a stick at back then—now cost a minimum of $1,700 if you buy online with a 15 percent broker's fee (not including all the other death accoutrements, which will easily heap on another $10,000).

Although Mount Hope is a lovely place, it's not in the safest of neighborhoods. In February 2012, a man was stabbed near the cemetery and left for dead. He was transported to the hospital, where he died a half hour later. Recently, the neighborhood received funding to install solar floodlights on peoples' homes to keep crime down. The area has beautiful Victorians of all sizes, and I expect that one day, in about forty years or so, the area will be gentrified like the rest of San Diego's outlying neighborhoods.

It's a beautiful setting, though, and one you wouldn't expect to be disturbed by the silent commuter trolley that glides right through the center of the cemetery on rails. The jam-packed trolley is in curious juxtaposition to the marble angels.

In the 1970s, six hundred tombstones were removed from Calvary Pioneer Park, dumped in Mount Hope's ravine, and bulldozed over (see Calvary Cemetery/Pioneer Park chapter). The headstones were left in piles for eighteen years until there was public outcry. Eighteen headstones were then cemented into the ground next to where the trolley passes by, at the foot of a steep cliff on the cemetery property.

My Ghosts Happen Meetup group held "family day" at Mount Hope, where members' friends and families could get to know each other, go through and learn the history of the park— and the kids could all play with each other and run through the grass, trees, and tombstones like in the good ol' days. In the 1800s, when the first large urban cemeteries were designed by gifted architects on the East Coast, the properties served as many major cities' first public parks and housed the finest American art of the time, created by now-famous names. Many cemeteries, such as Green-Wood Cemetery in Brooklyn, New York, founded in 1838, opened their grand gates to the public on the weekends and charged an entry fee for those wishing to hear band music, eat picnic lunches, and stroll through the grounds. For many, it was a welcome break from the crowded cities filled with garbage and pollution from burning coal. Today, Green-Wood still holds events for the public, such as tours, author lectures, and concerts, and puts those funds toward rehabilitating the marble tombstones and statuary being destroyed by lichen, slime, and sooty mold—a problem in all old cemeteries.

My husband, Jeff, and I brought our youngest daughter to play with the other children in the group. It was a beautiful day for a stroll through the park. Roadside Paranormal case manager and investigator, Leo Aréchiga, brought his four children along.

"Our group was having a family outing at the historic Mount Hope Cemetery. Carmen, my beautiful wife, came along and the grown-ups were in the children's section talking and looking at the older gravestones," Leo recalls. "At some point, two of my kids had walked off to explore by themselves when I heard my ten-year-old daughter call out for me. I looked over and she insisted I come quickly. I walked toward them and they came running to meet me. Both my daughter and her nine-year-old brother had serious looks on their faces. The story that followed still haunts my children to this day.

"According to my two kids, they were walking in the same direction on opposite sides of the street," Leo continues. "My son was heading toward a certain grave to read the inscription, and his sister decided to join him. Now, I don't know if *something* was drawing them closer, or it was just coincidence that both of them were walking to that same dead child's resting place, but as they grew closer to it, my son felt *something* stop him in full stride and push him back! It scared him to the point were he couldn't speak while he tried to make sense of what had just happened to him. The sensation he felt was that someone or something pushing back on his shoulders so that he couldn't take another step! He wasn't only stopped, he was pushed back and fell. As I listened to him tell me his story, I'll admit I was a bit skeptical. But, my daughter had witnessed the whole thing. She saw an invisible force stop her brother dead in his tracks, then watched him fall back. When my daughter ran to him, with fear on his face he said, 'Something pushed me!' I strongly discourage my children from lying, and I'm convinced that they truly had a paranormal experience that day."

In my own experiences, I've found plenty of paranormal evidence during the day at Mount Hope, and I find it much easier to keep track of the equipment instead of looking around in the dark for it. Apparently, it's also much safer. One day, one of Roadside Paranormal's lead investigators, Jennifer Donohue, and I went out to the cemetery. We were walking through the parklike setting when she and I broke off in different directions. I went over a hill by the headstones that have been placed by the trolley car rails, and she was on the hill above conducting EVP sessions. It was an overcast day, and what I've noticed on days like that is that sound travels oddly when copious amounts of negative ions are present.

I was taking pictures at the bottom of the cemetery's bluff, and all of a sudden I heard what sounded like a woman's jovial laughter. I thought someone was right behind me. But no one was there. Then I thought maybe Jennifer had run into some kind of crazy, laughing woman wandering the cemetery. Just then, Jennifer called down to me, but I couldn't quite hear her. I called up I'd be right there.

"I heard a man's loud laughter behind me. It was so loud and random. I nearly jumped over the bluff when I ran up to the edge and called down," Jennifer says of the incident. "I looked over the bluff and shouted out. I wanted to know if anyone else had heard it."

I went up the bluff to see what was up. Jennifer asked me if I'd heard someone laughing—it took us a minute to figure out I'd heard a woman laugh, and she'd heard a man. The spirit I heard just sounded like she was having a really good belly laugh, but it did scare the hell out of me—sounded like it was right behind me. We looked around—the park had just opened, no one else was anywhere near where we were.

"I had my recorder on," Jennifer says. "I was doing EVPs. I headed back to the tombstone I'd left my recorder on—I just kept thinking, *Glad I had my recorder on!* I went to play it and found out my recorder went off—right in the middle of my sound file. I'd not been holding the recorder at the time; it was propped up on an old tombstone. Neither of the laughs was audible.

"I pulled out the batteries and checked them," Jennifer continues. "They're the kind that you can touch and it tells you how much battery life you have left. The batteries were fine. I'd just put them in *that* morning. They were new and had only been running about an hour. The recorder had not been turned off, the recording had been ended, pretty tough to do, as I usually have to be quite precise in ending a file. Were they mocking us? Maybe. Were they trying to scare us? Perhaps. All I know is that the laughter I heard sounded genuine. As long as they were having a good time, I think it's all good. They made contact with us, so there was certainly something they wanted to convey. I've been doing this a long time, and the EVPs I usually get are so morose, mad, sad, or pathetic sounding—they're looking for help, or giving one-word answers. This was something special. I like to think they're having a good time wherever they are, and this gave me food for thought about the subject. Maybe death isn't so bad after all."

Roadside Paranormal investigator Michelle Myers was at Mount Hope with people from some other teams when they became aware of something much more disturbing than the experiences Donohue and I had.

"During our walk through the cemetery, we kept getting glimpses of low shadows darting between bushes and behind tombstones," says Michelle. "At one point, we heard a low growling. Later we broke up into two groups, my group set up with digital recorders and a video camera next to Kate Morgan's grave [see Hotel del Coronado chapter]. About twenty minutes into the investigation, my lead investigator stood up to meet the other lead investigator, who was walking toward us, then stopped next to a tree. I saw the figure she went to meet and didn't think anything of it until she hurried back to us and grabbed her walkie-talkie. When she'd reached the place she thought others were standing, there was no one there. She radioed the other lead, and he reported he had not left his investigation site on the other side of a hill, which his group members confirmed. When both groups met back together, the other group also reported having seen and heard figures around them as well."

Despite the paranormal activity here and the sometimes disturbing aftermath of Santería rituals (sacrificed animals and candles), I've found walking the rows at both Mount Hope and the cemetery next to it, a lot of residents still enjoy the parklike atmosphere during the day and go for walks there. It's ideal for kids: green grass, shade, and mysterious gravestones to read— and you won't usually find pedophiles there like you have to worry about at the parks. My daughter and I stopped by one day to take photos. I'd gotten her a point-and-click camera easy enough for her five-year-old hands to use, and she was eager to get to work. She walked up to a mom with two children and asked her how old her children were and if she could take pictures of them. The mother told her one was six and the other seven, and encouraged her to play with them.

I introduced myself, and she invited me to sit down and have a juice box and almonds. She told me that she'd lived nearby in a house that belonged to her parents. Four generations of her family had lived nearby since the early 1900s. The house where she was living was an older, smaller Victorian, and when her parents moved to Santa Clara, they asked her family to live there until they decided to come back.

I asked her if she'd ever seen any ghosts in the cemetery and she laughed. She told me when she was a child her grandparents would take her there to play; apparently on nice days some of the old-timers would bring chairs and a table and set up a chess game. The women would come over later with a late lunch, and the children would play all day there. Her great-grandmother had always given them plenty of warnings not to run around the tombstones and always made her bring her rosary in her pocket when she went to the cemetery . . . she'd always wondered about that. One day she asked her great-grandmother why.

Her great-grandmother told her about a child who'd come with his mother and her friends from New Town, now San Diego's downtown, in the late 1800s by wagon. They had friends in the area they would visit every so often. One day the boy had been roughhousing with some of the other boys. The boy's foot hit a tombstone as he ran, and he flew over the tombstone, hitting his head very hard on the corner of another tombstone. His mother was tending to him with a wet towel on his head to clean up the blood and bring down the swelling. She put his head in her lap and he fell asleep. No one knows why, but the child died in his sleep within an hour or so. The cemetery director felt so badly for the mother that he gave her a grave, coffin, and tombstone free of charge. The mother was consumed with grief, and a month later she rode her horse out to the cemetery and hung herself.

The mother had been a poor single parent whose sailor husband had died on a ship and had been buried at sea. The cemetery director recognized the dead woman as the woman who had lost her son the month before, so he gave her a secret burial in the children's section in the same plot as her son. He did not supply a tombstone, however, as it would have enraged other parents if they found out that a suicide had been buried in the children's section.

The woman told me that she'd not seen any ghosts at the cemetery. She mentioned that when her daughter was about three, she told her mother that she saw other children in the cemetery all the time and would talk about her "friends" to her father when they got home. When her mother mentioned that she'd not seen any other children that day, her daughter was adamant about them. The woman said that her daughter stopped seeing them around the time she turned five. She called the children over and gave them all juice boxes, and she showed me what her daughter was wearing around her neck. She laughed and pulled out what was on the cord. It looked like a vintage rosary. "I guess old habits die hard," she said and tucked it back under her daughter's T-shirt.

CHAPTER 7

Cabrillo Bridge
SAN DIEGO

Dirt hiking trails go beneath the underbelly of the Cabrillo Bridge, where there is reported residual and intelligent paranormal activity.

The sumptuous proportions, the proud dignity of the bridge, encourage great expectations, and one is not disappointed. While admiration is aroused for the engineering skill that made this bridge possible, the thought persists that the real architect of this colossal concrete viaduct was a much higher power than the official engineer.

—Eugen Neuhaus, Professor Emeritus,
UC Berkeley and San Francisco Art Institute,
from the book *The San Diego Garden Fair*, 1916

IF YOU LIVE IN SAN DIEGO you're no doubt famil-
iar with the Cabrillo Bridge that extends from Balboa Park and
serves as an overpass to the major freeway. Visible from Highway 163, the majestic high arches were stunning feats of civil
engineering for California in 1915. I couldn't imagine the route
to Balboa Park without it. One of San Diego's few iconic structures, the bridge has survived earthquakes, fires, reconstruction,
and even the increased weight of constant traffic; the bridge was
originally built for pedestrians.

The engineers could not have foreseen the auto traffic that
would crowd the bridge, nor could they have envisioned the suicides that would take place there with leapers' bodies hitting
oncoming traffic below. The bridge's safety railings were not
installed until 1950, and even today they don't cover the entire
span. Determined jumpers who want the San Diego city skyline
as their last view still jump from the bridge—or at least hold up
traffic for several hours until they are coaxed down.

Although you'd never guess by looking at the bridge, it seems
to have been a magnet for bad energy over the years. Some places
are like this—the Golden Gate Bridge, for instance. People on
the ledge about suicide seem to tempt fate by going to places
with easy access to a big drop that will end their excruciating
dilemma, although survivors of Golden Gate suicide attempts
all say they regretted the action the moment their hands let
loose of the rail. There are only two people who survived a jump
from the Cabrillo Bridge. One survivor landed in the man-made
lagoon below (before Highway 163 was built under it), and the
other became a paraplegic. In 1935, after hearing there had been
survivors, one man who didn't want to take chances on surviving actually hung himself from the bridge.

Built at a cost of $225,154, the bridge is 1,505 feet long and
roughly 120 feet high and was constructed in anticipation of the
Panama-California Exposition, a two-year event that took place

when San Diego's population was only 36,000. The bridge is the main access across Cabrillo Canyon, land formerly known as Pound Canyon, where horses and cows grazed in the late 1800s. The Laguna de Puente, a lagoon that once pooled underneath the bridge, was created by city workers and supported wildlife, including deer (I've lived here for eight years and have not seen a single one within the county) and small animals. It wasn't long before the Department of Health drained the lagoon because of the incredible amount of mosquito larvae found there.

Entering Balboa Park from the west on the bridge, visitors are greeted by giant century plants and San Diego's coat of arms mounted on the crown archway entering the inner park. The archway is designed with reliefs of Doric-order architecture and icons of the Atlantic and Pacific, which represent the joining of the two oceans by the Panama Canal. Everything you see at Balboa Park today was saved due to the philanthropic hearts (and deep pockets) of San Diegans who invested heavily in restoration. The world-class San Diego Zoo was created by one of those mitzvahs—a dentist heard the abandoned animals roaring for food (their keepers had just left them locked up when the exposition ended) and designed a plan to create the zoo. Big-name help also came to the aid of the park. Before Balboa Park was built, this area was home to the Tipai-Kumeyaay tribe. The Kumeyaay tribe now owns the US Grant Hotel—Ulysses S. Grant, Jr., the president's son, was on the board that commissioned Balboa Park for the exposition. Indeed, things do come full circle.

Cabrillo Bridge is a beautiful site in the daytime, but night is when things from the other side of the veil are noticed more frequently, only because most of the tourists have left and traffic has slowed. I believe paranormal activity can be seen all the time, as I often catch evidence during the day. I suggest visiting this location, at least for the first time, during the day. I won't hide the fact that this bridge has seen more than fifty suicides in her time, a few tragic murders, and even an airplane crash. This is a dodgy place to hang out after the sun goes down, so think personal safety when you're there and be aware of your surroundings.

In my paranormal investigations, I've found if there's any Native American residual energy, it's usually peaceful. It's not only the spirits of jumpers we were looking for during my team's investigations. People are murdered in and around Balboa, and accidents occur. In addition to several workers killed during construction of the park, "Sky Dragon" Joe Bocquel died in the crash of his pusher biplane beside the Cabrillo Bridge on November 4, 1916, while performing at the Exposition. Fatal car, pedestrian, and bike accidents are common on nearby Sixth Avenue and on Highway 163. So, is this bridge/park a beacon for negative energy? Did something occur on this land so long ago that it caused the area to forever be a portal for unnatural deaths? I do get a sense of dread just walking across the bridge, and walking under it is one of the most depressing feelings I've ever had.

In May 1994, a young actor from The Old Globe Theatre was killed in a random drive-by shooting as he walked across the bridge with his girlfriend. In the 1930s, a young woman was stabbed nine times by a culprit believed to be the Coast Fiend Serial Killer in the nearby Balboa Park parking lot, close to one of the investigation sites we set up.

On September 14, 1984, two San Diego police officers, including the first woman in the department to die in the line of duty, went into "end of watch" status—a phrase emergency workers use to describe death on the job—where far too many of our police officers go.

The officers removed two girls, aged fifteen and sixteen, from the company of two men in their mid-twenties. The men were drunk, and a later investigation showed that they had also

The last view for many is the San Diego downtown skyline and oncoming traffic on Highway 163. The guard railing on this bridge (visible on the right) ends before it spans the entire length of the bridge. Many have campaigned to have it extended. The Cabrillo Bridge has seen too much tragedy.

asked the girls to take methamphetamine that they provided. Making sure the girls were safe in their unit car before they went any further, the officers went about checking the men out and were in the process of writing misdemeanor tickets when the older of the two men, Joselito Cinco, wanted for several outstanding warrants, shot and killed the officers at point-blank range. Cinco tried to take the teens from the car, but they ran to the safety of an overturned picnic bench where an older couple was hiding. The second suspect, who was unarmed, became frightened and tried joining the group hiding under the bench, but was turned away by the couple. Police backup arrived and the officers apprehended the men. Cinco was held without bond and charged with two counts of first-degree murder with special circumstances, making him eligible for the death penalty. He was convicted and sentenced to death but decided to commit suicide before justice could be served.

A 1986 cold-case murder (which happened not too far away from our investigation site), was recently solved in 2007 when four men were arrested for the rape and murder of a thirty-seven-year-old woman. The incident occurred when a woman and two male friends were approached by seven men who attacked, robbed, and tied them up. The men dragged the woman off to a canyon south of the golf course, where they raped and killed her. The women's two friends survived. In 2007, the murderer was tracked via DNA that finally matched one of the men when he was put into the system for a crime. The men were arrested and charged for their crimes. The crime rate inside the park is infamous and was even highlighted in the opening scene of T. Jefferson Parker's novel *The Fallen,* in which a San Diego Ethics Commission director is found murdered in his SUV on a dirt road near the bridge.

"I didn't know anything at all about the Cabrillo Bridge in San Diego when I set out to write *The Fallen* in 2005," says T. Jefferson Parker. "All I knew is that it was stately and elegant, and it was built as part of Balboa Park for the [Panama-California] Exposition in 1915, and that I'd drive under it every time I went to the airport. I read in the *San Diego Union-Tribune* that a homeless man had been found living within the bridge and of course evicted. I didn't know about its haunted, bloody past at all. It's a beauty, and I love it even more now that I know about its shady, spooky history. Maybe it was just a gut-level instinct that made me set that murder under the Cabrillo Bridge."

Balboa Park is visited by thirteen million visitors a year and is patrolled in the day by San Diego Police—unfortunately, its loyal horse patrol was auctioned off to the highest bidder and replaced by ATVs. In the daytime, you rarely have the chance to be alone, as many buildings house more than a dozen museums, and others are the headquarters for organizations such as the San Diego History Center, where you can find more background on just about all the San Diego locations listed in this book.

My Ghosts Happen group conducted several investigations here, including two outdoor-safety-certification events (certification is vital to be included in private investigations). Our goal for this particular certification was to note the ability of the candidates to remain calm and see how members responded when confronted in uncontrolled locations. The second goal was to investigate and make note of any paranormal activity—and, of course, to be able to capture any useful evidence in such an area. The third part of the training was all about safety during a night investigation in rugged terrain, as the pathway gets quite rugged, especially if you're not wearing the proper footwear.

Just before you pass over the El Prado entrance from Sixth Avenue is Nate's Point Dog Park, filled from sunup to sundown with the happiest dogs in San Diego. On the backside of the dog park from the bridge is an unmarked, unlocked gate that leads to the dirt hiking trails that take you under the bridge, adjacent to Highway 163 (the highway is fenced off from the area where the trail goes). Homeless people frequent this area, and it's believed that one of them started the fire inside a hollow bridge column that could have destroyed the entire bridge. The fire smoldered for several hours but was extinguished when firemen drilled holes into the bridge and filled them with water. The bridge's old wood was finally removed and replaced with steel.

The area is noisy even in the early-morning hours. It has an incredible creepy factor. I once found a dated, crumpled note that could have been a suicide letter. When I looked up the date later, I could find no record of a jumper on or near that date, so I assume whomever it was just decided to live instead. Perhaps the words weren't strong enough to be a *goodbye world*, but maybe he was a passive, would-be jumper. I primarily thought it a suicide note because of its obvious location. It read, "You knew you shouldn't have started what you started. It cost a lot more than you could have imagined." Then it had some expletives and was simply signed—Mark.

The team picked up some EMF spikes and some eerie sounds on their recorders, but the digital audio couldn't even be enhanced enough to single out what we thought were noises because of the traffic constantly swooshing by. As a medium, I did pick up a whole lot of anguish and anxious emotions, as did the other sensitives who were with us. Some inaudible voices made a few of us turn around and say, "What?" and find that no one had said anything.

Megan Meadows, a Ghosts Happen assistant organizer and Roadside Paranormal member, says, "There sure is a difference from walking through Balboa Park at night and in the day. You can really feel the weight of suffering under that bridge."

Once you investigate under the bridge and go into the area on the other side of the bridge, there are several sloped canyons where you can definitely feel you are no longer alone—remember, at Balboa Park, it's not the dead who can hurt you.

"Our team conducted a late-night investigation of Cabrillo Bridge when the car traffic and noise would be at its lowest," says Michelle Myers, a member of Ghosts Happen and Roadside Paranormal. "We did not have any visual experiences, but we did take time out to conduct EVP sessions to pick up any spirits that may be lingering in the area. We did not hear anything at the time of that investigation, but when reviewing the recordings later, distinctive drumming was audible in the background. None of the team members heard anything that sounded remotely like it during the actual investigation."

The drumming sounded like music that would be made by Native Americans and was clearly audible under our conversation. On another investigation, I captured an EVP with an odd sound that sounded like a voice saying "Hup!" several times. I attributed it to a hiccup, or some sound from our team, but no one made note of it, and I make an audible note if someone else making a noise during an EVP session does not. What I found in doing later research (thus proving you can never do enough research) is that the Mohave Indians, associated with our local tribes, did a tribal dance that had the word *hup* in it. The Tutomunp dance song originated with the Mohave Indians and was sung at sunset. *Hup* translates to "We are going on. We have a long way to go."

CHAPTER 8

Proctor Valley Road
CHULA VISTA

Shadow people (see Spotlight On: Shadow People) are a common
paranormal phenomenon on Proctor Valley Road. I imagine that they
are either created or drawn to the substation next to the lonesome road.
Either that, or we're all suffering from hallucinations due to the high
EMF, which is just as probable as shadow people existing.

PROCTOR VALLEY ROAD . . . the name doesn't sound
all that frightening, but day or night there are really weird
things happening on this particular stretch of lonely road. The
surrounding McMansions built in the last decade have pushed
the wildlife farther into the county's open spaces, and when the
county built trails in those areas, lots of people hiked and biked
there. Now, most creatures only come out at night.

I'd heard plenty of urban myths about the area before going out there—*lots*. Stories that go back decades in Southern California's gestalt about Proctor Valley Road and chupacabras, Bigfoot, the Proctor Valley Monster, UFOs, aliens, and the mysterious glowing lady who flags down cars driving on the dirt road. There's also the woman wearing the blue nightgown lying in a fetal position on the road until you slow down, and she gets up to frantically flag you over. The part of Proctor Road I'm telling you about is only a mile-long dirt road connected on either side by paved sections of Proctor Valley Road, but you never know what's around the next blind curve.

It's an infamous place for teenagers to neck and is also a popular location for gang members to hang, if the tags on the underbelly of Highway 125 and Proctor Valley Road are any indication. This part of Proctor Valley Road is short, but there are other pieces of Proctor Valley Road that don't really connect with other pieces of the same road. Even if you planned it, you couldn't have made a more confusing road; it's all quite random. The GPS in the car, my two handheld GPS devices, my cell phone GPS app, and the Google map on my iPad were all taking me in different directions. After 9/11 many GPS blackout locations were declared around the country, and this is one of them. It can't be located with Google GPS because of its proximity to the San Diego Gas & Electric power substation on the road. I'm probably on some government list right now for looking at it so intensely from satellite devices, especially since I was looking at how close it is to the Mexican border. To get there, you must pay a $3 toll twice on Highway 125, unless you know a shortcut that bypasses the toll road. There are no signs posted on Proctor Valley Road other than NO DUMPING.

Before you go, study Google Maps and note the overpasses in the area on Highway 125 in Chula Vista. Also Google the Miguel SD&GE substation and you'll get a general location, but without street names. Zoom in to street level and you'll be able to locate a gravel road somewhat close by.

I'd seen the strange Proctor Valley Road videos on YouTube, which have really grown those urban myths to full bloom. I finally decided to see what was going on and arranged a pre–team investigation scouting with Megan Meadows, fellow team member of Roadside Paranormal. Late one weeknight we headed out there with Bulova, former canine agent wounded in crossfire (he now lives with me), who comes along on many of our dodgier investigations when the likelihood of meeting up with danger-ous humans is far greater than finding anything paranormal.

The odds of actually finding some sort of wildlife, including cougars and coyotes, are actually pretty good, considering the nearby food source of small groomed pets in the posh gated com-munities nearby and the water supplies in the Sweetwater Reser-voir and Lower Otay Lake only a few miles away. The trickle of a tiny creek on one side road (on the open-space side) can be heard if you're outside your car. On part of the road by the bridge, wildlife sounds are replaced with the hair-raising buzz of five-hundred-kilovolt lines going into the substation from Arizona. There are lots of blind turns on this loose gravel road—and cars exceeding the speed limit—not to mention potholes. If you find a car, you'll be lucky if it has its lights on, as people often go out here to neck and turn all the lights off and are completely oblivious to their surroundings. Both day and night, the likelihood of being hit and killed by a car if you're either a pedestrian or driver is high if you're not very careful. If you are prone to any kind of EMF-sensitivity headaches, bring your Motrin along. The EMF along this road is high, and if it doesn't give you headaches, or even if it does, there is a chance of it causing auditory and visual hallucinations. Or it may be that the things you are feeling and hearing are real.

"The area was pretty desolate and very dark," Megan says of the road. "There is a lot of chaparral growing beside the road, and as we drove away from the overpass the road turned to gravel. We spotted the carcass of a goat in the headlights, although we weren't really sure what it was when we first saw it. We got out of the van and Bulova went directly to it. I took a closer look with our flashlight, picking out the golden-white coat of the goat. The carcass was flat, devoid of any blood, muscle—anything. It looked like something had sucked everything out of it and left it flat and missing some pieces. We both felt like were being watched by something in the trees located in the open-space area."

Bloodless goat carcasses are said to be the calling cards of the chupacabra. When Bulova started growling at the trees, we hightailed it back inside the van and locked the doors. It almost felt like the goat had been put there to make us stop and get out. They say high EMF (you know, that whole "fear cage" theory—the physiological effect of electromagnetic fields on the mind and body that causes agitation, fear, paranoia, headaches, and even hallucinations) makes you paranoid, and we were definitely feeling it.

We went out again for another night investigation and took ten members of my Meetup group Ghosts Happen. There was no traffic, and we walked as a group. Many members of the group reported that they saw shadows dart in and out of the moonlight by the substation.

"It's along this gravel stretch that evidence and reports of chupacabra activity have been made," says Michelle Myers, a member of Roadside Paranormal. "We went to find evidence of chupacabras, and though we did not encounter a goat-sucker, we did witness a spectral figure advancing toward us on the road. Several of the team, including myself, saw the same image of a tall, hulking man in a dark shadow form walking slowly in our direction, coming out from a freeway underpass. In turn, we shone our flashlights in its direction, but the light seemed to be

Michelle Myers and I examined several of these primordial-looking creatures after I dug them out of the gully and flipped them onto the road. What on earth were these huge creatures doing in the desert? Proctor Valley Road holds many secrets.

absorbed into it. Some of the more daring team members tried chasing after it, but it would disappear each time. The shadow figure didn't seem threatening and moved slowly. The image of those broad shoulders and thick arms stay rooted in my mind, though I don't recall having a scared or anxious feeling from the sighting."

I also saw that same figure and I felt that it was pursuing us. This solid figure would just disappear from the center of the road with all of us watching. We tried to record it, but it was about sixty feet away from us, and our IR wouldn't shoot that far. Later on that evening some of the team, including myself, went out to explore the desert area between Otay Ranch and Jamul, where we four-wheeled out into the desert and found piles of big, empty TV boxes and bricks. We also found some kind of strange dragon statue sitting on one of the boxes. It looked like the perfect setting for a meth-maker's dump, so after opening one of the boxes, I decided it probably wasn't a good idea after all.

On a recent daytime investigation to Proctor Valley Road, Michelle and I went to find further evidence of the elusive chupacabra. What we found was almost as weird as what we'd been hearing. Off the road, under the bushes in a gully, we saw what looked like spines, but they also looked like palm tree debris. I went into the ravine and dug them out and tossed them up to the road. They were huge skeletons of six fish that would have easily weighed more than sixty pounds with flesh on them. The fish had teeth, and there was no natural source from which they could have come from in the area.

You never know what you're going to find on Proctor Valley Road. So give up your expectations of anything specific, and I think you'll find something worthwhile. It is truly the Twilight Zone of Southern California.

Spotlight On:
Shadow People

Some researchers believe shadow people are evil entities, often found at the scene of "bad hauntings." These same people, for the most part, also believe in demons that have the ability to harm and kill people. Personally, as a Spiritualist medium, I believe in dark energy, but I don't give that darkness a name such as the devil. Other investigators contend that shadow people are visitors from other planets or parallel universes studying our behavior. I believe this theory ties in with their ability to time travel and traverse through parallel worlds.

So why do we notice shadow people at night? Let's just say they are visitors from another parallel universe, or even outer space, who come to observe our behavior. In reviewing digital video of shadow people, I've noticed that what gives them away is when they step into the smallest amount of light, even into a shadow that is only slightly lighter—their disguise is completely blown. And somehow, they always know they've been detected and quickly dodge behind something else. We've all seen the YouTube videos capturing shadow people (if not, Google them). Perhaps they're even smarter than we think and revealing themselves on purpose . . . now there's a thought to ponder.

Scientifically speaking, creating reflection is much easier than creating absence of light (darkness). For instance, you can hide in a room where the lights have all been turned off, but you may only be able to partially hide in that same room when a shaft of light is coming through an open door. It's hard to make that light go away unless you create a vacuum of darkness and close the door. There are no flashlights that create darkness. But in that same room—let's say it's a ballroom—it would be easier to hide during the day.

So many people walk into a room where there are mirrored walls and actually believe it's a larger room. For this next example, I need you to think like a magician. If you wanted to hide in this mirrored room during the day (and perhaps only stay hidden for a fraction of a second like shadow people do), you could probably just put a well-placed mirror up in front of yourself. It would probably just cause the person walking into the room a split second of confusion, but people wouldn't go out of the room screaming they'd seen an alien. They wouldn't know what they'd seen, and that would probably be the last time they thought about it . . . the rational mind at work.

Think of Harry Potter's invisibility cloak as I describe the technology involved in actually creating an invisibility cloak of sorts. How would it work? It has to have ease of movement and be nearly weightless. The battery it uses must have a large storage capacity (graphics take up a lot of processing, which in turn uses battery power like crazy) and not be too heavy. It must be loaded with supercomputing processing ability but still be light. It must be able to detect any surface area (color, pattern, texture) near you and translate it instantly onto your cloak. It would also need to keep out heat or dispel it naturally so as not to be detected by thermal imaging. These qualities and abilities transfer into what shadow people would need if they were time travelers or aliens and wanted to get around to spy on us.

My technology-based work brings me in contact with many interesting scientific projects and the brilliant scientists creating them. Creating physical anonymity—the ability to become invisible—is a dream for the United States government, which would use the technology to conceal soldiers and their transport. In working with technology organizations after 9/11, I saw Homeland Security and InQtel (the CIA's venture arm) funnel many, many millions into companies such as DuPont and organizations such as NASA to create superior weapons of war, but they don't seem to have come as far as they'd hoped in a decade. There was beta technology that showed promise—fabric embedded with billions of nano-cameras that detect and emulate a pattern in a background and reflect it immediately as its camouflage—but the devil is in the details.

Shadow people also seem to be able to camouflage physical characteristics such as temperature. For instance, a paranormal investigative team may detect a shadow person on digital imaging equipment but not temperature-sensing devices. Shadow people seem to be able to hide thoughts and emotions. As a medium and psychic, I have never picked up anything from a shadow person (that I know of), and I have stories from at least another dozen mediums/psychics who claim no telepathic contact from the shadow people they've encountered. However, I have spoken to many mediums and psychics who believe in the devil and evil and have become quite fearful in places where shadow people have been seen. Whether their minds are projecting the fear or they are actually sensing something is anyone's guess.

Physiologically speaking, our eyes detect nuance in color because our primordial lizard brains and peripheral vision have been honed over human evolution to detect and warn us of things that might be an oncoming threat. Our eyes also catch movement, especially fast movement. Across the board, people who've seen shadow people say they are damn fast. So we are able to sense shadow people because they cannot travel undetected against lighter shades, and they move quickly enough to trigger our survival instincts. By the way, some believe shadow people's speed is due to their coming from parallel universes, traveling at much faster speeds than our own.

Some theories about shadow people state that they are not residual energy at all. Nor are they the spirits of once-living humans, visiting aliens, or time travelers, but rather elemental creatures. Elementals are mythological beings that first appeared in print in the alchemical works of Paracelsus, a respected Renaissance physician, botanist, alchemist, astrologer, and occultist. In Paracelsus's belief system, there were four types of elemental energies: *gnomes* (earth elementals), *undines*, such as water nymphs (water elementals), *sylphs* and *fairies* (air elementals), and *salamanders* (fire elementals). During his time, the salamander was believed to have magical traits that allowed it to regenerate from fire.

Although many of his ideas may seem far-fetched today, Paracelsus was no quack. He's credited with identifying and naming *zink*, the element we now know as zinc. He held high positions at universities, wandered the world in search of hidden knowledge, and is now given credit for providing the first clinical/scientific description of the unconscious.

I feel that individuals should search their own belief systems, knowledge databases, and experiences to develop their own unique thoughts on shadow people. Only by sharing these ideas can we keep this research moving forward and learn scientific ways to capture the phenomena.

Northern and Eastern San Diego

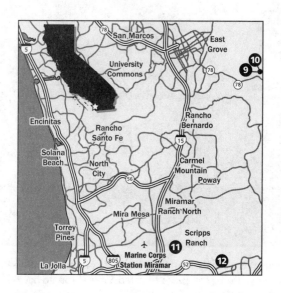

Lakeside
Ghost Rider of State Route 67 **(12)**

Poway
Los Peñasquitos Creek Arch Bridge **(11)**

San Pasqual Valley
San Pasqual Battlefield State Historic Park **(9)**
San Pasqual Cemetery **(10)**

CHAPTER 9

San Pasqual Battlefield State Historic Park
SAN PASQUAL VALLEY

The San Pasqual Battlefield memorial has a lot of paranormal—and wildlife—activity. It's a great place to catch EVPs if you go back far enough (to get away from traffic sounds), but be careful of the heron that guards the place (he's under the large oak). This is the entrance that can be seen from Highway 78.

PEOPLE DON'T OFTEN ASSOCIATE the state of California with bloody battlefields, yet they pass by them every day. The San Pasqual Battlefield State Historic Park is one such location at the crossroads of Highway 78 and Ysabel Creek Road in San Pasqual, the battlefield is marked by a stone wall dividing it from the highway. It consists of a museum, monuments, and a battlefield, and many who go to visit are schoolchildren learning about California history. I'd passed by the battlefield at least twenty times before I realized there was something really wrong with the energy in that area. Having visited historic battlefields on the East Coast, I recognized that there is something *different* about the energy where young men have been slaughtered and left to bleed out, alone, and die in the name of a cause. Something really *terrifying*.

I decided one day as I drove by and caught wind of this energy yet again that I would stop and see what seemed to be pulling me over. I parked on a dirt pullout off the two-lane highway and found the San Pasqual Battlefield State Historic Park (there's not much signage, and it's off the road and difficult to see). The park honors the soldiers who fought in the battle between United States and Californio forces on December 6, 1846, in the midst of the Mexican-American War. The park was hosting an upcoming reenactment, so I knew why the energy was so active; no one could ever be laid to rest as long as these memories were relived over and over. Do any of you battlefield fans ever wonder why battlefields are so haunted? How would you like your *excruciating* death reenacted on a regular basis? Most Civil War reenactors don't understand this concept. I've had friends who were reenactors, and whenever I would visit their homes I'd immediately be able to tell if they'd recently been in a "battle"—their homes would be filled with battlefield souls that would eventually leave. When I'd mention it, they'd tell me about the poltergeist activity going on in their dwelling. *Really?* Folks, these soldiers go home with you!

On the East Coast, one reenactor had a stroke on the battlefield and no one had noticed—they thought it was part of the reenactment. When the battle was over and he didn't get up, others ran to him. He lived, but he told the story of the *real* battle going on around him, seeing others being blown up by cannon fire and dead bodies stacking up. He described the souls of dead soldiers walking around him, pulling at him to get his soul out of his body. He fought them off. Understandably, he was terrorized by the experience and gave up reenactment all together, giving away all of his costly equipment and clothes and not wanting anything to do with it ever again. Others talk about realistic dreams of battles while sleeping at their reenactment camps. Those aren't dreams; those are spirits sharing their memories.

I was uncertain about what happened on the battlefield, and I was actually drawn to another property nearby. I walked into the fields opposite the area that had been previously described to me as the battlefield by one of the docents and found an area of sand; I imagined it being a riverbed at some point. There has been a lot of flooding in the middle of the valley. All of a sudden, as I looked out at the fields, I felt the wind knocked out of me. I fell to my knees. I closed my eyes and heard battlefield noises and guns firing and shouting that just consumed me. My heart was pounding loudly in my ears, and I felt compelled to hold my throat; my mind's eye saw blood pouring out of a wound. I leaned forward. My hands fell out before me and reached into the sand. Physically and mentally, I felt the terror those boys had gone through in California's bloodiest battle. Since that time, I've heard moaning, shouting, and even the sound of metal against metal, like swords hitting each other, that have made me physically flinch. I've also had lots of moments of nausea, but still I've returned. My experiences there are now much less traumatic, but I can't shake the feeling I'm being drawn there for a reason. As I write this, I can't help but think that many of the men there on both sides were Christians. Although it's not my own religion, perhaps next time I go back I will bring a minister to read some words over the field and perhaps bring them some closure.

What I felt in that sandbar that day felt like the terror of lost souls who would never be recognized and their torment never ended; the incident gave me nightmares for years until this month when I reached out to someone who would tell me why—oddly enough, that news would come from France.

Like many in America who have sought a better quality of life elsewhere, historian George Hruby became an expat and moved to Bordeaux. Before he became a Bordelais, he worked in San Diego law enforcement in many capacities, not only serving as a homicide detective but also finding and identifying the bodies of illegal aliens buried in deserted locations. He had heard about a soldier thought to be buried on Mule Hill in San Pasqual and brought to the search his skills in law enforcement—including his ability to sort through witness accounts and arrange them in priority by reliability. He searched through records written since 1846 to breathe life into the battle and the events surrounding it. I'd done some research on the San Pasqual Battlefield, but I'd not gotten too much help regarding why the area beyond the designated battlefield had such an emotional impact on me. In Hruby, I found an ally in my search for answers.

I described the location that I'd been drawn to over the years and its emotional effect on me in an e-mail to Hruby. To my relief, he wrote me back:

> The area you "felt" such things at is in the identified areas tagged as SLP-TS-7 and SLP-TS-8. [You may see the maps on his website, **sanpasqual.org,** to refer to the numbered locations]. I took the first psychic I encountered in my research involving the San Pasqual Battlefield to the location. Without her knowing any of the details about the location, she took off in the direction of sites seven and eight on her own. She reacted very emotionally while in these areas and very much

like you described—panic and terror at this location. The reason the both of you feel this way is because the American soldiers swept around the point into section SLP-TS-6 but were quickly overwhelmed by the enemy (120 Californios to less than 40 Americans). The Americans, on tired and broken-down mules, ran in retreat headed across identified sites 7 and 8, and broke up, all fleeing in different directions while being pursued by the Mexicans on outstanding horses. The pursuing Mexicans in the early morning darkness and fog followed with long lances, and almost four Mexicans to every one American. Each soldier was on his own and literally fleeing for his very life. Seventeen were killed in this area and another approximately fifteen wounded. That is why you picked up on this area.

Based on the history of what really happened to those boys on the battlefield, Hruby's research did a lot to both affirm and help me understand my emotional reactions to the area.

The Mule Hill Historical/San Pasqual Valley Agricultural Trail, at the crossroads of Ysabel Creek Road and Bandy Canyon Road, is a ten-mile open-space trail that gives visitors public access to parts of the battlefield. On a recent beautiful sunny afternoon, I arrived there to take pictures. There was a guy sitting in his old, creepy car staring at me when I got out of the Jeep with Bulova. He kept staring at me. Bulova sensed his hostility immediately and began growling and eyeing him back. He strained against his leash to make me aware of the threat. We walked over to the trailhead, and I began taking pictures of the area.

The guy gave me the creeps; his eyes never left me. Intuition kicked in. My rule is: *never* ignore intuition. So I walked toward his car and took a picture of him in his car with his license plate with my cell phone and messaged it to my husband, Jeff, letting him know where we were. My phone rang immediately, with Jeff calling to make sure we were okay; I kept him on the phone as the guy shouted some expletives and started getting out of his car. I gave Bulova the hand signal for *secure*—to him, that means get rid of the threat. He ran over to the car, and the guy backed right back into it immediately. Before he had a chance to close his door all the way, Bulova slammed his powerful front paws and nearly one hundred pounds of body weight against the door, slamming it shut, and viciously barked at the stranger with bared teeth through the open window. The man frantically rolled up his windows. I whistled Bulova back and the guy drove quickly away. Had I not had Bulova there, I don't know what the guy would have tried to pull. A paranormal investigator's best friend? A properly trained security dog.

The trail system of the open-space property goes to directly to Lake Hodges, where a convicted serial killer murdered teen Chelsea King in broad daylight on a much heavier traveled trail. You can never be too safe in any kind of deserted area.

At the start of this trail are a plaque that states YOU ARE HERE on the map and an *X* stating A SOLDIER IS BURIED UNDER THIS TREE. There is no longer a tree, but I imagine the spot is somewhere within fifty feet of the trailhead. I've been on this trail at all hours and have heard what sounded like gunfire, and I've been with others who've heard the same thing simultaneously. Since it's a rural area, it could have been gunshots. Perhaps neighbors shooting at trespassers? I've heard many disembodied voices while walking down the trail in this area, as have others I was with. There is a lot of agriculture going on in the surrounding the area, and sound travels oddly in the San Pasqual Valley. The voices most convincing to me have sounded like they'd come from within five feet of where I was walking. Bulova has also heard them. He has stopped, and, instead of following his instincts, which are to investigate, he has refused to go on in several places on the path, pulling me back toward the car with his leash.

Be aware that much of the land is privately owned and—without barriers or fence lines, or even homes—it's difficult to tell who owns what. I suggest using Google Maps with Street View (the little person icon you can place on the map). If the property is private, sometimes the roads will show just a blur instead of a street entrance, but this is usually the case only if someone has requested that Street View access be removed. I highly recommend formally asking for permission in areas that are not designated as open space, as private property offers many surprises, including but not limited to unfenced dogs that may take a bite out of you—and people with guns.

On the same side of the road as the San Diego Wild Animal Park is the San Pasqual Battlefield Memorial. There are several plaques placed there, including some that carry the names of the Americans who died in that battle. There is enough room for a few cars in the pullout, and a short stone wall surrounds the area. You can Google "San Pasqual Battlefield" and get down to Street View to see the place for yourself. When I last visited, the sun was going down in a brilliant golden light. A strange heron kept rushing me wherever I walked, and when I'd turn to face it, it would turn the other way and walk another direction. Then it'd chase me again as soon as I turned around. It's a great location to do an investigation in, and I've recorded EVPs here that have made my flesh crawl. None of them were understandable, but the tones of the voices gave me the willies.

Janine Haynes, cofounder and paranormal investigator at S.P.I.R.I.T. SoCal, visited the San Pasqual Battlefield recently with cofounder Chris Oliver. "Our team was investigating the Presidio mission museum when we came in contact with a male spirit through question-and-answer via our EMF detector," says Haynes. "We set up a system of 'blink once for yes and

two times for no' with the spirit. When I began to read off locations on the map hanging in the museum, the EMF detector
was silent—until I spoke of the San Pasqual Battlefield. Every
time I mentioned the battlefield, the EMF went crazy. We visited
the battlefield the next weekend.

"We have been investigating the San Pasqual area for only a
short time, but have found amazing activity there," says Haynes.
"Down by the war memorial, we heard what sounded like a group
of people running towards us and whispering. After investigating the area, we found we were the only ones there. The whispering continued off and on the entire time we were there. We
also caught an EVP that sounded like gunshots, which was cool
because we didn't hear them with our ears at the time. It was very
late and extremely dark, and as we began to walk up through the
stone gates, it had a sad feel to the area. We began to take photos
of the area and the monument that had been placed there. Suddenly, we heard what sounded like a group of people marching
down the hill towards us. The marching sounds became louder,
and I heard a voice say, 'Watch yourself.'

"When we went over our EVP session for the night, hoping to
have caught the voice on tape, we found the voice was not recorded,
but there were sounds of the marching as well as what sounded
like gunfire, yelling, and groaning sounds. We continue to investigate this location for more evidence. Most of what we experienced
seemed to be residual. Down the road by the museum portion
of the battlefield, we also heard very similar marching sounds.
It was very dark and as we walked up the hillside, we all came to
an immediate halt when we heard rustling in the bushes. Terri-
fied we were being stalked by a cougar, we stayed very still. We
decided to come back the next day before it got too dark so we
could make ourselves more familiar with the area. We descended
the hillside, and when we looked back up, I saw a man wearing
dark clothes and a black hat just up the hill where we'd just been.

Just as we made eye contact he disappeared. It was an amazing full-body apparition that was so real we thought it was a docent from the museum until he disappeared."

The area has been noted for its paranormal activity for a long while, and it is not just limited to soldiers who fought in battle. Native Americans had made the valley their home, and generations have lived and died there. To the unaware pass-erby, the San Pasqual Valley may be quiet and still except for the occasional traffic, but if you take the time to really feel the energy around you, I think you'll be surprised about what goes on around you.

CHAPTER 10

San Pasqual Cemetery
SAN PASQUAL VALLEY

San Pasqual Cemetery sits right off of Highway 78 near the Santa Ysabel Creek bridge. The cemetery is sandwiched between ranches where people do not hesitate to come over to see what disrespect is being done. Sound travels well here, so anything you say may sound like it's coming from only twenty feet away to them. I highly recommend visiting this site during daytime hours.

THIS CHAPTER PERFECTLY ILLUSTRATES how dangerous an investigation can be. How you can go off to an investigation and end up in a life-and-death situation you have no control over. Outdoor investigations are like that. This was my very first investigation with my fledgling team. We decided to go to San Pasqual Valley, an area near Escondido known for a bloody battle between Mexico and California in 1846.

Michelle Myers, Kim, and I met near the Wild Animal Park around 9 p.m. one summer night. The cemetery is difficult to locate in the dark if you've not been there before and have only vague directions from the Internet. The little store on Highway 78 burned to the ground in the last wildfire (our Internet directions told us how to get there from the store), so we didn't have too many landmarks to go by. We drove to and fro a few times over a two-mile stretch, and then the car in front of us swerved off and pulled over about half a mile ahead. We soon found the driver had left behind a mountain lion he'd hit while speeding. I stopped in the road, put my flashers on, and asked Michelle and Kim to wait in the car—after all, someone had to pull me back in the car and drive me to the hospital if the mountain lion decided to lash out at me in pain.

I approached the badly injured lion. I wanted to see if there was some way we could lift it and transport it safely. As I rested my hand on the lion's chest and told her it was going to be all right, the large cat opened her eyes, sprang up, and dragged herself into the bushes, disappearing into the night. In a matter of seconds, the encounter was over.

By then it was about 10:30 p.m. The guy who'd hit the cat had gotten out to see if his car was okay, got back in, and fled the accident scene . . . an illegal act in California. We looked up a fire station on a GPS and decided we'd get more help if we went there in person rather than calling a dispatcher. We needed to find the mountain lion and get her to an emergency wildlife hospital. We were hoping that the Wild Animal Park would have someone on duty who could help us. It was dark inside the firehouse, so I pounded loudly on the door of the fire station to wake up the firefighters. A woman came to the door first; she was the lead commander, and she and her battalion were training new people. Although it was late and we'd woken the firefighters up, she saw our situation as a good training opportunity; they were quite helpful and enthusiastic.

She woke her entire team, and they brought a thermal imaging gun—which I envied—with them. We rode in the fire trucks so we could show them where the accident had happened. They blocked off a large section of Highway 78, allowing only one lane open where they could flag people through. We walked the highway and off-road areas, and the firefighters went off into the gullies. I had my night-vision goggles on, but I couldn't find any trace of the lion. I imagined since the thermal gun couldn't locate the cat either, that she might have already gone into shock and died. Her body had probably lost heat quickly and was somewhere in the dry lower ravine area, where the temperature was still about 70 degrees; the thermal image of her, if she'd died, would be hard to differentiate from the warm weather.

They flooded the area with searchlights and two hours later, we still hadn't found the lion. Our night ended about 1 a.m., a miserable failure all around. I imagined the only way we'd be seeing the lion again is if we saw her ghost on the road at some point.

After the mountain lion incident, we'd gone out during the day and scoped out San Pasqual locations, and even stumbled upon what looked like an abandoned slaughterhouse above the road with the firehouse. We pulled over and looked around the old, vacant building covered with graffiti. We found the building intriguing. There were no NO TRESPASSING signs posted. There are a lot of gang tags in the small valley, and I'm not quite sure if they have any territorial significance, like you'd find in a large city, or are just art created by bored teens. About an eighth of a mile away is the San Pasqual Academy, a large cluster of buildings that make up the first-in-the-nation residential educational campus designed specifically for foster teens. The population of San Pasqual, as of 2010, was 370, with 23 people per square mile, many of them immigrant workers, children, and families.

As we explored the dark rooms of the slaughterhouse, the joke was on us. We continued looking around, and it became clear that the building had been used as some kind of Halloween horror house, or B-movie set; what we first thought were body parts were actually props (whew!). If we'd gone in at night, it would have made for a really terrifying scene, and we would have ended up at the fire department reporting a "murder."

Later, Kim and I went back to the building, which at sundown had seriously bad vibes. We heard something and she called into the building, "Is anyone there?" because it just looked like a good place for homeless people to squat. We heard a raised whisper inside that said something, not quite clear. Although the whisper didn't sound like a human, I wasn't going to rule out humans. Since we had neither canine security team members Bulova or Sparky with us to do a pre-sweep, we opted to leave.

I've been to the San Pasqual cemetery a number of times during the day doing photo shoots. It's on a hill overlooking the San Pasqual Valley, surrounded by orange orchards and majestic mountains. A few times I've gone in the evenings with Bulova, and I've heard what sounded like lots of voices coming from the valley where there are only a few scattered houses. I've heard this before about the valley, how people hear the sounds of the Mexican-American battle that took place there in the mid-1800s (see San Pasqual Battlefield chapter). It's a strange vibe at the cemetery, and sound travels oddly. I've noticed that when I think I'm hearing things not of this world, Bulova's ears go back instead of forward as they do when he's listening for predators.

There is a metal-pipe guardrail at the bottom of the hill to help safely guide people up the steep incline leading to the cemetery. There is no other fence or posting, except the unlocked gate that you can open and drive up to on the side of the hill. I imagine this is the service entrance (though it doesn't look quite safe) for hearses because they are still burying bodies in the small historic cemetery (please be respectful during your visit).

Michelle, Kim, and I first investigated the cemetery on a still night; it seemed like we could hear for miles. We set up detection equipment that would flash lights on a handheld control pad and give us a little warning if our perimeter line was crossed. We set up our equipment and began recording movie and audio. We also set up our K-II and EMF meters. We recorded for about two hours and took a ton of photos, but for the exception of a few sound anomalies that couldn't be heard clearly or explained, we didn't get much. The perimeter alarms went off several times that night, but that could have been explained by the wildlife in the area, although most animals remained hidden.

I've had some curious experiences with the metal-pipe guardrail that goes up the hill of the cemetery. One of the posts has become detached from the top rail, and there are a few inches of space between the two, leaving the horizontal guide rail flexible. While I was walking up the hill to take photos one day, the guide rail slammed down a few times on the post. It was sudden and loud enough to make me jump. I looked around for a big-rig truck going down the narrow road, thinking that could have somehow caused movement in the ground that shook the rail. Nothing . . . I started walking up again, and the rail repeated the action. As I've had a number of paranormal encounters that began with the entity using whatever was handy to communicate, I began asking questions. Two curious little boys walking home from school to a nearby ranch stopped to listen and I waved at them; they broke into a run for home.

I asked whatever was using the pole to communicate by using a one-and-two-bang system for yes/no. Immediately, it began answering questions.

From what I gathered, the entity was a Native American woman from a tribe that had lived where I later found out was right there. When I asked her what year she lived in and gave groups of years she could answer yes/no to, she seemed confused and didn't answer. Apparently, a bear injured her when she was getting water from the creek. Later, I looked up bears in the Escondido area, and at one time the area was a natural habitat for grizzly bears—lots of them. I asked her if she was buried in the Native American cemetery at the San Diego Archaeological Center down the road. She answered, "No." I asked her if she could see what I was doing; she answered, "Yes." So I began pointing in different directions. We clarified that she was buried in the orchard nearby, so it had to have been before the Native American cemetery was established, perhaps many centuries before. She told me her children were with her. So maybe she'd been born in the valley before the Kumeyaay were relocated there by the Mexican government.

I found on the website **sanpasqualtribe.com** that the ancestors of the San Pasqual Indians lived for many thousands of years in the valley of San Pasqual near the present Wild Animal Park.

Stories of investigation teams hearing gunfire and battle sounds from the cemetery are constant. Janine Haynes, cofounder of S.P.I.R.I.T, a Southern California paranormal group, recently went to the location with the group's other founder, Chris Oliver.

"As we began to make our way up the hill, I heard what sounded like a baby crying," says Haynes. "We looked down on the farmhouses below, but there were no lights on in any of them. We heard it again, and stopped to get our bearings on where it was coming from. We were drawn to a grave. Once we approached, it looked like a crib. On further inspection, it was the grave of a baby. The sounds stopped and we continued to investigate around the area.

"In the middle section of the cemetery, I heard a man say, 'Hey.' I turned quickly to see that Chris Oliver and I were alone, and no male was present. I have started to hear the voices with my ears to what I only used to get during EVP sessions . . . I hear this tends to happen to investigators. This male voice kept talking about loving his car and asking where his car was. I quickly began an EVP session in hopes of capturing what I heard on tape. We started to listen to the recording in the car, but decided to wait until we were more awake the next day to listen to them. When we went to review them, the recording was gone. It takes holding down two buttons at the same time to delete files, so it was odd they were gone. We went back today for some daytime photos and heard the crying once again."

Having driven through this area in the midnight hours, I've sensed many paranormal activities on this route where many have been killed. Highway 78 is one of America's most dangerous highways. It goes through the San Pasqual mountain ridge and on to Ramona, Julian, and Anza-Borrego, and meets Highway 86 and then Highway 95 before continuing on through to the Salton Sea and eventually reaching Las Vegas (it's a much better route than the more traveled Interstate 15).

This small two-lane highway full of hairpin turns has an astounding death toll due to car crashes and cars running over pedestrians and bicyclists. I've never felt alone driving this road in the dark, early morning hours. Being a medium is both a curse and a gift; on this road it always feels like I've picked up a spirit or two, and I've seen shadow people shifting around in the back of my van in my rearview mirror. I'm never shy about telling them to get out.

One night I was on Highway 78, going toward Julian about midnight, when what looked like a giant buck jumped down from out of nowhere on the road in front of me. I stood on my brakes, gripped the wheel, and tried not to career off the road and over a sheer cliff. I braced for the impact of the deer going through my windshield, but it never came. I slid around the blind turn and came within inches of hitting a woman whose car had run out of gas and had nowhere to go. She had her flashers on, but I couldn't have seen them from the other side of the road. I quickly backed up, hit my flashers, and lit some flares to throw on the road to warn oncoming traffic that drove around us. I gave her the gallon of gas I had in my vehicle for emergencies. She was hysterical, had twin babies screaming in their car seats, and was shaking realizing how close we'd all come to dying.

Before picking up the flares and putting them out so I could follow her back over the hill, I asked her if she'd seen the deer. Still crying, she shook her head. I looked up the hill and saw that it would've been a sheer drop for the deer—it definitely would have broken a leg in the fall. I tried to remember the last time I'd seen a deer in San Diego County. I'd lived there about six years and had only seen a few on the Pauma Reservation. I'd not seen a single one in San Pasqual until that night. I wanted to look over the cliff, but there was no safe way to do so. I wasn't so sure I'd actually seen a real dear. Thinking back on it, it seemed very otherworldly to me.

Months later I went into the store in San Pasqual and talked to the owner about the near-accident. She was a fan of the paranormal and sold "alien" rock lamps there. I asked her if anything like that—with deer—had ever happened. A retired highway patrol officer was in the store and overheard us. He told me that he'd been up there himself the night an accident happened with a "big ol' buck" nearly forty years before. A woman had been driving home from work, and a deer had come out of nowhere and must have miscalculated its jump and fell on top of the car. The woman lost control of the vehicle and went over the cliff. She died instantly . . . although they couldn't get to her for a while.

He said they found the deer as well, and it had more points on its antlers than he'd ever seen before on a buck in that area. He mumbled something about what a shame it was to waste all that venison. He told me they got the woman's body out by lowering a body basket and two firefighters down from a fire truck line, but as far as he knew, the car had been left down there because it was unsafe to remove—and that those "beautiful antlers" were probably still down there as well. Was the guy having one on me, or was he serious? He sure was convincing, but small-town people do seem to have fun at an outsider's expense. He sure told the story convincingly, After what nearly happened to me, it sure gives me pause to think about the speed I'm going every time I drive around a blind turn on that road.

CHAPTER 11

Ghost Rider of State Route 67
LAKESIDE

State Route 67 on a stormy afternoon. This is one of America's most dangerous two-lane highways, responsible for taking many lives since its construction. This is the bend in the route where we saw the specter of the bicyclist disappear.

CALIFORNIA STATE ROUTE 67 is a two-lane ribbon of highway that winds from Interstate 8 in El Cajon, to Santee, Lakeside, and Poway. It runs through the center of Ramona before becoming Route 78 at the end of town going toward Julian. The twenty-five-mile road, nicknamed "Blood Alley," is filled with steep inclines, fast slopes, and blind hairpin turns. Recent statistics report forty-six deaths on Route 67 between 1998 and 2008, many of the dead being bicyclists and head-on collisions.

Highway 67 has its share of ghost stories, including one about the immigrant worker who'd been riding his bike home to Santee one night after a hard day at work at a construction site near Mount Woodson. Apparently, the man had no lights on his bike. The man who hit him with his car had been working with him on the job, and the two of them had been drinking earlier. It's said that the cyclist ghost of the immigrant bicyclist swerves in and out of traffic to run drunk drivers off the road before they can hurt anyone. He's supposedly already killed half a dozen people since the mid-1980s. This story has a Mothers Against Drunk Driving (MADD) public-service-announcement ring to it, but there *might* be some truth to it. Fact or urban myth? In any case, I heard this story from friends who grew up there; it's the story parents tell teens in that neck of the woods when they get their driver's licenses.

There is a ghost-bicyclist story I do know is true because it happened to me.

One weekday spring morning at about 10:30 a.m., I was driving from Highway 15 (San Marcos) to Santee to stop on an errand before taking my daughter on to Balboa Park. It was a nice day for a drive. My daughter was three and highly alert. She's intuitive and has often been visited by her "special friends" and angels since before she could speak. She's also very communicative; at the time she was reading at a first-grade level, and people used to mistake her for a small, smart seven-year-old. I'm not telling you this because I'm a doting mother; I'm telling you this because she made a credible witness to the events that were about to happen.

Being a Spiritualist medium, I'm usually prepared for anything my daughter sees or hears. I'm used to seeing all kinds of spirits in different situations. But, some spirits "bleeding through" to this world look so solid I can't even tell whether they're human or spirit until something "otherworldly" happens. Such is the case in this next story.

We were coming down Highway 67 toward Lakeside. About four miles past Scripps Poway Parkway, there's one sweeping turn before you get to Griffith Road at the bottom of the mountain range. It's a turn you could easily loose control on—especially if you're riding a bike.

My daughter and I were singing with the radio when we both saw (she from her car seat in the back of the van) a bike going around the turn. From where we were, a few seconds lapsed before we'd be able to see around the blind turn again. I'd already moved over to give him room as we passed. Two seconds later, when we could see around the turn where he should have been . . . he was gone. As I realized what happened, my daughter let out a loud shrill scream and cried, "He's gone over!" That's exactly what I thought, too. At the speed he was traveling, he could have easily lost control of his bike, hit the railing, and gone right over, taking his bike with him.

I raced to Griffith Road, where I could stop and call police. There's a gated business right where the cyclist would have come down. I found someone in charge and told him a bicyclist had gone over the railing onto their property. I asked for the address to call into the police. The guy was lackadaisical, and both my daughter and I were quite hysterical.

He said, "Lady, you and your kid need to just settle down. He's all right; don't worry about it."

At that point I let the expletives fly, got back in the van, and went to another nearby business. We flew into an office of a large company, and I grabbed one of the business cards off the front counter and called the police immediately with the address. We waited outside to flag the police car down. An officer asked my daughter and me questions, as one of the fire trucks blocked off traffic on the highway. The crew walked up and down the road looking over the hill to find the biker. The other truck went down to the bottom. A search-and-rescue helicopter swooped in and began what it anticipated would be a critical rescue. Forty-five minutes later, they had searched the entire cliff area several times over. They couldn't find *anything*. Again, I described the biker to another officer. "He's wearing those biking uniforms with logos and has one of those bike caps. . . ."

"What caps?" the young officer asked.

"You know, those hats they used to wear in the early '80s."

"He wasn't wearing a helmet?"

"No, those hats—like a cloth baseball cap—like a painter's cap . . . with a short bill. . . ."

It struck me midsentence. My daughter and I had both seen the same residual haunting. I guessed that the lackadaisical attitude of the guy at the first business we'd gone into had this happen before, or maybe they see him too. After what I'd said to the guy, I was in no position to follow up.

That's when I realized the full impact of having a helicopter, fire trucks, and the police at an accident scene . . . with no accident. Had we not been so hysterical, they may have given me a ticket for a false accident report and billed me for the time and equipment resources. The cop shook his head, "There's no one down there, ma'am. We're going to leave now."

He suggested that the biker raced to the bottom of the hill and turned somewhere before I came around the corner. It wasn't possible, but I tried to feign relief. He radioed and sent everyone back to their appointed stations. I watched them leave, the helicopter whirring away, my daughter waving after them.

"He was a ghost, huh," my daughter said, more as a statement than a question. I'm glad she'd held off to state the obvious.

"Yep," I answered, securing her back into her car seat.

"What did he want us to see?" she asked, always on the lookout to help a lost spirit.

"Honey, I think he just wanted to make sure someone still cared." It's hard to explain residual energy to a three-year-old, especially when her guess might be as good as, or even better than, mine.

"I'll send my angels down to find him; they can take him home," she said, helpfully.

"That's a very thoughtful idea, honey. Have them come back quickly; I don't like driving on this road without them."

Residual hauntings at accident scenes are not rare. I imagine it has something to do with the sudden impact of a life torn away, just like that, that somehow rips a tear in the fabric of time, so to speak. I've seen similar things happen at murder scenes. It's like a scratch in whatever records time. There doesn't seem to be a way to stop a residual occurrence from continuing to replay over and over, but there also doesn't seem to be any harm in them either . . . unless you're getting billed for their attempted rescue.

CHAPTER 12

Los Peñasquitos Creek Arch Bridge
POWAY

SAN DIEGO HAS A DARK SIDE that doesn't like to be turned belly-up for the public to view. This chapter is one that illustrates San Diego's dangerous, violent, and unpredictable side, where young people are particularly vulnerable. I think what's most unsettling about this story is that it could have happened anywhere and to anyone, but it took place in my own city, and the police officer who was supposed to be protecting the young woman involved was actually her murderer.

If you look under the Mercy Road/Scripps Poway Parkway/ Highway 15 overpass in what borders on Poway, a suburb of San

Diego, you'll find another nearly forgotten bridge that you don't see from the highway: the Los Peñasquitos Creek Arch Bridge. Built in 1949, when Poway was little more than a small town, the bridge sits in the shadow of the overpass. It's 434 feet in length, with an arch span of 220 feet. The overpass above it was built in 1966 and then entirely replaced by today's overpass in 1976. Through all the construction and deconstruction, the old bridge remained.

On Dec 27, 1986, Cara Knott, a twenty-year-old San Diego State University student with a promising future, was taking care of her sick boyfriend in Escondido. She called her dad, Sam Knott, to let him know she was headed home. Cara drove a VW Bug over the long stretch of lonesome highway (there's been a lot of expansion since then) that wound in and out of mountains and canyons in a southerly direction. I imagine her immediately checking her large speedometer when she saw California Highway Patrol Officer Craig Peyer's light bar reflect red, blue, and white in her rearview mirror. Her thoughts probably went from panic to confusion, as she knew she wasn't breaking any laws.

It was about this time that Cara's family was watching *Sleeping Beauty* on TV. All of a sudden, Sam became extremely distressed. He'd later say it felt like "a call to his soul." Not knowing what else to do, he began a frenzy of phone calls to four different police agencies that went completely ignored; they told him to call back in forty-eight hours, when he could make a missing-persons report. Cara was probably fighting for her life at that very moment, or possibly even dead by the time he made his last call. He and one of his daughters and her husband went out looking for Cara, while Cara's mother waited by the house phone, the only real means of communication back then, for any news.

I can imagine how the scenario probably unfolded— Peyer pulled over the young, beautiful Cara Knott and sexually harassed her. The situation escalated, and Knott, who was probably very scared, may have intuitively seen that Peyer was on a path to murder, and did everything to get away. Peyer bludgeoned her with his California Highway Patrol–issue flashlight and strangled her with a rope he carried with him. Then the coldblooded murderer dropped her body from the Los Peñasquitos Creek Arch Bridge.

Nine hours after Cara made the call to her family, her body was found below the underpass. It wasn't the police who originally found Cara's body; it was Sam and his family who found Cara broken, strangled, and dumped at a time when the police hadn't even began looking for her. The murder shocked the county, and women avoided going anywhere alone. In a ironic twist, Peyer was interviewed by local TV station KCST in a ride-along about tips for protection when women are driving alone. During the taped interview he was quoted as saying, "You never know who you could meet along the road. You could even get killed."

Cara had recently taken a self-defense class and used those skills to scratch at his face and eyes to fight him off. Her scratches were visible on his face during the media ride-along. After the telecast, dozens of calls came in to authorities by women who'd been sexually harassed by Peyer—many on or near that same exit where Cara was murdered. Detectives working on the case put two and two together, and Peyer became the prime suspect. DNA testing was not yet available at that time, but an uncommon blood type found on Cara's boots matched Peyer's. Twenty-one days after Cara's death, Peyer was arrested for her murder.

Was this Peyer's first murder? He seemed a little too confident in his work as a killer. Serial-killer profilers from the U.S. Department of Justice say when sociopaths/psychopaths cross the line and commit a predatory murder, they just look for another opportunity to do it again. I believe that Cara was not his first victim. Apparently, his superiors had knowledge of his behavior, as several women had made official complaints against the officer before the escalation. Unfortunately, the warning signs that should have removed him from the CHP before he killed Cara Knott went ignored. When all was said and done, twenty women had their day in court testifying against him.

Unbelievably, Peyer's trial ended in a hung jury. He was convicted on his second trial and given twenty-five years to life. Peyer, who has been kept segregated from the general prison population and has become a model prisoner with special access to offices outside of his cell to practice his trade as an electrician, was turned down for parole in 2004, 2008, and 2012. The Knott family spearheads an ongoing effort to make sure that Peyer stays behind bars where he won't be able to do any more harm, and asks people to write letters to the district attorney and the parole board on their behalf. He's up for parole every four years.

Peyer has claimed his innocence the whole time that he's been locked up. More recently, when DNA testing was offered to clear him, he declined without any explanation. Cara's family, like so many murder victims' families, has never been given closure about what really happened in the last moments of Cara's life.

Today, on the left side of the short road near the bridge where Cara's body was found is a memorial with a gazebo, a bench, and hundreds of *descansos* (small memorials) under a stand of beautiful oak trees still in their early youth. Going just a little further, the road dead ends at a locked automatic gate with day/night surveillance cameras trained on it and the surrounding area, protecting some kind of city government building. Trucks pass in and out of the gate at all hours. Police cars are a constant; the area is frequented by just teens hanging out and dodgy homeless people living under the bridge. Although the area is secluded, there seems to be a fair amount of security.

My first visit to the site was accidental. I'd always had a creepy feeling about the area since I moved here, but I had no idea why

I avoided the off-ramp. One day my husband asked me why I avoided what should have been a shortcut home. I told him the whole exit just gave me a feeling of anxiety. He'd lived in the area more than a decade before I did and knew what happened there. He told me about Cara Knott. I was shocked, but I'd kind of put it in the back of my mind until one day while trying to avoid traffic. I turned down the street to park until an accident was cleared. I kept driving down the road, fascinated at what I was seeing . . . and feeling. I'd done some research on the case via the Internet, so I knew a lot more than someone just making a wrong turn.

I pulled up in a dirt parking space and took in all the rocks with names and birth and death dates—some painted, some engraved, or scrawled with a Sharpie. It was heartbreaking. I wrote down many of the names to research them; it turns out a good many of them are cold-case murders, including one that was recently solved after many years.

The garden, once tended by Sam Knott in memory of his slain daughter, is now a memorial garden for many hundreds of people who were killed. The location is connected with the non-profit Survivors of Violent Loss program. Having had friends and family members who were murdered, I know such a program is a much-needed service in any community. I've volunteered with grief and suicide programs, and was lucky enough to have worked with the founder of one of the first programs in the country. Half of the work I do as a Spiritualist medium is consoling the grieving. When I give messages from those passed on to the living with affirmation of details no one else but the person receiving the message would know, it can be a great source of closure for people. When working as a paranormal investigator for murders or missing-persons cases, I try hard to get any evidence that might lead to useful information I can give to the authorities and family members—especially information that can be verified in some way.

I hiked up to the area on the bridge/bike path from which I believe Peyer threw Cara's body. An overwhelming feeling of grief just took over at that point. I didn't even feel like I could breathe. The sprawling garden was quiet except for the creek rushing by and the traffic driving rhythmically above on the overpass. I definitely got the impression of brute force and violence. For a moment, I felt like I couldn't walk. I sat down and took measured breaths as I watched the crows take flight from the oaks below while a bicyclist rode across the bridge. He stopped and asked me if I was okay. I nodded, thanked him, and told him I was just taking a rest. I got up and walked back toward the memorial garden. I definitely felt an emotional imprint of Cara's murder and those who've spent time grieving for the young woman on the bridge. You really can't erase the imprint of the events that happened that night; I believe her spirit remained with her dead body and she was instrumental in psychically calling her family to the spot where Peyer threw her body over like a bag of trash.

I scanned the area where Sam Knott had taken his last breath during a heart attack while he cared for the oak trees—the Victorian funerary symbol for strength and eternity—just yards away from where his daughter's body had been found. The oaks he planted from acorns memorialize his dead daughter and bring life and beauty into this place of remembrance.

After Cara's murder, her father turned his grief for the loss of his daughter into crusade; his efforts caused law enforcement to ease up on the forty-eight-hour waiting period to look for missing people, and to put devices in police cars to monitor officers' whereabouts at all times. Thanks to Sam's lobbying, an $83 million communication system now links all county emergency agencies. He also worked with legislators to bring about change in laws to give women greater protection from potentially dangerous situations. Sam Knott is my hero.

The next time I visited, I took my mother and daughter. A patrol car followed us all the way back to the garden, and the male and female officers parked and watched our every move. Considering what happened there, I found this disturbing, and my daughter was freaked out because she knew the story of the rogue officer. She hid behind me as we walked over to Cara's memorial. The officers still watching us, decided to interact. They pulled out what looked like a sticker badge and called my daughter over to their car. There was no way she was going, and I shook my head, told them she didn't want the sticker, and waved them off. Finally, they left. My daughter finds it a peaceful place, and even now she asks to go to the garden and brings flowers from our yard to leave on the children's memorials; Cara's memorial is also a special place for her to say a few words and let her spirit know she's remembered.

Please don't use any provoking techniques here; be respectful of other people—remember that the people who visit this location are more than likely mourning a family member who has died under violent and tragic circumstances—and just leave them alone. Also, please leave the area as you found it.

My Ghosts Happen group has investigated the scene twice, and there have been several visits with Roadside Paranormal members. The purpose of these investigations is to possibly communicate with entities that may be trying to get information to investigators about any murder cases that are still open. After all, if ghosts have no concerns about traveling through time and space, why not tell us something that might help their families have resolution about their murders? I believe that once you pass over, a great many details of your death are made clear to you, so maybe by reaching out, something will reach back.

"There are people out there killing with no motive, and just waiting for some random person to come by," says Eugenia Swingle, a Roadside Paranormal investigator and member of

Ghosts Happen. "Just nine miles down the road is where John Gardner killed Chelsea King, his only motive being to rape and kill her. You never know when these killers are going to pick someone out; you always need to be prepared."

There were about fourteen members of the Ghosts Happen group investigation one evening, including Eugenia and a former member of our group who is a veteran in recording EVPs. I didn't think there was any chance of capturing EVPs that night because of the highway noise and the winds. What we found was that it is much quieter under the highway overpass. When we were wrapping up the investigation in that area, we asked whoever was there if they could let us know if they had anything to tell us before we left.

Our former member captured the three-word EVP of what sounded like a little girl saying, "I'll miss you," that he didn't catch until he was reviewing his evidence and put the audio through Audacity (a free software program available at **audacity .sourceforge.net**). You could clearly hear us talking in the background, and the recorder was in clear view while the EVP was recorded. It was a very chilling but sweet piece of evidence. The voice didn't seem lonely, just stating a fact.

The area beneath the overpass—all the way to where the bridge's pillars meet the dirt in the upper area and all the way down to the creek—had amazing and lively energy. I imagine the shift in mood is due to the swift flowing water and the high negative-ion count created by the creek's movement. We stayed on the bridge for a while, and Eugenia collected a few EVPs that sounded like white noise over our discussion, which is really strange because none of our equipment makes noise like the sound on her recorder.

"The energy on the bridge seemed very oppressive to me," says Eugenia. "It's the only way I can describe it. It felt uncomfortable. I think the fact that there's a freeway above it made it seem like everything was okay, but it was a false sense of security."

Roadside Paranormal's Eugenia Swingle with the Los Peñasquitos Creek Bridge in the background.

We went up the path back nearer to the bridge, and all of a sudden the K-II meter started going off with strong yes/no answers to questions we were asking. There weren't many and there wasn't much detail, and pretty soon the energy was exhausted and that was it. Swingle and I constantly heard someone behind us—we were in back of the group—and that was strange because we couldn't tell if it was otherworldly (although no EMF signal was coming up on our tools), or if we were being stalked by someone human hiding in the shrubs.

"I think it's sad," says Eugenia of the energy that remains at the location. "I know if I was Cara, I wouldn't be able to get any peace. It's not like someone stalked her and finally found her—it was a random incident. I hope if she hasn't passed on and left this place, that she will one day be able to come to terms with what happened and that her father, if he hasn't already, finds peace and his daughter as well."

Spotlight On: Communicating with the Dead— ITC and EVP

The human ability to communicate with the dead and unseen have long been thought possible. People have reached out to appease the spirits of those who've gone before for thousands of years. For instance, traditional Chinese religion and culture are based upon ancestor worship, whereby respect is paid and offerings given to the family's dead, and requests made by family members for health, happiness, and material wealth are taken into consideration. The Celts reached out to communicate with the spirits of the woods and worshiped elemental beings in nature. Christians have always had a close relationship with Jesus, who is said to have died on the cross for them. Spiritualists believe they can communicate with the dead directly and deliver messages of comfort to the living. In houses of worship throughout the world, people go weekly—sometimes daily—to worship and connect to the unknown and unseen. I ask you, what could be more paranormal than this?

It seems as though the entire world has a connection with the dead and invisible. We live in a paranormal world. Is there really any difference between Pat Robertson claiming to have a direct link to God or a paranormal team getting EVPs? As I see it, the only difference is that I've never heard Robertson play back the voice of Jesus on a digital recorder. So why, then, is it so hard for people to believe the evidence they hear? It's not like the Ghost Hunters are constantly asking people during their TV show to call in with their pledges. People have nothing to lose if they maintain an open mind, but most find it more comforting to be open-minded in a house of worship or among others in a religious setting. I find this curious, but people are complex.

For now, believers in communication with the dead are a suspect minority, but their numbers are growing every day, even as those in organized religion plummet. A 2009 CBS poll points out that 48 percent of people believe in ghosts, with 45 percent counting themselves as nonbelievers. How many of those nonbelievers believe in a religion with a faith-based, nonphysical entity? I'd say about 95 percent of paranormal investigators I know also have a religious or spiritually based faith.

Mark and Debby Constantino, the paranormal powerhouse couple seen on *Ghost Adventurers* and *Paranormal State*, are among the superstars in the field. They are amazing electronic voice phenomenon (EVP) experts, and I've seen them in person on the *Queen Mary* gather live EVPs in response to their questions. Recently, I asked Debby Constantino how they got to be so good at collecting audio evidence.

"Sally, I think we are 'so good' because we have respect for the dead. Truly, I say this because I believe the dead can literally see right through you. You can't lie to them, and they can see your vibration. I also pray for their souls. We also leave them material things—anything to make them more comfortable. They are our friends and have done more for us than most of the living. The EVPs that surprise me the most are those coming from dolls as well as antiques." The Constantinos have captured a storehouse of EVPs, many of which can be found on their website (**spirits-speak .com**) under "Galleries."

Another celebrity of the instrumental transcommunication (ITC) world—and one of the first—is Frank Sumption, creator of Frank's Box, a name stolen by many to identify their own ITC devices. I own an original Frank's Box #55—each box is made from different parts Frank gathers, and every box seems to have a different feel and personality. Sumption is a reclusive inventor who tinkers with each creation until it's done. But do his boxes work? I've gotten stunningly accurate answers from my box, which oscillates radio frequencies (see Creole Café and Cobb Estate chapters).

"Of course they work—the concept is simple," explains Sumption. "Just like using white noise, you have to supply a raw material that can be remade into voices and images." So how does the Frank's Box capture audio phenomena? "*Capture* is the wrong word—it implies some kind of accident; there's really a much bigger reality and awareness to the voices coming through the box. They talk and make images because we are listening and looking. As far as I can tell, they need some kind of raw material to communicate, like white noise which contains speech frequencies, and bits of speech in the boxes or EVP-maker. That's just a guess at why the boxes work—it also seems to be the nature of higher beings to reach out to fellow beings in the universe."

In a curious juxtaposition, Sumption is outspoken on the subject of ghosthunting but is considered an expert on the subject of ITC in the community. "I stay away from ghosthunting and the standard paranormal paradigms because they don't make sense," says Sumption regarding how his box relates to paranormal investigation. "Why would any intelligence be in dark, moldy, nasty abandoned buildings? Why would they only communicate in the dark? Why does anyone think that where you drop dead is where you are stuck forever? What if you drop dead taking a crap—you have to sit there forever? There are no stuck spirits, and there are no accidental captures. This paranormal *whatever* seems to lead people around by the nose till they wake up. I didn't intend this stuff to be a for-all-mankind thing; I do it for my own curiosity. I don't know how it relates to the world."

April Slaughter, author of *Ghosthunting Texas* (Clerisy Press), has traveled with TV's Ghost Hunters investigating many haunted locations, and she has some advice for those seeking to record EVPs. "EVPs can be defined as any sound on a recording that does not seem to have any plausible explanation for being there. It does not have to be an actual *voice*, as the term implies. While voices are common, so are recordings of things such as music, animal sounds and so on. These anomalous sounds are not generally heard in real time, but rather upon playback of an audio recording.

"In all my years of investigating the paranormal, I have learned that EVP recordings can be intelligent responses and reactions from those on the other side of the veil," explains Slaughter. "However, I think it is important to note that EVPs can also be recordings of residual activity, meaning that they are not always actual spirit voices communicating directly with us, but actually audio of something repeating itself in the environment . . . sort of like a broken record.

"Any device with the ability to capture audio can be used to record EVPs. Both digital and analog voice recorders are most common, though camcorders are also equipped. The clearest and most credible EVP audio I have personally captured has been on the ZOOM brand of digital recorders, widely available in many retail electronics stores. Keep in mind, however, that what works best for one individual or group may not work well with another. The best advice to be given is to try various recorders and find which one works best for you."

The Anza-Borrego Desert and Surrounding Area

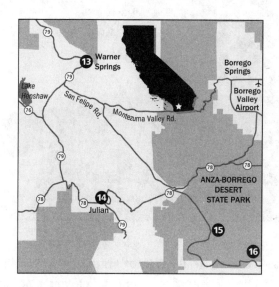

Anza-Borrego Desert
   Blair Valley and Pictograph Trail **(15)**

Julian
   Julian Jail **(14)**

Vallecito
   Vallecito County Park **(16)**

Warner Springs
   Warner Springs **(13)**

CHAPTER 13

Warner Springs
WARNER SPRINGS

THE TAR-BLACK RIBBON of Highway 79 travels the out-lying San Diego County desert and takes you places you nor-mally wouldn't end up otherwise . . . places like Warner Springs. This area seems to be a vortex for strange activity of all types. During the 1800s, the area was known for a serial-killer Big-foot; now it's known for ghosts and UFO sightings. Even the chupacabra is believed to have traveled up through Mexico to get there. The spirits that haunt this area more than likely had tough lives trying to survive the environment.

A few likely suspects for a haunting include two stagecoach drivers shot down in holdups where they bled out slowly and alone, destined to continue searching for help in death. There are several stories about ghosts appearing in the fashion of the old West and trying to flag down cars on the highway. When drivers slam their brakes to help, they are unable to find anyone of flesh and blood on the dark highway. Warner Springs seems to have it all, so I went there to see if there was any truth to the stories I'd been hearing since I moved to San Diego.

Warner Springs is sacred Native American land, once belonging to the Cupeños, who settled there more than one thousand years before. The Spaniards arrived and forced them into the missionary system, and they lost control of their land. There were skirmishes and even an occupy movement that predates today's (as the term comes from this era and can be found in writings of that time), but in the end the Cupeños people who'd lived there in peace for more than a millennium were sent to the Pala Indian Reservation.

For many years Warner Springs Resort, built around a natural hot spring, seemed to be the main commercial business in town (if you don't count cattle and agriculture). The resort/spa was a far cry from the dangerous Butterfield stagecoach stop it once was. The resort has since closed, perhaps due to the success of the Pala Casino Resort Spa that sprang up on the Pala Reservation about thirty miles down the road, offering Chevy Camaro giveaways, Zumba fitness, and live entertainment. I checked further into it, and it's rumored that the Pala Indian band of Native Americans may be buying the Warner Springs property. I tried checking with both the resort and the Pala Reservation, but neither was able to confirm or deny the rumors. If true, sometimes what goes around comes around—it just takes about a hundred years.

I'd been introduced to the area in 2003, at about 2 a.m.—and hadn't ventured back until recently to do research for this book. I'd gotten lost driving back from an observatory event at Mount

Palomar. My headlights pierced the foggy, pitch-black night. I was passing the Warner Springs post office and slammed on my brakes as a white wolflike creature ran out in front of my car and froze in my headlights. Although I came within ten feet of hitting it and my wheels laid long strips of noisy black rubber behind the car, the creature stood its ground in a posture of defiance. It was much larger than a coyote—more like a large wolf, and completely white except for dark markings shading its face. Its eyes found my eyes. The creature's eyes were glowing a piercing blue (that could have been a reflection from my headlights) that struck me as odd; I was in awe. It also had a sparkling shimmer to its coat (which could have been the dew from the night shining in my lights). Then it was suddenly gone, as though it had never been there at all. It all seemed somehow mystical.

Since then, I've spoken to my friend Susan, who has Native American ties. She laughed when I told her the story, because she said she couldn't imagine me stopping long enough to take notice of something in such detail—I led a pretty fast-paced life back then. She suggested that the creature stopped me physically to give me pause to reevaluate how I was spending my time. It was interesting, as at the time my husband and I were making the decision to have a midlife baby. She also told me that she'd also seen her totem animal—a bear—on Highway 79 one night while driving back to Borrego with her family. Bears have been extinct in this area for about one hundred years. She told me the only real way to tell if an animal was sending a spiritual message was that something about them would make them stand out—the way they looked at you, or something about them that seemed unearthly.

When I asked Susan about any paranormal stories in Warner Springs she may have heard about, she told me a story from her childhood. When she was eleven and her brother fourteen, her mother packed their bikes and luggage in the back of their truck and brought them to visit her grandmother. At their grandmother's they decided to ride their bikes, but promised to meet the rest of the family at the Chapel of St. Francis of Assisi at Warner Springs for Sunday Mass. The building, constructed in 1830, is rumored to be haunted. The chapel is where the Cupeño Native Americans worshipped once they adopted Christianity. It's known as the starting point of the Cupeño tribe's trail of tears, as they were forcibly evicted from their land from that point. After Mass, the kids rode their bikes around until it started getting dark, and then they got caught in an unexpected storm. They rode back to the chapel for cover and decided to wait it out until their mom started looking around for them. It was about 8 p.m., dark, cold, and pouring rain. The rain let up, and they went down the back road where they'd ditched their bikes before running up to the chapel.

Both Susan and her brother stopped in their tracks, as there was a glowing bundle lying on the ground near the cemetery. At first they thought the figure, wrapped in an Indian blanket, had been left to be buried. She described a dim orange light surrounding the covered figure but could see no source of light. Her brother, being a boy, began tossing rocks at it, but the rocks weren't hitting it—they just seemed to be sucked into it. Although they could hear the rocks hit the ground, they didn't see them bounce off the mysterious figure. The form never moved. Just then, their mom came up the road and headlights flooded the ground. The image disappeared. She said she and her brother began wondering if the figure was ever there at all.

Intrigued, I planned a visit to the chapel. I tried to call earlier to ask permission to investigate there, but an exhaustive Internet search found no contact information. The woman at the Warner Springs Ranch did not want to speak about anything to do with the property. I'm still not sure who owns it. I called the Pala Band of Mission Indians but did not receive a response. I even called the Warner Springs sheriff station to see if they had an emergency contact for the property, but they also did not know whom to contact. I drove out, and although the chapel was open, there was no docent. I'm always very respectful when entering sacred spaces, as I don't wish to dishonor or anger the spirits who are there.

I had seen a YouTube clip posted by a team of paranormal investigators. They went into the chapel using a K-II, and one of the members went up to the podium, read from the church's bible—and got results. For me, touching sacred artifacts falls into the "provoking" category, something I don't do. I put the K-II meter on a seat and turned it on, as well as an EMF meter and recorder. I scanned the area for any electrical interference and found none. What I did find was a responsive and critical ghost. It responded to every question I asked: "Can you see me?" *Yes.* "Do you mind me being here?" *Yes.* "Are you always here?" *Yes.* "Were you a priest?" *Yes.* "Is there more than one of you?" *Yes.* "Is there a nun here?" *Yes.* "Is there more than one nun?" *Yes.* "Do you still love?" *Yes.* "Do you love me?" A definite nonresponse. "I'm going to give a sermon—do you mind?" *Yes.*

I started to walk slowly to the podium, with no intention of actually getting close to it. As I walked away, the K-II meter pegged the full light scale and stayed there. It even made the buzzing sound it makes when it's under a substation tower. My EMF reader did not originally respond at all to what was happening to the K-II. As I began walking back, the lights dimmed accordingly until I was back in the seat. Later, I found that an EVP had been captured—the single word, *Go,* in a woman's voice that spoke under my question, "Do you want me to leave?" Although I hadn't heard the *Go* until later, let me tell you—I could definitely feel it. Although ghosts usually create one- or two-word EVPs, they seem to choose their words well.

It's not surprising that there are ghost sightings and encounters in the Warner Springs area, as it's had quite a violent and
tragic past. There have also been sightings of cryptids (creatures
studied in theory by cryptozoologists because no specimens exist)
in the area going back more than a hundred years. A Bigfoot-like
creature was spotted in the Warner Springs area in 1876 and
reported in the *San Diego Tribune,* where it was described as "a
large relic hominid covered with hair."

While cruising the Internet for leads on the Warner Springs
area, I came across the Monster of Dead Man's Hole. The area
this monster is believed to inhabit has been dubbed Dead Man's
Hole, a former stage stop on the Butterfield route. The Butterfield stage-line route was desolate with few opportunities to water
horses. The trail took coachmen directly past what is referenced
as Dead Man's Hole, a mythic source of cool, safe water. A stop
here and at other watering holes along the route was essential
for the horses, since the heat and dehydration could kill them.
Once the horses died, people were soon to follow. It's been said
that the canyon behind the watering hole was deep, dark, and
filled with insurmountable challenges to navigation.

The first "known" victim of the Monster of Dead Man's Hole
was discovered when, in 1858, a stagecoach driver made a stop
there and found a corpse in the water. Soon others began to
notice men of all backgrounds disappearing. The corpse was
later identified as a prospector who had a camp nearby. Dead
Man's Hole was the scene of another man's death in 1870. Six
year's later, a passenger resting from a stagecoach ride screamed
and claimed to have seen "a naked *thing* covered with long black
hair" staring at him from nearby bushes; the creature vanished
into the canyon. In 1872, another man's body was found near
the hole. He'd been choked until his windpipe was crushed.
That same year, the body of a teenaged Native American woman
was found, also choked to death. On the heels of that murder,

a forty-five-year-old woman was found dead, but her murder was different—she'd been shot in the back. Twice. All of these crimes are still unsolved.

In 1888, it's said that two Van Helsing–like hunters of local notoriety boasted they would find the Monster of Dead Man's Hole, and off they rode. Apparently, they chased it back into the cave area and shot it. They searched the creature's lair and found between five and eight human skulls (depending on what you read). Their description claims the creature was large like a giant bear, at least six feet tall, and it looked like a vicious gorilla, covered in dark-brown hair with a human face. They brought it back to Julian, but that's where the physical records of a newspaper trail end. Some say it was an April fool's prank, but that doesn't explain the constant carnage at the watering hole or the ghostly figures that have been seen in that area since.

A trusted associate recently introduced me to Linda Bare, who lives in the Warner Springs area. She gave me the details of her encounter with a chupacabra.

"I remember the day of my sighting of the chupacabra very well," recalled Bare. "It was midday, probably around 1 p.m. as I was driving southeast on Highway 79, just outside of Temecula, returning to Warner Springs near Vail Lake Resort. I caught sight of this creature on the left side of the road. It was running and crossed in front of my truck, continuing into the brush. It was gray in color and tall—about the size of a small miniature horse.

"Its chest and hindquarters were slim with shorter hind legs. The front legs were much longer, and its paws were very large, and its ears, jaw, and nose were pointed. It also had long fangs. The entire sprint in front of the truck probably took a matter of seconds, but I studied the features—as this was the strangest thing I'd ever seen."

Is there a Bigfoot, chupacabra, or giant wolf living in or near Warner Springs? I got Alex Boese, professional "hoaxpert,"

The area known as Oak Grove, near where the legendary Monster of Dead Man's Hole is believed to exist.

author, and curator of the Museum of Hoaxes, to join in my search for the Monster of Dead Man's Hole. We followed the vague Internet directions, consulting our live satellite readings on the iPad—that showed pools of water. We found a swimming pool and a lot of private-property signs. We asked people, but they either didn't know or weren't interested in giving directions. I offered a kid twenty dollars; he looked toward his house where someone was watching us through the curtains, hesitated, and then shook his head.

We drove off-road on a dirt road near Warner Springs for a few miles until we reached the end. We were losing sun quickly. I cut the engine. Boese brought what some consider an authentic recording of a Bigfoot call. I opened the Jeep and popped the CD into the player, cranked the speakers up, and strange calls blasted across the twilight horizon. Crows circled above, cawing loudly. There was no other response, and with only my high beams to get us back to safely, we headed back.

"Photos frequently surface showing misshapen creatures found washed up on beaches or lying in desert sands," said Boese of cryptids. "Their eyes are out of place, staring glassily at nothing, and their limbs twisted and bent. They look like nothing from this world. "Photoshopped!" the online skeptics soon cry out, or "It's the work of a taxidermist!" Sometimes they say, "Hoax!" It's easy to slip into knee-jerk skepticism, so I step back and recognize that just because something is strange doesn't mean it's not real. This is particularly true of anything relating to nature, because nature can and regularly does produce specimens of unparalleled weirdness. It swaps limbs around, moves organs about, and turns bodies inside out. Most of its mutations don't survive for long. But some do.

"So when people ask me if Bigfoot, the Loch Ness Monster, the chupacabra, or the Anza-Borrego Sandman [see the Vallecito chapter] are real, I'm not willing to come to any conclusion," continued Boese, author of *Electrified Sheep*. "I think their existence is very unlikely, as I find it hard to believe that if these creatures really existed, someone in their Hummer hasn't run over one of them yet, producing a specimen that biologists could poke and probe and finally pin up in a museum. I also know that the idea of these creatures has long been an irresistible lure for hoaxers and attention-seekers, but I also recognize that nature can always surprise us. So maybe these creatures are out there somewhere, lurking at the edges of our cities. It's not impossible. But if this is true, I kinda hope they're not found, because they're better off remaining hidden rather than ending up in a zoo or on reality TV."

Spotlight On:
The Curse of Warner Springs

The Saint Francis Indian Cemetery lies behind the Chapel of St. Francis of Assisi in Warner Springs. It's unclear how many Cupeño Native Americans were interred in the small piece of land, but at one point sixty-two markers were counted; most are without names now. The Cupeños felt close ties to the place where their ancestors were born and buried—they wanted to see the land where their bodies lay under the earth every day; they wanted to pay homage to their dead and the spirits that remained.

In 1880, John G. Downey, California's seventh governor, acquired the nearly forty-five thousand acres that included Warner Springs and beyond, using it primarily to raise cattle. The Cupeño tribe was outraged, as they knew they would soon be asked to leave the titleholder's land. Where would they go? They were taxed for using the land, and rumors of retaliation began.

In 1883, Downey and his wife, María Jesús Guirado, the daughter of a prominent Spanish gentleman of Sonora, Mexico, were on a train that wrecked in Tehachapi Pass. Due to slumbering staff and untended brakes, the train derailed and plunged into a ravine. Downey was pulled out of the train, but his wife's body was never recovered. Shortly thereafter, a friend introduced him to Yda Hillis Addis, a pretty twenty-year-old journalist to whom he immediately proposed. His sisters tried to prevent him from marrying her, as they were worried about his fortune. While they were doing everything possible to keep them separated, he married his housekeeper, Rosa Kelly.

Downey threw himself into his work and assets and began thinking about parsing off his Warner Springs property, especially the valuable land around the natural hot spring. He became critical of the Cupeño people, which he thought of as "squatting" on his land. Although many of the tribe were employed by his ranch—and they'd been there at least a thousand years before he stole their land—in 1892 he took legal action against the tribe to evict them.

The Cupeños challenged the eviction in the U.S. Supreme Court. Many were critical of Downey's decision, and he was feeling the stress of his actions. Downey died at home in 1894, some say by his own hand. Friends discussing his frame of mind had said that ever since his former wife's demise and the shock he suffered from the train accident he suffered from what we now recognize as post-traumatic stress disorder. Downey was constantly dealing with his fears and nervousness. With the sisters in charge, Rosa Kelly mysteriously exits the story, and two years later, Downey's adored sister, Annie Donahue, heir to his fortune, met a tragic end at age sixty.

The U.S. Supreme Court decided the *Cupeño v. Downey* case in 1901. The court ruled that the Cupeño people had rights to the land, but in one of the most unfair moves the U.S. Senate ever made, they told the Cupeños they'd waited too long to file their case.

In 1897, the Cupeño tribe refused to move off their land. Teddy Roosevelt saw trouble brewing and tried negotiating property rights with the heirs of Downey's estate. They wouldn't even entertain a discussion. Roosevelt offered to purchase land for the tribe to relocate to.

Cupeño chief Cecilio Blacktooth refused Roosevelt's offer and reportedly said, "You see that graveyard over there? They are our fathers and grandfathers. You see that Eagle Nest Mountain and Rabbit Hole Mountain? When God made them, he gave us this place. We have always been here. We do not care for any other place. It may be good, but it is not ours. This is our home."

In 1903, the nation was watching, and reporters were sent to follow the story as the army hired locals and their wagons to carry the members of the Cupeño tribe to their new home, where no preparations had been made to receive them. The night before they were to leave, one hundred armed, newly deputized men, many who'd been Downey's employees, arrived and awaited word to put the plan into place. The tribe would be combined with four other tribes (using different languages and customs) that had already been relocated to the reservation with limited resources.

The newly elected chief of the Cupeño people, Juan María Cibimoat, and his wife and daughter were the last to be loaded into wagons in the forced evacuation under armed escort to the Pala Reservation. It's said by some that everyone saw Cibimoat kick three times and spit three times upon the land they were leaving forever— apparently placing the ultimate curse on the property before they headed out. He reportedly told the white landholders that their lives would be ruined and that they could eat sand from that day on, although it seems as though from the moment Downey purchased the property karma had already begun to play itself out.

In 1906, cattle baron Walter Vail leased the Warner Ranch property and was crushed between two streetcars in Los Angeles.

Death wasn't the end of the curse for Downey, whose body was exhumed from the Los Angeles cemetery in which it was originally buried and then shipped unceremoniously to Coloma, where he was reburied, alone.

Many attribute the recent financial troubles of Warner Springs Ranch with the curse. The property should have been doing well in these troubled times, as it was cheaper to stay there than at most other luxury locations in San Diego. Flanked by the Los Coyotes Indian Reservation and Anza-Borrego Desert State Park, the ranch touts two Olympic-sized pools and a natural hot spring that the Cupeño people still mourn losing to this day, as they bathed in it daily to keep themselves healthy and to revive their spirits. The Cupeño tribe believed the spring's water held medicinal value and their people would never be healthy again without it. Sadly, when they were moved to Pala, many became ill, passed into the spirit world, and were buried on land not their own.

The property is currently entangled in litigation involving a bankruptcy, the Pala Band of Mission Indians, and the last owners of the Warner Springs Ranch. It's hard to say which way things will go. Will Warner Springs Ranch come full circle with the Pala people and finally end up in the hands of the tribe it was illegally taken from, or will some financial or legal miracle come through for the last owners, allowing them to keep the property? It's difficult to call at this point. The property could be closed for years before the case is settled. Curse or no curse, I foresee a winner and a loser—and perhaps a time when people will once again gather in peace and use the sacred springs again.

CHAPTER 14

Julian Jail
JULIAN

This jail has been rebuilt time and time again, but finally this cement building replaced the others that did not withstand the tough desert heat and cold. This jail never seems to be locked, but I wouldn't walk in unannounced. I've heard of people walking right on top of people sleeping in the dark corridor that loops around the two jail cells.

JULIAN, CALIFORNIA, is located in a physically rugged part of the state where the roads are narrow, the cliffs are steep, and the weather is either too hot or too cold most of the year. If you hear about Julian in the news, it's usually because a wildfire has nearly destroyed the town and a miracle shift of wind or a brave fire battalion has saved it from complete devastation. It's been this way for more than one hundred years, and nothing much about the town is likely to change in the future.

In 1869, A. E. Coleman, a.k.a. "Fred," a former slave who lived with a Native American family in the nearby city of Wynola, discovered gold in Julian. He started two mining companies after he first noticed gold while riding his horse through a local creek. Others followed suit, and mineshafts were soon dug into the mountains. Litigation about land grants and mineral rights continued on until all the gold was pulled out, miners moved on, and further litigation was a moot point. The region was lucky to survive the exodus of miners and suppliers (and money) that left in the mid-1870s. Instead of becoming a ghost town like so many abandoned mining towns of the time, the community survived because an industry had sprung up around the orchards planted during high times. In its gold-mining heyday, there were close to 600 people in the area—now that number is around 1,502.

Julian today is a far cry from the rough-and-tumble town it once was, with eight bars and fighting in the streets. Now, restaurants with music wafting out of doors can be found open during the early evening, but the town rolls up its sidewalks soon after sundown. And that's when the town gets dark . . . very dark. You can see all the stars and crisp wisps of vapor form around your every breath with the evening chill. This is the time of night when all of those stories about walking wolves (mythic man-wolf creatures) and the last surviving bear come to mind.

Julian is cradled in a mountainous area with an abundance of apple orchards and a mix of older and smaller Victorian homes. Highway 78 cuts through the center of the little town; blink and you're on the way to Anza-Borrego, Kumeyaay Native American country, and BLM property.

Fall brings an avalanche of visitors to Julian because of its Apple Days Festival. During the winter the small town is decorated for Christmas, and people come from other states and even other parts of the world to get very cold and sometimes wet, eat hot apple pie, drink warm cider, and buy baked goods and locally handcrafted gifts.

The summer and spring weekends bring packs of motorcyclists that ride through to the Salton Sea and on to the annual Laughlin River Run. Weekdays, after the winter holidays, Julian gets kind of quiet.

There was the feeling that what happened in Julian stayed in Julian until 1952, when the Julian Jail was closed for business and fugitives from law—innocent, or otherwise—would be housed in a county jail. The once very busy two-room jailhouse, built in 1914, still stands today. I've heard that at the time it was built, it boasted the only indoor toilet in Julian. The tiny building is perched on a hill with a beautiful view. Not bad housing for criminals. A plaque on the outside of the cement building reads:

JULIAN JAIL

1914

Run by a citizen constable whose wife cooked for prisoners, this jail held suspects, often involved with whiskey and/or fists, for trial and, if found guilty, for short terms imposed by the justice of the peace. Long terms were not served here. Designed and built for the County of San Diego for $1,075 plus $62 extra for overlooked grating and door, this reinforced site mixed concrete jail ended the escapes common to the three wooden jails that previously existed on this site since 1872. County ownership ended in 1952.

Another plaque is dedicated to the service of Daniel and Dee Baker, whom I assume were the original caretakers. The building is nothing fancy, nor is it locked at night, and no sign mentions restricted hours. I imagine that having drunks in a tiny building without heat or stove of any kind could have proved fatal to those drunks susceptible to hypothermia, but I could find no evidence anywhere of anyone actually dying in the jail.

But I did read about a man who was murdered just outside of the jail in 1870. During that time there were (and still are) several Native American reservations in what's now San Diego County. Back in the day, race relations between whites and Native Americans were at an all-time low. I did read about lynch-mob tactics where yahoo riders thirsty for trouble would go out and "collect" suspects, from the reservations, give them a "court hearing" that was never fair or civil, and "prisoners" would be lynched, shot, or beaten.

What happened to a Native American man now known only as Jose is only a footnote in the book *Ambiguous Justice: Native Americans and the Law in Southern California, 1848–1890* (Michigan State University Press), by Vanessa Ann Gunther. According to Gunther, Jose was abducted by a mob, charged with larceny, and held in prison for the night until his case could be heard the next day. During the night, he was mysteriously dragged outside and beaten to death. There was no sign of breaking and entry, and no investigation was conducted to look into his murder.

A man was also murdered on August 29, 1890, in front of the newspaper office—and the editor refused to look into it or even print it because he'd been threatened. The paper soon had another owner.

A woman who prefers to be known only as Sandra, whom I met in a retail store in town, told me about an incident that happened during her teen years when she worked in Julian as a waitress. Her parent's house was near the restaurant and even in inclement weather she'd ride her bike to work. Her ride took her past the Julian Jail.

During the winter, she'd often have to stay late at the restaurant to clean up after the cook had gone home.

"This one night," she said, whispering low so the women who were shopping in the store couldn't hear us talking. "I cannot begin to tell you how I felt—it was really something. There was no moon that night, so it was super-dark except the small area where my bike light hit on. All of a sudden, as soon as I turned onto the street the jail is on, it was like the temperature dropped twenty degrees and I hit an invisible wall. There was no reason for it, but my bike just kind of bucked me off—like what happens when your tire runs into something. I thought I'd hit a car. I fell off and took a minute to gather my wits.

"I stood up slowly to make sure I was okay. There was nothing around I could have run into. Well, I stood up and shook the dirt off my clothes and made sure I wasn't bleeding. I was—I'd cut my knee wide open and hit my head a good one—so I sat down on the side of the road. I left my bike on the side of the street. It only took a few seconds for all this to happen. That's when this car went by gangbusters—you know, *really fast!* His front tire crushed my front wheel and my handlebars. Had I been riding where I would have been a minute before, I'd have been killed for sure. I don't know what it was, but whatever it was saved my life. For no reason, I looked over at the Julian Jail—the door was open. I've always felt that whatever happened to save me was connected to that jail. Sounds completely weird, but that's what happened. I think a guardian angel must live there."

I'm not quite sure what to make of this story. The woman seemed perfectly sane and a credible witness. She showed me the goose bumps that had sprung up while she recalled the story. She even showed me a small scar on her knee from the incident. Physical poltergeist activity (see Spotlight On: Poltergeists) rarely happens, especially in an outdoor area, but I've often heard stories of people in peril being rescued by beings they believe to be their guardian angels.

I looked high and low for other locals who'd had a personal Julian Jail experience, but I found only a lot of myth built around the jailhouse. There was the story about the lady in white who can be seen opening the jail door every Friday the thirteenth, and the story about the wino who fell asleep and froze to death one night and can still be heard moaning for help in the wee hours of the morning. One woman claimed her grandfather had gotten locked in the jail as a kid and slept in one of the cell bunks only to be woken by a man screaming for help outside. The door was locked, and the boy couldn't get out. In the morning, he found the door open. Unfortunately, the woman's (who told me the story) grandfather is no longer alive to interview directly.

One weekend I took my husband, Jeff, out to Anza-Borrego, where we camped out with some of my friends in the desert. There are hundreds of square miles of BLM land with fire rings scattered around. We spent most of the days climbing the mountain trails. It was beautiful and so clear at night that we could see stars all the way down to the horizon. The desert flowers were blooming. On the way back home, we stopped at the Julian Grille and had dinner and perused the shelves at the Julian Book House next door. We were ready to head back home when my friend Susan (who'd flown in with her husband, Frank, from North Carolina) asked where they kept the dangerous people—she wondered if a small, seemingly peaceful town had such a need.

It was nightfall already, but I had a flashlight in the Jeep. We walked over to the Julian Jail, and I told them about the man who'd been beaten outside and how it was supposed to be haunted.

We walked around inside where we looked at the two cells—both are locked—and down the corridor that wraps around the jail cells. The corridor is pitch-black. I half expected to walk into some drunk who had passed out—someone could have been there lurking and we'd not even have known about it until we walked literally right over him. Walking through the corridor was the creepiest part of the evening.

Just for the heck of it, I did an EVP session and caught nothing. But Farrington Paranormal Investigations (**fpighosts.com/evps .html**) managed to get a Class-A EVP at the jail that said, "Kill."

Although I sensed nothing in the area, it still seems as ripe for ghosts as Julian's apples in the summer.

CHAPTER 15

Blair Valley and Pictograph Trail
ANZA-BORREGO DESERT

This Blair Valley trail takes you to the pictographs where shamans would speak to spirits and translate the communication into pictographs still seen today. This is an amazing place of Native American energy. Please, if you visit, tread lightly and take out what you bring in, or you may have more than a ranger following you home.

WHILE MY HUSBAND, JEFF, AND I were dating, we spent many long weekends camping in the deserts of California and Nevada. Although I'm not really a nature lover, the beauty of the desert landscape is awe-inspiring. With the exception of Hawaii's least populated islands, Vietnam, and some parts of Africa, I'd never really gone camping in a place where I was so alone with nature. Frankly, nature and I don't get along. In Africa I had a close call when bitten by a Gaboon viper, in Hawaii I fell twelve feet down into a damp and unstable hidden hole, and in the jungles of Vietnam I was robbed at gunpoint.

When I first visited Blair Valley in Anza-Borrego, I immediately appreciated the difficult circumstances the Kumeyaay Native Americans overcame while they lived in the area for thousands of years. The pictographs and *morteros* (deep man-made indentations in boulders where the community ground acorns, seeds, and other food staples) along the trails are reminders how the tribe once lived as one with nature. Under a moonlit sky, you feel the presence of a people who connected with nature in a way you and I will never know.

It's a moderately rough off-road journey to the valley, but the scratching bushes lining the dirt road aren't really your only worry—don't do this with a car that you baby; paint jobs and tire alignments will suffer. Once I got to Blair Valley, I was filled with spiritual energy that seemed elemental in nature; the closest I've felt to that kind of energy was visiting the sacred vortexes of Sedona, Arizona, the ceremonial areas in Hawaii, and the old abandoned temples in Southeast Asia.

It was nearly dark when we got to the primitive campsite and set up the tents. We'd brought our friends Becky and James Rollins, who were visiting us from Australia; we thought they might like a change of pace from the Sydney shore. There was an amazing full moon that evening, and we couldn't have timed things better. Becky and I had met in Maine when we taught at a summer camp together in our freshman year in college; we managed to keep in touch, and once in a while our vacation plans allow us to holiday together. My husband brought his guitar and another for James; they're both avid musicians and we had a musical evening filled with laughter under the night sky. The mountains and desert floor were bright with moonlight.

I told them a little about the Kumeyaay people as the coyotes raced across the desert chasing rabbits and mice, competing with the owls that snatched prey right out from over the hunt. Night in the desert is when everything that was hidden and remained still during the day is revealed.

I've read about the Kumeyaay tribe prior to the arrival of the Spaniards, who disconnected them from their land and religion. I am no expert, but at one time the Kumeyaay seemed to have a central god whose prophet, Kuuchamaay, sent messages to the people through red-tailed hawks, eagles, and ravens. Their spirits lived in sacred places, such as the nearby mountains where shamans painted the pictographs, telling the Kumeyaay story. It was said that the supernatural beings who dwelled there were available to aid the people if they asked for help, often the job of the shaman. The Kumeyaay cremated their dead in a ritual that would help the spirits into the next world and practiced what we now call animism, a belief in spirit beings that are thought to animate nature.

At about midnight, the guys said goodnight and went off to their tents to sleep, while Becky and I kept talking and catching up on our news over the last year. We were the only people camping in the area, and we enjoyed the quiet, which was broken now and then with coyote calls and screeching owls.

We sat listening to the noises of the desert, and I told Becky about the trails we'd be hiking the next day. All at once, Becky, who'd been looking through binoculars, put her hand on my arm and pointed up toward the pictograph trail. I looked to see what kind of wildlife she'd spotted. I looked and looked and tried to figure out what kind of matrixing games my eyes were playing. Not sure what I was seeing, I took the binoculars and looked again. We watched for about thirty minutes at what seemed like a dozen ghostly shadows moving around on the mountains. I gave the binoculars to Becky.

"Holy Dooley! What the hell is that?" Becky whispered in amazement.

"I don't know," I answered, as the figures had no recognizable features. "Maybe goats—sheep?"

"But, they're *gliding,* not gittying about like goats do," she said, pointing out the obvious. Had it been a night without a moon, we wouldn't have even seen the figures. "Should we wake the guys?"

"No, let them sleep. Whatever it is, it's not going to hurt us. Let's get the flashlights and put our boots on—and go check it out. It looks like some kind of natural phenomena to me."

"As you can see, I'm not feeling all rapt about the situation here," Becky said, meaning that it wasn't exactly a rapturous moment, and going up the mountain to check things out didn't sound like a good idea to her. "Why don't we just call a trooper to come check on it?"

"*A trooper?*" I smiled; those Australian rangers sure must be efficient. "Oh, yeah, there's lots of police out here in the middle of nowhere," I answered, sarcastically. "It's hard enough to get them out in a *real* emergency. I can't imagine giving 911 this description and not having them ask if I'm drunk, on medication . . . or in need of medication."

She hesitated, but we were soon on our way, and the closer we got the more apparent it was that what we were seeing were not animals or tricks of the light. The long, narrow projections of darkness were about eight feet long, three feet wide, pitch-black, and moving around the mountain in a group, going from one area to the next as if in search of something and checking all the nooks and crannies.

My first thought was that they were aliens because the figures we saw were so unearthly. Then, I thought about the rich culture of the Kumeyaay people and about the spirit stories of other Native American cultures I'd heard and read, including the stories of my own Apache grandmother and her ghostly stories of Superstitious Mountain that scared the hell out of me. I'd recently met author Antonio R. Garcez, an amazing modern storyteller who writes regional Native American paranormal books. He travels to interview Native Americans and finds the ghosts stories of each culture. These were no aliens; they seemed to be some kind of spirits who once worked with the Kumeyaay when they called this home. Perhaps these shadows were the spirits of the Kumeyaay themselves still watching over their sacred homeland.

My mind was reeling with the possibilities. I took many photos with no flash and a high-speed ISO, but I knew, because of the distance, that the only things I'd get were grainy images at best. We moved slowly, keeping our flashlights turned off and sticking to the bushes so we wouldn't be seen. The shadows seemed to have some kind of joined intelligence in the way they moved as a group with some kind of system. Without warning, Becky beamed her LED flashlight on the shadows; they scattered and regrouped at the base of the mountain, and then they stayed there, unmoving.

"Uh-oh," I said, wondering what the next move might be.

"What do you suppose they are?" Becky asked, curiously. We stood still and watched, wondering what we should do. We watched for what seemed like forever, not wanting to move in case our retreat would encourage some kind of reaction from them.

"Didn't that one just move?" Becky said for the hundredth time. "I'm feeling a bit wonky," she finally concluded after about an hour.

I wasn't feeling very well either. Between standing so still I was barely breathing, my stomach being in knots, and every muscle in my body feeling taut, I was ready to go. We'd thought about calling out but opted against it. I felt for my phone in my pocket, but I remembered that it was charging in the Jeep. The day's heat had given way to the desert's nocturnal chill. I'd taken the bandana from around my neck and covered my nose and mouth to keep the cold air from giving me a headache, but it was too late. Becky had her hoodie zipped up to her eyes. We were quite the pair.

The shadows seemed to lighten up or to lose energy. We decided to make a break for it and quickly made our way back to the camp, looking over our shoulders to make sure they— *whatever they were*—were not following us. Neither one of us could sleep that night; instead we sat in our folding chairs just staring at the mountain to see if the shadows were advancing. I tried to take pictures, but nothing came out. We had our backs to the fire we'd been sitting behind earlier, but the brightness of the flames made it too difficult to keep an eye on the shadows. They seemed to remain standing still, but finally disappeared in the sun's first rays. We could no longer see them at all and began to question whether they'd been there at all.

We finally went into our tents and fell asleep until noon when a Boy Scout troop showed up to set up camp. When we woke, we told the guys what we'd seen, and they both asked us why we didn't wake them up, as we really should have just for the sake of having more witnesses. Later in the day we hiked up to the pictographs, where we met up with a group of the boys and their Scoutmasters who were flying remote-control gliders from the top of the mountains.

One of the Scoutmasters asked if we had a screwdriver. He borrowed my husband's Swiss Army knife to tighten some screws in a plane that had hit a rock. The Scoutmaster asked us, in all seriousness, if we'd heard voices the night before. I shook my head and told him what we did see. In exchange, he described the last campout they'd had. Apparently, in the middle of the night, when the boys were sleeping, he and another Scoutmaster were awakened by the sound of whispering voices. When he got up to quiet what he thought were Scouts, he found them asleep. The two quietly waited to see if the voices would start again. There were no other campers around where they heard the voices. The low whispering continued. He described it as going in and out like a radio station. The other Scoutmaster woke up the remaining adults and asked them to participate in a prayer circle; he was not a Christian, but since he was outnumbered, he agreed. He said the whispers began to dissipate, but the sun was already coming up by then. He admitted that he found himself frightened by the phenomena and noted that he was the only scoutmaster in the group who'd returned to the area.

We camped for another two days. Two more campers showed up the last night we were there and went night hiking up the trail. We'd passed them on our way down the narrow pathway between boulders. Becky asked the two women if they'd gone night hiking there before. "Plenty of times," one of them answered. She bluntly asked them if they'd encountered anything . . . supernatural.

Both women laughed and shook their heads. Then one of them thought about it and said that about ten years earlier they'd heard a woman screaming from her tent. Everyone ran to her, thinking she'd either been bitten by a snake or was being attacked; they unzipped her tent and found her cowering in a corner, screaming. She noted that the woman was visibly shaken by what she described as a dark figure sitting in her tent watching her sleep, and she claimed it disappeared when she screamed. The tent had not been unzipped, nor was there another way to get out. "She asked if she could bring her VW Bug over to our campsite and sleep in it. We told her no worries—and that's where she slept until dawn, doors locked and windows up. She left without even waking us up. Personally, we don't believe in such foolishness."

We nodded in agreement, as if the thought was utterly ridiculous. I was relieved to find that they didn't ask us why we'd originally asked the question.

"It scared the hell out of me," Becky now admits about our experience with the strange shadows. "I don't know what I thought I was doing shining a light on them—I just didn't want them to be real and thought it would make them disappear. Boy, was I wrong. I was really frightened they were coming for us, but they just stayed there for about two hours or so until the sun came up. They really seemed to be standing sentinel, or something."

Since that time, I've checked the Internet regularly and posted in hiking wikis trying to find anything similar. A guy contacted me who'd been in one of the mining holes in the mountains nearby. He climbed in seeking shelter from the heat. He fell asleep in the cool shaft and woke up as the sun was going down. He sat up, feeling there was someone else in the tiny cave. Bolting upright, he took his pocket flashlight out and lit up the tiny cave; there were dark shadows sitting all around him. He was in such a hurry to get out that he gave himself a concussion as he crawled out the narrow passageway. He drove himself to the ranger station where they called an ambulance, as they thought he was completely nuts. "I've never been so scared in my life!" he summed up in the post.

I couldn't help but think the shadows we'd seen might have had something to do with the Kumeyaay mythos, so I began searching for clues in their stories and found what I believe to be the Kumeyaay word describing a shadow spirit: *temeshaa*. I remembered what I felt when I saw the shadows—it wasn't fear *exactly*, but more respect and awe. There was something so old and watchful about them. I began thinking that they seemed to continue on a path just as the seasons do, regardless if any humans are even participating. The shadows did not seem to even know of our presence until Becky turned on the flashlight. We seemed to interrupt their partaking in a ritual that they might do every night for all we know.

Once in a while, by happenstance, we have the opportunity to observe the paranormal in action. As investigators, we need to grasp this concept—the things we see and hear and the supernatural events that take place around us are probably not occurring just because we are there to witness them. It's self-centered to think that the spirits around us perform only when we're there pointing a meter at them. The spirit realm is always around us, and like the Native American people who honored, worked with, and cherished the spirits in their world, we must also see the bigger picture and work toward understanding who they are, why they are here, and how to best work with them. I think we need to heed the Native American respect and awe of the unseen world around us, because one day we might find out we need them a whole lot more than they need us.

While doing research for this chapter, I found a beautiful story about a compassionate shadow spirit and its interaction with a woman who needed help desperately. It's from a book titled *Indian Legends of the Cuyamaca Mountains* by Mary Elizabeth Johnson, published in 1914. The story is "Ah-ha' Wi-Ahha' (Water Colder Water)." An excerpt follows:

> *When she reached the spring she sat on its brink, and filled her basket with its cold, refreshing water. Gazing into the crystal depths she caught a glimmer of a shadow quickly passing, and at once knew it to be that of the good spirit of the spring.*
>
> *She beseeched and plead with it to save her from the clutches of Hum-am' Kwish 'wash (Whip to Kill People); and as she leaned over farther and farther, trying to get one more glimpse of the shadow, the waters rose up and gently engulfed her.*

CHAPTER 16

Vallecito County Park
VALLECITO

The Vallecito stagecoach stop where just about anything—hold-ups, shootouts, death . . . hauntings—could and did happen. It's great for a weekend investigation; your team can spend some time together at the venue and then just fall asleep afterward.

DO YOU WANT TO GO on a paranormal investigation where just about anything can happen, and it's pretty much you versus the elements? The Anza-Borrego Desert is the place. It's a long haul out to the desolate area, and once you're out there, you're pretty much on your own.

In the old days, passengers paid a few hundred dollars to ride the Butterfield Overland Mail route stagecoach without any guarantee they'd actually arrive at their destination—actually many did not. Trains made the dangerous and costly travel obsolete. More than one hundred years later, the Butterfield Stage Station now is Vallecito County Park's centerpiece.

Back in the day, the stage station wasn't much but it was a place for stagecoach passengers to stretch their legs, eat, and sometimes sleep. Butterfield Stagecoach drivers carrying mail and passengers from the East Coast to the West, and vice versa, took this opportunity to water and rest their horses and get some sleep. There were no real amenities at the stage stop except for the shelter from the brutal range of temperatures outside and protection from the wildlife and sneak attacks from bandits who robbed passengers and stagecoaches at gunpoint. Overnight guests slept on the floor with blankets.

Throughout the years, the Vallecito station was occupied by one tenant after another. In 1884, James E. Mason purchased 160 acres that included the old, abandoned station. Mason died and was buried on the property in 1931. The state ended up with the land, and in 1934 San Diego County began restoring the stagecoach station. Today, only one room is part of the original structure.

The current cemetery has three graves, although some claim the real graves are somewhere else on the property. In addition to James Mason's grave, there is another belonging to John Hart, one of the first attendants of the historic Butterfield Stage Station, who died at age thirty-one in 1867. The most interesting grave—and the one with the best story—is that of a woman identified as Eileen O'Conner, a woman traveling from back East to meet her husband-to-be in Sacramento in the late 1850s. When she got to the stagecoach stop, she stayed to rest and missed the stagecoach's departure. The station manager put her in a bed in the backroom for several days, as she assured them she would soon be ready to travel, but she died inside the building.

According to local lore, this grave belongs to the specter of the "White Lady," whom people claim to have seen walking the grounds in a wedding dress. Newly wedded women leave their bridal veils on the grave to receive good luck from the ghost, who never made it to her own wedding.

No one claimed her. The womenfolk at the station rooted around in her luggage and found an expensive wedding dress folded at the bottom of her bag, so they dressed her body in it and buried her in the desert. During one of my recent day visits to the park, I discovered a bridal veil on her grave, which I found rather odd. *Shouldn't that be inside the grave?* Later that day, I met a woman who was also spending some time at the park that day. I asked her about the veil, and she said it's an old tradition with local women who, after their weddings, place the veils on her grave for luck. Apparently, the spirit of Eileen O'Conner—who never had a chance to see her true love again—blesses the couples with a life of happiness.

The first time my team went to Vallecito, there were other campers, but it was pretty quiet and we were pleased with the experience. The whole area has a creepy feel, especially when driving down the lonesome roads where one is reminded of the makeshift graves of criminals shot holding up the coaches and the men protecting the coaches whose decomposed bodies dot the route. Today you'll see *descansos* with photos and plastic flowers commemorating deadly vehicular crashes that have taken place more recently. Lots of pictures of guys with motorcycles. Here, death is a natural part of desert life. I can only imagine how they crashed, considering how I've swerved many a time while driving that narrow highway as dark shadows pass in front of my headlights and off the road.

Before the American settlers arrived, Spaniards came to "conquer" the Native Americans of this area. The earliest people to live here were the Hawi; later, the Kumeyaay occupied this area from about AD 1000 to 1906, when they were placed on reservations. Before their removal, many of the Native Americans died protecting their homeland where, for centuries, their people had been born, raised, and died.

As a medium, I definitely felt the influence of the Native American spirits present. For many years the settlers and people who passed through—and people today—have seen and made note of UFOs in the Anza-Borrego Desert. As recently as 2011, a YouTube video titled "Amazing UFO Sighting Southern Anza-Borrego Dec 2011" shows a UFO having encountered what looks like a county helicopter doing a rescue operation. What some call "ghost lights" are reported low to the ground and hovering without a sound, rushing toward people and then disappearing.

Strange sightings don't end there; in 1939 a prospector told of being attacked by several large, upright creatures covered with hair near the Anza-Borrego Sink. Locals nicknamed a Bigfoot-like creature the "Borrego Sandman." Miner Harold Lancaster encountered the creature in 1964. As the beast approached him, he took out his .22 pistol and fired warning shots into the air to scare it, and it took off. Reports of the "ghost lights," UFOs, and the Borrego Sandman have been reported by military personnel, locals, and tourists alike.

The "White Lady" has been seen rising from her grave on full-moon nights and walking to the stagecoach building. Some observers claim she is the dead bride-to-be, Eileen O'Conner. Others claim to hear and see a stagecoach and horses roaring through the area and then vaporizing. According to sketchy sources, two Texans shot each other over a game of cards in the building, and there are Internet rumors of these two spirits haunting the place.

I once had a strange experience in the one-person bathroom of the station during a day when I was alone there. The half-gallon of Julian apple cider had caught up with me. As I pulled up my pants, the doorknob shook violently like someone knew it was locked and they were trying to break it open. It was a very deliberate movement. I texted my husband and told him if he didn't hear from me in a minute to call the police. I opened the door quickly to see if anyone was there. The parking lot was empty and there was no one around. I checked all of the other bathrooms. Empty. No one was in the park.

That same visit, I was taking pictures of the children's playground and all the swings were still. Then, as I started taking pictures, one swing began to move to and fro and the others barely moved in the gentle breeze. The moving swing kept going higher and higher, as if someone was pumping their legs and propelling it. The second swing began moving a little, and the third baby swing was still. It swung like that for about twenty minutes and then slowed to a stop. At that point, I heard someone clear their throat in back of me. Unfortunately, I did not

The swing in the children's playground started swinging on its own without any wind while I was there. It looks like there are some very playful spirit(s) at the campgrounds.

have any other equipment except my camera with me, even my cell phone was dead in the car. It was getting dark and clearly time for me to leave.

On one visit with my team, there was a lot of activity at the stagecoach-stop building itself and a little at the graves. We had an E-Pod-AMP that detects the e-field which surrounds static electricity—we placed it on Eileen's grave and asked questions. It responded to our questions by changing colors. It was difficult to know if the machine was really working or if it had been picking up the dry static electricity coming up from the desert winds. We did catch a few illegible EVPs that sounded like the whispers of a woman when we asked her if she wanted some treats we'd brought.

"The pre-hunt research for this site didn't prepare me for what we found," recalls medium and Roadside Paranormal investigator Jennifer Donohue. "At most, I expected some images or EVPs from the cemetery. The evening started simply enough as we unpacked our gear and set up tents before losing daylight. I headed up the hill toward the bathroom, and a man's voice called from behind me, 'Look here.' I didn't think anything about it until I turned around and no one was there. Retracing my steps, I rounded the corner of the locked and deserted stagecoach station, but still found no one. I shrugged it off and moved on.

"The group spread out around the site after sunset to take readings—I started at the station with Sara," says Jennifer. "As I passed the dusty, empty room at one end of the building, a vibrating pulse of energy seemed to pass right out of the building. I saw the waves you see when it's hot and you're looking out over a tarmac. It went through me, which gave me quite a case of goose bumps. The energy felt sickly and left me feeling nauseous and wanting to take a shower.

"Working with a digital recorder but wanting immediate feedback, I called Sara over with her K-II Mel Meter. She said she hadn't gotten anything yet, which surprised me—the area felt alive . . . magnetic. She walked next to the building, scanning it with the meter and shook her head. Nothing. Meanwhile, my sense of unease ratcheted up a hundredfold as we both heard a man's voice say, 'Kelly.' I didn't hear anything on the recorder except a sharp breath I don't remember Sara or I making. When Sara put the meter up against the window shutters, all five lights immediately lit up. We asked the usual questions—if it wanted us there? Did it want us to leave? Did it know it was dead? The lights did not change. They stayed fully lit until we asked, "What are you?" The indicator lights went dark. After that, we didn't get any more readings on the K-II around the building.

"After the investigation, we all sat around enjoying the campfire having what I call the After the Hunt gathering to let off some steam [watch for our live online *After the Hunt* shows coming to ghostopedia.com]. At the end of the night, Sara and I went back to use the bathroom, and the energy had gotten a little crazy around the stagecoach building. We had to go by it to get to the bathroom, and it felt like someone was watching us—and not in a good way. We gave the building a wide berth and picked up the pace.

"On our way back, Sara and I heard some knocking coming from what sounded like the inside of the building. We thought somebody had gotten inside. We went around to the doors and they were all still locked—from the outside. They leave the lights on inside, and we were looking through the cracks in the wooden shutters and kept seeing black figures quickly moving around. We wrote them off as bats. When Sara knocked on the wall, we heard a faint knocking like it was coming from the other side of the building. We went around to the other side and knocked. Then we heard it again: a response from the other side. We knocked again, but there was no response, like it wasn't going to play unless we chased it around to the other side of the building again. We did it again, but this time, Sara waited on the other side. There were no further responses.

"I remember on one of our trips, as soon as we'd finally got in our sleeping bags and started falling asleep, an earthquake hit—it was pretty big. We all just waited for aftershocks, but it stopped. That's the most frightening experience I've had there."

Roadside Paranormal case manager and investigator Leo Aréchiga was part of an experiment with a new piece of equipment.

"The Vallecito Stage Coach adobe is a place filled with stories of valiant settlers and unfulfilled dreams," says Leo, romanticizing the reason that the place is haunted. "Our team made a point of investigating the claims that the old building and surrounding area may be haunted, so an overnight stay was in order. We arrived at the campsite Friday evening and set up camp and planned the night's investigation.

"The sun settled behind the surrounding mountains as we sat around the campfire preparing our equipment and loading batteries and fresh flash cards. The adobe stagecoach building, which was only about one hundred feet away from our camp, disappeared into the darkness. We headed toward the gravesites where three stone-covered graves stand alone as reminders of the frailty of life in the desert. The following is something that many of you will be able to relate to; others will simply laugh and tell the story, *Did you hear the one about the guy* . . . Sara brought a new instrument to test on that particular investigation. It wasn't a high-tech device, nor is it a widely accepted paranormal tool. Sara brought a microwave. That's right, *a microwave*. I'll give her credit—it was a brand-new one. Right out of the box. The theory is that a microwave blocks out environmental 'noise' that interferes with equipment including EMF, and keeps the recorders in a soundproof environment—free from our shifting shoes in the desert sand and any whispers or noise our clothes made. Simply put, a nontechnical Faraday cage.

"The idea was to place voice recorders inside the microwave, so if an EVP was caught, it would not be from an accidental source, rather a conscious attempt from a spirit to communicate with us. Even today, I think it's a great theory. I have to admit though, the team wasn't as thrilled. It seems no one wanted to carry the heavy box to the investigation area. No one except me, that is. The giggles and snickers were plenty as I hauled that microwave over to the graves. We set up K-II meters, voice recorders, and other equipment around the graves and inside the box. My camera was recording, and we began to ask questions. At one point some of the instruments on the headstones lit up and there was a slight blip on the K-II meters. We took pictures. Then it stopped. After a few more questions it happened again. We continued our attempts to communicate with the spirits, but no results were had.

Roadside Paranormal team members (*left–right:* Jennifer Donohue, Leo Aréchiga, and Kim) relax and get warm after the investigation at the After the Hunt fireside gathering.

"After another group of campers near the gravesite answered us with mild profanity when we asked if anyone was there, we packed up," says Leo, clearly remembering the incident with humor. "We returned to our own site, microwave in tow. Later that night we walked to the old adobe stagecoach that stood directly behind us. The wing flaps from the bats could be felt as they swooped past us. We took pictures, video, and had EVP sessions. One of our members did capture voices on his recorder. Voices that did not belong to any of us. Voices that did not belong to any *living* person either. There was our flicker of proof. On many occasions, that flicker is all you get."

Coastal Southern California

Coronado
Hotel del Coronado **(19)**

Oceanside
Hunter Steakhouse **(18)**

San Diego Harbor
Star of India **(17)**

Santa Catalina Island
Santa Catalina Island **(20)**

Summerland
Summerland **(21)**

CHAPTER 17

Hunter Steakhouse
OCEANSIDE

The Buena Vista Lagoon is said to be the place where developers pushed what was left of the cemetery off the cliff into what is today's wildlife sanctuary.

WE COULDN'T HAVE IMAGINED a more perfect trifecta—paranormal investigation, good food, *and* history. Hunter Steakhouse, built on the Oceanside bluff that was once the sacred burial ground called Buena Vista Cemetery, has it all. So how does a cemetery become a haunted restaurant? As with all investigations, we need to review the history to get the gist of who today's spirits are and why they might be communicating with us.

The cemetery swung open its gates for business in 1885, after the property had been divided into 160 plots. Its first interment: Sarah Francie Parry, fifty-one years old, who died from "heart dropsy." Burials continued until 1906 with only forty-four bodies interred—less than a third of the cemetery's capacity. I'm not sure what happened, but I imagine the city just lost interest in this piece of property and so gradually abandoned it. Newspaper stories claim that in 1955, a schoolteacher who lived nearby on Stewart Street purchased the land to maintain her view of the lagoon. Apparently, it was a wise investment, as both the extension of I-5 that took a chunk out of the property and greedy developers who saw the land as a good opportunity took it off her (or her heir's) hands. I have to say one of the biggest mysteries about this property is why, with such a beautiful view, the builder didn't situate the building to take advantage of it.

My sources say that only ten bodies were removed (others say seventeen) from the site and interred in surrounding cemeteries, though the developer was given instructions to relocate up to forty remains. The low number removed is no surprise, given that the construction company had a deadline and there were no advocates for the dead overseeing the work. To do the job properly, archeologists would have been needed. Although graves today are far more standardized than they used to be—six feet under, with a cement vault encasing the coffin that encloses the embalmed body—back then it was a guy with a shovel and no oversight. Maybe he'd dig four feet down but wanted to get home before dark. On another day, maybe he'd get enthusiastic, lose track of time, and dig down seven feet. For the most part, bodies were placed in simple wooden coffins not meant to withstand time, with some dirt over them. Death reports were not required by the city until the 1906, as the San Francisco earthquake and fires demonstrated the necessity for paper trails. Before that time, there were no laws surrounding the practice of burial, and the funeral industry didn't have nearly the choke-hold monopoly it has today.

The Buena Vista Cemetery was the *nearly* final resting place for many working-class immigrants. There probably weren't too many fancy coffins—probably about four or five. Others would have been made of thin wood, and the bodies weren't always embalmed, as one had to have the means to pay for the expensive process. Most people were busier worrying about the next month's expenses than paying for embalming when "dust to dust" would do just fine. Digging up a coffin more than fifty years later would just about guarantee that not much of the body would remain except for femur bones, jewelry, and a skull—if that. Only the well-to-do with the good coffins and embalming would be found relatively intact.

One such body was that of a woman who spooked the demolition crew, as they could see her through the leaded-glass "window" in her coffin. Her hair was still red, her skin pale, the rest of her well preserved. The other body in such stellar condition was that of Doniphan Blair Frazee, whose surname was a famous one in San Diego history. According to a newspaper report, his body was eerily preserved to look still alive, and even the flower he held in his hands still showed color, which raises the question: did the embalmer put the fresh-cut flower in a vase of embalming fluid so it would suck in the liquid before placing it into the casket?

Whatever happened to spook the workers on the job left some of them feeling guilty about dumping the bodies. Even today, the historical society reports a person having recently called to give them the details of the desecration during that job. According to some, coffins were shoved over the bluff with a bulldozer, to be covered with dirt and debris from the site. Others were said to be sunk into the lagoon.

Notable pioneers once residing on this plot of land include John Henry Myers, entrepreneur, builder, and brother of Andrew

Jackson Myers, Oceanside's founder (who built the first home in the city after receiving a patent from the U.S. government for the land); and Marshal Charles C. Wilson, whose brave heroics were talked about long after he was shot down in the streets of Oceanside by John Murray on July 4, 1889. Others buried there were integral in the small city's survival.

What was the land like before it was the city of Oceanside? It would have been a good place for the Native Americans who lived there, because antelopes, bobcats, deer, elk, foxes, mountain lions, rabbits, river otters, ground squirrels, oysters, albacore, halibut, bass, tuna of all kinds, and thresher shark were plentiful. The Luiseño Indians are believed to have been the first people on this land for close to one thousand years. The Luiseños are part of the Shoshonean tribe—they called themselves the *Payomkowishum,* which translated means "people of the west." It's said that the Oceanside population of this tribe once soared at ten thousand. I imagine a beautiful property such as the Buena Vista bluff overlooking the lagoon was a great lookout post for enemies coming by sea, and it probably offered something of a shelter from the elements. Chances are this piece of property was inhabited at least a thousand years before it was even made a cemetery.

It seems as though the settlers learned the same lesson as the Native Americans did—nothing is permanent, especially when there's money, greed, and apathy connected with the situation.

The Hunter Steakhouse is a paranormal investigation–friendly location, and it's hopping with energy. I've used its large banquet room for my larger Ghosts Happen Meetup group meetings. We have a speaker come in, enjoy dinner (at great group rates!), and then do an investigation inside that later spills into the eerie moonlit lagoon area below.

On several occasions, I've taken investigators out to the lagoon in the early morning hours when the traffic on I-5 has slowed. The lagoon is a 223-acre wetland habitat managed by the California

Department of Fish and Game. At least 103 bird species, 18 mammal species, and 14 amphibian and reptile species live in and around the lagoon, and many more birds visit during spring and fall migrations. Altogether, more than 200 bird species have been observed—which means that many of the strange animal sounds heard here may be odd to us because we've not had a chance to hear them before. People normally enter the sanctuary from the Coast Highway 101 on the Carlsbad–Oceanside border instead of sliding down the bank. This steep hill "entrance" is a good way to experience your first good fall, and the area is littered with rubbish, including plenty of liquor bottles and condoms from the teenage wasteland that seems to have been created there. Wear boots and long pants. Please watch your step, and try to walk where the land has already been cleared so you're not disturbing any of the wildlife—I've also seen snakes in this area.

I've had a number of extraordinary paranormal experiences in the lagoon area, including witnessing "ghost lights," which look like globular lights about five feet in diameter traveling above the surface of the water. As they come in toward shore, they submerge without leaving a trace except for the light that seems to get swallowed by the darkness of the lagoon. This has happened twice. There is also an area in the lagoon by the water where you can actually feel a vibration late at night; it's like a low-level hum I've heard in EVP sessions here, Some nights it's there, some nights it isn't.

I've taken my Frank's Box #55 down to the lagoon, and it's caught a Native American radio station that carries all-night chanting, and instead of oscillating through the stations it just sticks there. Although there are more-powerful stations closer to Buena Vista, this tribal music seems to come from KOPA, owned by the Pala Band of Mission Indians, which is at least twenty-five miles away. Other Frank's Box ITC messages (see Spotlight On: ITC Technology) we've received include "Do not follow me" and "My own children hate me."

Capturing shadow people on digital displays inside the Hunter Steakhouse has been a learning experience. While shooting a series of more than three hundred images from the same place within seconds of each other with 3200 ISO, I captured a shadow person walking across the inside balcony and down the stairwell, where it finally disappeared about halfway down the stairs just as one of the team members walked into the room.

In the women's bathroom, where a lot of paranormal experiences take place, I came out of the stall, and the door next to my stall was closed. I clearly heard a woman's voice saying, "I'm here," and I waited, thinking it was one of my team members. I waited about three minutes and finally said, "I'll meet you outside," but there was no response. I asked who was in the bathroom. No answer. I knocked on the stall door, but it opened to reveal no one else in the bathroom. This was later in the evening after most of the staff had left and all of the patrons had been gone for hours. When I left the bathroom, I found my team was outside, and only the manager, a man, was left in the building.

I got an EVP from a session in the bar after nearly everyone had gone home. One of the team members had asked, "Why don't you show yourself?" Later, the recorded EVP response replied, "Take off your shirt." The voice sounded more than lecherous, it sounded like a command.

"There have been several reports of a man sitting in the lower bar area," says Michelle Myers, one of the lead investigators and case managers for our group, Roadside Paranormal. "I have not seen him, but there is a clear feeling of tension and uneasiness in that space. While conducting EVP session in the upstairs dining area of the restaurant, team members and I heard rustling sounds coming from a corner booth, and couldn't find any physical source for it. Some of us also had feelings of anxiety and tingling while in that space. One team member that is sensitive felt the presence of an angry man there, and from what I recall, the residual stress of a couple having a heated argument. Outside the restaurant, some of us heard strange animal-like sounds coming from the lagoon behind the restaurant and followed them, but could not find the origin of the sounds."

Jennifer Donohue, a lead investigator for Roadside Paranormal and medium, is one of several who have heard the "moving furniture" upstairs. "Our investigations at Hunter Steakhouse are never disappointing," says Jennifer. "Pushy voices through the PX are fairly common. One night, as the restaurant cleared out and we geared up, we heard someone moving furniture upstairs. It sounded like employees were moving tables back and forth across the room. Needing the space quiet before we could begin, we sought out management to ask how much longer before they would be finished. The confused manager showed us the space above—a dark storage area in the rafters where clearly no one had been moving anything, certainly nothing that could cause the loud scrapings we'd heard earlier."

Nearly all of the teams I've come in contact with regarding this location have heard the "moving furniture" sounds from above.

"Many ghost researchers have noticed an apparent spectral law of cause and effect: desecrate a cemetery and you often create a haunting," explains John J. Lamb, author of *San Diego Specters* and former homicide detective. "We don't really know why this is so, but proof of the rule can be found at the Hunter Steakhouse. Episodes from the Hunter cover almost the entire gamut of spectral phenomena. Employees and diners have seen full-figure and partial apparitions, heard disembodied voices, and experienced ghostly touching. There's also poltergeist activity, spectral rapping originating from the locked attic, and the bar is home to what could be a teetotaling spook that sometimes knocks bottles from the shelf.

"The Hunter is also one of the few places I've investigated where I actually saw something strange occur. Back in October

1999, a reporter from a San Diego television station was inter-viewing me at the restaurant when the topic somehow drifted to the Amityville Horror. I laughed scornfully and said that the supposedly true story of Amityville was a complete fraud. Then I gestured toward the dining room and added, 'You want a *real* haunting? This is the place.'

"At that very moment," Lamb continues. "Every light in our portion of the restaurant went out. The reporter squeaked with fright and ran from the room while I began to applaud the ghost's perfect timing. Investigation revealed that the electrical breakers for that portion of the building had somehow tripped. But how, no one knows. The electrical panel was in a locked room and the restaurant manager—who was present during the interview—had the only key. The manager also claimed that this was the first time in his memory that the lights had behaved that way. So, if you're ever in Oceanside, make reservations at the Hunter Steakhouse. It has a deservedly fine reputation for its steaks, seafood, and *spirits*."

When the cemetery land was first purchased by the school-teacher protecting her lagoon view in 1959, it had already been damaged by a fire that had consumed all of the wooden grave markers—the only records of life and death before records were implemented. A few marble markers remained, and one caught the eye of someone who made sure it was recorded by the San Diego History Center before it disappeared altogether. I believe the epitaph kind of sums up what these spirits must feel as their final resting place was destroyed and their coffins shoved off the bluff in the name of progress:

Our household circle is broken
A voice we loved is still
A place is vacant at our hearts
That never can be filled.

CHAPTER 18

Star of India
SAN DIEGO HARBOR

The *Star of India* in all her glory as part of the MMSD armada

WHEN MY HUSBAND AND I WERE COURTING, he lived in San Diego and I lived in Las Vegas. We camped in Red Rock Canyon in Nevada and spent time at San Diego Harbor when I visited California. When I flew in on Friday nights, we'd have dinner at one of the harbor restaurants then stroll over to the promenade where the Maritime Museum of San Diego's (MMSD's) armada of ships, boats, and submarines are anchored.

The *Star of India* is the oldest active tall iron ship in the world and a California state and national historic landmark. It's difficult to imagine, but when she was conceived, horses were the main method of transport. The once state-of-the-art beauty has survived many eras of technical achievement. Boarding her now, one can easily imagine the absolute freedom ships once provided. She's everything and more, but there's just something unsettling about the antediluvian artifact from the mid-1800s that gives me chicken skin when I pass her berth on a dark night.

When I moved to San Diego, we joined the MMSD and I also found a great many Meetup groups for making new friends with similar interests. I joined San Diego Ghost and Paranormal (SDGAP) and found Dave Hanson, the group's leader—a great resource for this Southern California paranormal neophyte. SDGAP is also where I met several people who became core members of my own paranormal-investigation team, Roadside Paranormal, and the backbone of Ghosts Happen, my Meetup group.

Hanson is known as an expert on historic and modern ships, and he clearly loves being on the sea. The ship's history is amazing, and it will help you understand what spirits may be walking her wooden planks for eternity.

The *Star of India* was built as a full-rigged iron windjammer ship in the small city of Ramsey (population currently 7,309), on the Isle of Man in the Irish Sea. In 1863 she was first christened *Euterpe,* the Greek muse of music and poetry, by the whimsical and well-read wife of Captain R. H. Brown, one of the ship's shareholders. No expense was spared when building the vessel, as Ramsey and the investment company's investors were trying to establish a reputation for building large, quality iron ships.

Dave Hanson and Cheryl Bailey of San Diego Ghost and Paranormal aboard the *Star of India*

On November 14, 1863 there was a substantial luncheon with tables set for sixty. Amid great celebration, the 202-foot ship glided off the blocks she'd been built upon and surged into the harbor. A promising life's journey seemed to stretch all the way to the glistening horizon for the stunning *Euterpe*, but it wasn't long before a curse took over her future.

The *Star of India* has had several reincarnations, mainly because she's been on the sea for nearly 150 years and the lifetime of companies proved much shorter than those of the boats they built and purchased. During her first three decades as *Euterpe*, she navigated twenty-one round-the-world trips.

She began her new career sailing to India with Captain William John Storry, who crashed her into a brig off St. David's Head. Later in that voyage, members of the crew refused to work unless the ship was docked for repairs (more likely, the men had lost faith in Storry's ability to lead and wanted to jump ship). The situation soon turned into a mutiny. Storry docked and had the magistrate jail seventeen of the thirty crewmen. The men were sentenced to two weeks of hard labor to set an example, and the ship left the dock with a more cooperative crew. She was repaired at sea and her goods delivered to meet the captain's slip time.

On her next voyage, also led by Storry, a cyclone hit her in the Bay of Bengal. Suffering substantial damage, the ship made it back to port for expensive repairs. She made four more passages to India as a cargo ship for her shareholders and even outlived Storry who was buried at sea from her deck. Then, with the death of her captain and her sale to a new company, her luck seemed to change.

Shaw, Savill & Co. saw the ship's potential and purchased the *Euterpe* in 1871. She spent the next quarter of a century transporting immigrants to New Zealand, Australia, Chile, and California. The long journeys were rough on crew and passengers and often included burials at sea.

In 1897, the Pacific Colonial Ship Company of San Francisco acquired her and sent her on voyages from the Pacific Northwest to Hawaii and Australia, transporting sugar, coal, and timber.

The Alaska Packers' Association, San Francisco, purchased her in 1906 and changed her name to the *Star of India*. She was one of the association's six iron ships and carried fisherman, cannery workers, coal, canned salmon, supplies, and equipment from Alameda, California, to Nushagak, central Alaska. As the *Star of India, she* spent the next twenty-three years going to and fro from Alaska to California. A slump in salmon sales proved completely fatal for the fleet, and she spent many of her later years docked. Steam power became favored over wind, and then petrol-propelled engines become the standard. The *Star of India* became obsolete. Without the wind in her sails and the movement of waves under her bow sending her forward to faraway destinations, she fell quickly into disrepair.

Jerry MacMullen, a San Diego waterfront reporter and visionary, along with a group of investors, purchased the ship in 1926 for nine thousand dollars. The Zoological Society of San Diego became involved and planned to turn the ship into an aquarium, but that didn't work out. The idea of a museum of nautical artifacts from the ship's era came to mind when one of the *Star of India*'s rooms became a dedicated library used by MacMullen. There he stored the books that he'd bought for the sole purpose of learning how to make the ship sea-worthy again (it had been towed to San Diego from Alameda). During the course of the *Star of India*'s resurrection, MacMullen, enamored with the ship, wrote his own book about her—*Star of India: Log on an Iron Ship* (Howell-North, 1961).

Money became tight during World War II, and plans of raising funds for the ship's repair failed miserably. The *Star of India* was again mostly forgotten and became MacMullen's pet project until 1956, when the *Star of India* Auxiliary formed and attracted funds for the old ship's restoration. MacMullen lived to see her become the crown jewel she is today before he passed in 1981.

Knowing a location's background is key in determining the candidates for a haunting. Perhaps the ship's ghost is Jerry McMullen himself, protecting her from harm, as he did during a good deal of his lifetime. There are the others—Storry, the captain who died onboard during his service when she was the *Euterpe*. The immigrants and crew members who didn't complete their journey because of illness or accident, the suicides, and even a child who perished because of dehydration could be prime nominees for the spirits who seem to be attached to the ship.

"The ship has had quite a few deaths onboard over the course of her long career," says Hanson about the *Star of India*'s darker past. "I work at another historic-ship museum, and from what I can tell most all of the vintage ships of any size are haunted in some form or another. They vary in the amounts of paranormal activity from residual hauntings—nonconscious psychic imprints and ghosts—to earthbound spirits that have crossed over, but decided to return to stay or visit for one reason or another. There is something about having moving water underneath the keel that seems to provide more energy for the ghosts to physically manifest, or otherwise make their presence known."

There is a theory about the negative ions produced by the ocean (see Spotlight On: Negative Ions) acting as a feeding trough for spirits who need this kind of high-level energy to manifest. Other than high negative ion count, why are ships haunted?

"Ships typically experience a number of deaths onboard," explains Hanson. "Unlike a home, deaths occurring on ships were, for the most part, unexpected and sometimes quite violent."

A violent, sometimes quick death has a way of manifesting a spirit that may not even realize it no longer has a physical body. If you put yourself into that situation, I imagine you can feel how frustrating that would feel.

One accidental violent (and not-so-quick) death that occurred during the mid-1860s was that of a passenger who was an army captain who'd lost his men to war, and perhaps some bad decisions, as he was very depressed and cut his own throat. The medic onboard sewed him back up the best he could, but three days later he'd managed to rip the stitches out and finish the job of doing himself in.

"When I was in high school and college, I'd sit at the table in the saloon area and do my homework," says John Merrill, chief engineer of the MMSD armada, and someone who has been on the *Star of India* since 1977. "I'd see this full black apparition with a hat [describing an abolition-style hat] come right through a locked door, turn and go into the first mate's cabin. It started to happen more frequently. At the time I didn't believe in ghosts; since that time I've learned to accept them."

MMSD maintenance supervisor David Burgess, who has been onboard the organization's vessels since 1978, has also had some ghostly experiences aboard the ship that he cannot explain. "Between 1978 and 1982, I worked the night watch onboard the *Star of India* from four in the afternoon to about seven in the morning. One night after everyone had left and I'd locked up, I was reading in the first mate's cabin where I slept and sitting in the corner on the bed reading. I noticed that my feather pillow got an indent like someone had put their head down on it. Then about forty seconds later it just fluffed back up again back to normal. Well, I took my book and went out on deck for a while and then switched beds when I came back down—I did not want to be sharing a bed with anyone. That was the only thing I've *seen*, but I've heard things.

"About every three or four weeks I heard heavy-duty boot steps striding across from the sail locker like someone was carrying a heavy load," Burgess continues. "The first time I heard it, I ran up to see who was onboard and found no one. A few times I was eventually able to get up there and follow the strides—yeah, really strange stuff. Three times between 1978 and 1982, I heard what sounded like a party on the 'tween deck—I heard lots of people talking and what sounded like dice, and I'd go to see what was going on—and there was nothing. The sounds would stop. I'd look outside and there would be no one out there either.

"When I was staying in the cook's quarters and getting ready for bed," Burgess says of a particularly strange incident, "I heard the sound of the anchor dropping—and that makes a hellacious amount of noise—I thought someone had figured out how to get onboard the locked-up ship and let the anchor down and let the mechanism free. But when I immediately went to see what happened, the anchor was up and there was nothing out of place. I ran up on deck to see if there were any other ships around, and there wasn't."

James W. Davis, first mate, chief rigger, events general manager, and chief engineer on *Medea,* began working with the armada in 1975 and has not only heard all of the stories, but has also seen and experienced ghostly encounters on the vessels. "The sound of the chain dropping makes an incredible amount of noise—it makes a sound like no other. David [Burgess] isn't the only one to have heard it. Jim Brink heard the same thing. Each ship has its own unique sound of an anchor being let down—there is no mistaking it.

"I used to work in the gift shop when it first opened on the *Star of India,*" says Davis. "I was sitting in the store when no one else was there, and all of a sudden the spring-loaded brass locking mechanism turned and opened, the door opened slowly ninety degrees, and then took about the same amount of time to close. Then I watched it lock itself. It was enough for me to go up on the deck and walk around for a bit. When we first got the infrared alarm system that picks up movement, I got a call between one and three in the morning two weeks straight to come in and check the *Star of India.* Finally, I just sat in the saloon and spoke out loud to John Campbell, the teen stowaway who fell from the loft and died. I said, 'John, you have to get used to this alarm—setting it off every night is killing me.' After that, the calls to come in and check the ship stopped abruptly."

The ship certainly does seem to have a number of apparitions with individual personalities. Davis notes that most of the activity on the vessel seems to begin after one in the morning, and it seems like nearly anyone who has worked the graveyard shift has had some kind of paranormal encounter. With modern alarm systems and cameras recording night and day, the need for people sleeping on the boats has cut back, though the roaming patrol also has its own stories . . . those are for another book.

For the staff of the *Star of India*, there's no better job than being on the sea on some of the country's most legendary vessels during the day, and being able to go home at night. *(Rear, left–right)* James W. Davis and David Burgess. *(Front)* John Merrill.

During an investigation on the *Star of India* with SDGAP, our group split into three smaller groups, one group for each of the ship's decks. Beginning at 9 p.m., each group spent an hour or so on each deck, and then switched decks until all three groups had an opportunity to investigate each deck. As a medium, I noticed quite a bit of energy around us on the ship, but trying to capture it on electronic devices proved difficult. We did hear unexplained footsteps, but it was difficult to get a bead on where they were coming from. The K-II picked up some activity. I got several hits on the mid level of the ship when I asked questions.

"Are you with us?" [Light at 5] *Yes.*
"Can you leave here?" (Confused responses)
"Are there more than one of you?" [Light at 5] *Yes.*
"Can some of you leave?" [Light at 5] *Yes.*
"Are there some of you that can't leave?" [Light at 5] *Yes.*
"Are you dead?" [No lights]
"Are you hurt?" [No lights]
"Were you a passenger on the boat?" [Confused responses]
"Were you a crewman?" [Confused responses]
"Are you thirsty?" [Light at 5] *Yes.*
"Can you see me?" [Light at 5] *Yes.*

Then the device became unresponsive.

Trying to record EVPs, we thought someone was knocking in response to our questions, but it was just the pistol shrimp snapping their claws closed and making loud sounds. In the lower decks you can hear the shrimp going all night long.

As far as collecting uncontaminated EVPs on the ship—good luck! Chances are you will hear street noise the entire time, as the harbor is packed well into the early morning with rabble-rousers and drunks. You're also right next to an airport. Your best chance is conducting investigations on a weeknight.

During my investigation with SDGAP, the ship had an elaborate pirate exhibit on display so there were pirate mannequins everywhere, which made for a surreal lights-out investigation. There were places on the ship where I experienced a deep feeling of despair and I credit that feeling to the people who died onboard, as much of it is residual energy. In some areas of the ship, EMFs were relatively high, which made using a meter nearly useless. EMF could have contributed to some of my own morose feelings I experienced on the ship on the lower decks. I also felt several entities watching us, but dodging contact. These incidents I credit to "shadow people" (see Spotlight On: Shadow People). I don't believe any entities on the *Star of India* have malevolent intentions but are instead simply observing us. I had two episodes on the 'tween deck near the bow in which I felt someone poke me in the ribs and neck, although no one was close enough to me to have done so.

Hanson has conducted several investigations aboard the ship, and he's encountered some unique experiences working with a medium on his team. "I've heard some unexplained sounds, but not gotten anything definitive on any of my instruments," says Hanson of not being able to catch physical evidence on the *Star*. "I've been present when mediums in the group have reported that a spirit is trying to communicate with me, but as I'm not very sensitive to such things, I could only take their word for it.

"The most recent instance of receiving information while having a medium mediator with us was during my last investigation on the *Star*," Hanson recalls. "While the team was sitting in a circle in an EVP session on the lower deck, I was told by the medium that the entity there was getting rather hostile and actually threatened us with bodily harm. We weren't doing anything disrespectful to him, or to the ship—he just resented our presence during his quiet time. This isn't the first time he acted this way towards a team I was with, and I'm sure it won't be the last. I've heard from other teams that he has been this way for years.

"Similarly, I was present when a number of people in my group saw a shadow person on the 'tween deck—we were sitting near the aft timber-loading windows at the time. Several people saw the moving dark mass, and a few of them even made out certain features. I was busy manning a video camera, trying to capture it on film, but due to the lighting, or lack thereof, I wasn't able to see anything, and my camera picked up nothing usable.

"The experience that affected me most was having my recently deceased mother come through in the middle of an investigation on the *Star of India*," says Hanson of an instance that completely took him by surprise. "I wasn't expecting her, so I was obviously surprised that she would show up there—though I later came to realize that she checks in on me a lot, but I only tend to find out about it when I've got a talented medium around to let me know. Evidently, she just wanted to check up on me and let me know that she was fine and not to worry about her. We had a very interesting conversation via the mediums, and I learned some meaningful lessons about what it was like on the other side and the journey we continue to make even after death." (See Spotlight On: Mediums and Psychics for more explanation regarding the subject of guest spirits making an appearance in unexpected haunted locations.)

Hanson and Cheryl Bailey, assistant organizer of SDGAP, share an inspiring story. They met through the Meetup group and fell in love. They now run the group as a team.

"Keep your team small," advises Bailey—good advice for any investigation. "And set aside dedicated times for EVPs—meaning set times where all members of the entire investigation are quiet and don't move around. The ship makes all kinds of interesting noises—make sure to make note of those on your recordings."

The *Star of India* is an amazing ship that any paranormal investigator, novice or practiced, will appreciate. She is everything and more if you allow her to be. Instead of coming to the table with preconceived ideas of what you're going to get, come with an open mind and I think you'll be pleasantly surprised.

SDGAP is planning an annual paranormal conference, the first to be held on the *Star of India* and her nearby neighbor, the *Berkeley*. See Resources for more details.

CHAPTER 19

Hotel del Coronado
CORONADO

The Hotel del Coronado shrouded in fog on New Year's Eve 2012.
The Beautiful Stranger seems to be haunting the grounds as well as
the hotel.

THE HOTEL DEL CORONADO sits majestically in all
her Victorian glory on the shore of Coronado, overlooking the
Pacific. Opened in 1888, the monolithic hotel was once one of
the largest resort hotels in the nineteenth century and is one of
the largest wooden buildings in California. Those familiar with
the hotel just call her The Del, and she wouldn't truly be a grand
historic state and national landmark without at least one ghostly
resident.

Unlike today, the only people you'd find lounging in the common areas of The Del in the 1800s were guests and the staff waiting on them. Staying at The Del was a much more private experience than it is today with droves of tourists wandering the halls. Thomas Edison, L. Frank Baum (who did much of his writing of *The Wizard of Oz* series at The Del—believed to be the location that inspired some of the later attributes for the Emerald City), Humphrey Bogart, Rudolph Valentino, and Babe Ruth were all guests. None of the people I just mentioned seem likely candidates for the female specter seen in and around the hotel. So, who left their spirit to stay on as a permanent guest?

"I believe that the Hotel del Coronado is haunted by several ghosts and not the ones most listed," says California historian and author Richard Senate. "Several people have seen figures in turn-of-the-century outfits in the halls—a man and a woman. The man was said to resemble Teddy Roosevelt. I spent a night in the haunted room and had nothing happen. But the age and history of the inn is why I believe it's haunted. In those days, places such as hotels were used by doctors to perform illegal abortions, and every once in a while such operations resulted in the patient's death. When that happened the doctor would leave, and the hotel staff would find the nude body. Old hotels have seen both the best and the worst in the human condition, and as a result visible scars in the form of ghosts were left behind."

On November 30, 1892, the *San Diego Union* ran a story with the following headline:

By Her Own Hand: A Young Woman, Suffering from Incurable Disease, Suicides. She Wanders Out into the Storm to Die— Desperate Act of a Guest at Hotel del Coronado—A Revolver the Chosen Weapon.

This local Victorian tragedy soon developed into a nationwide story as the search expanded to identify the woman who checked in under the alias Lottie Anderson Bernard. The body was misidentified several times due to families eager for closure regarding their own missing family members. "The Beautiful Stranger," the nickname she's now known by, checked in on November 24, 1892, and never checked out.

The woman, believed to be Kate Morgan by most researchers, was given the official date of death of November 28, 1892, by the coroner. The location in which her body was found was described in the coroner's report as *Near the shore, feet pointed toward Pt. Loma . . . next to the ocean.* The Del's stated place of death is the western oceanfront corner of the hotel.

Apparently, The Beautiful Stranger made many connections and was quite active during her five-day stay. One account has her riding a horse for several hours, another purchasing a gun from a store in San Diego a few days before she was found (the gunsmith's testimony did not read all that conclusively). The stories that developed just don't add up. I imagine the only people who knew for sure what happened are now deceased.

The staff claimed she'd told several of them that she had incurable stomach cancer. The coroner found no sign of illness. Some claim she was so ill she had to be lifted to ride a streetcar, but her employer did not describe her as an invalid.

During her stay, court records show that the guest in question was constantly under the watchful eye of a young bellman. He testified that he gave her the matches (her personal correspondence had been burned), obtained alcoholic beverages for her, and hand-patted dry her hair with a towel in her room after she claimed to have fallen into the tub and submerged her head. It was later assumed by some that she'd tried to drown herself unsuccessfully. My Emily Brontë sensibilities red-flag the bellman's testimony, as the young woman whose body was found was around twenty-four years old. It would have been considered quite inappropriate for her and the young bellman to have been in the room for any period of time together . . . alone. If she needed an attendant, wouldn't a woman from housekeeping have been called up to help her?

When the inquest was completed, the body was officially identified as Kate Morgan, born Kate Farmer in Fremont County, Iowa. Her mother, Elizabeth Philamena Chandler, died when she was two, and Kate's only sister passed away at the same age. Kate was sent to live with her mother's father, Joe Chandler, and his wife. The story goes that Kate married Thomas Edwin Morgan (whose own mother passed away when he was a young boy) and they had a son. Unfortunately, like many infants in those days, he passed away after living only two days. Supposedly, Kate dumped Thomas and ran off with Albert Allen, a stepson of Thomas's stepmother. The two were believed separated by the time Kate became employed as a housemaid in Los Angeles.

Several witnesses noticed her having a bitter argument that sounded like a lover's quarrel on a train in Orange, California, where the man departed and left her to continue on without him. Of course, this testimony caused speculation that she was pregnant, alone, and probably suicidal. Could she have tried inducing an abortion herself? Perhaps she had a doctor perform the procedure in her room? Several strong tonics were available for such occasions, and it was also rumored that she visited a local pharmacist earlier in her stay.

This might explain why Morgan's employer, whom she'd seen only a few days before, said she was in good heath when she left their home. Then, while staying at The Del, she seemed to take on such health symptoms as one might have if she had incurable stomach cancer, as she'd told some of the hotel's staff members. Perhaps a botched abortion was to blame for her failing body and mind. Symptoms of a surgical, chemical, or herbal abortion of those times might have included pain in the arms and legs, vomiting, pounding headache, extreme abdominal pain, and muscle weakness. Of course, if there was proof of an unsuccessful abortion found during an autopsy, it might have been withheld from the report to keep scandal from befalling the hotel belonging to one of the most influential men of the time.

Amidst the excitement of the body being found and the coroner's investigation, the story was front and center in discussion and the newspapers. Other city papers outside of California had picked up the story until it landed at Morgan's grandfather's front stoop. He soon became a target for reporters demanding interviews. Unable to stand any further attention, he finally wired the funeral home to bury her and asked them to send him the bill. All other requests for more information from Kate's relatives, including telegraphs to George L. Allen and her husband, went unanswered.

During the hotel's initial inquiry regarding where her funds would be coming from to pay for the hotel, she gave them the name George L. Allen of Hamburg, Iowa. He was contacted and the funds were wired. Maybe he was responding in regard to someone he thought was Mrs. Lottie A. Bernard, how Kate had signed the guest register, not Kate Morgan. It seems to me that had he known it was Kate Morgan, the woman who'd dumped her husband, Thomas Morgan, and left with his eldest brother, Albert Allen, Thomas's own stepbrother-in-law by virtue of a common stepmother, his willingness to pay her bill might have been in question. Though if he did know that Lottie Bernard was Kate Morgan and wasn't responding to the coroner's request for information . . . well, that would also be very strange, indeed.

Some people do not believe Kate took her own life but had instead purchased the gun for her own protection. Others believe the woman was tangled in a blackmail scheme and that the bullets in her own gun did not match the one lodged in her head. If this woman was actually Kate Morgan, staying at The Del for five days was an extravagant expense and well outside of her means. Despite having a wealthy grandfather (whom she seemed to be estranged from), Morgan was employed as a domestic worker in Los Angeles. During her stay at the hotel, she was also constantly calling down to see if she received a telegram from her brother (Kate Morgan had no brother) named Dr. Anderson. No telegrams came at all for her. She'd left Los Angeles in good spirits, promising her employer to return on Thanksgiving (the day after she left) in time to cook the holiday dinner.

All of these facts put together do not make for a solved case. Could it be someone else other than Kate Morgan buried in Mount Hope Cemetery? Sure. There was never any in-person identification of the body. Could Morgan have been murdered? Absolutely.

And for every big, unsolved story there are conspiracy theorists who throw us a bone about what might have happened on a grander scale. "The hotel owner was John Spreckels, one of the wealthiest men of his time," says John T. Cullen, author of the novel *Lethal Journey,* which is based on the woman found dead at The Del. "Spreckels was a confidant of kings and presidents. I believe Kate Morgan was a grifter and organized a blackmail attempt against Spreckels that went horribly wrong. While Kate Morgan and her two accomplices, John Longfield and Lizzie Wyllie, were trying to pull off the blackmail, Spreckels was in the White House with President Benjamin Harrison, negotiating the future of the sovereign nation of Hawaii and his family's vast holdings in sugar cane fields. The monarchy fell just five weeks after Lizzie Wyllie [a name that also came up during the investigation], who I believe is the true Beautiful Stranger, died at the Hotel del Coronado. The mysterious death became a national scandal fueled by the telegraph, the Internet of its day.

"More importantly, the case was embedded within an international conspiracy by U.S. corporations to overthrow the Hawaiian monarchy and annex this sovereign nation as a territory," says Cullen. "Coincidentally, the monarchy fell just two years after another death connected with Spreckels and the Hotel Del. David Kalakaua, last king of Hawaii, stayed at The Del in December 1890 as a guest of John Spreckels. He was the first royal ever to stay at the hotel. He traveled north to stay with John's father Claus Spreckels in San Francisco, but died suddenly, and mysteriously, on January 20, 1891. My detailed analysis ties together myriad tiny clues, from embroidered hankies in the dead woman's hotel room and in a trunk owned by Kate Morgan in Los Angeles." Cullen believes that his research blows the lid off a 120-year-old cover-up designed to shield John Spreckels and his Hawaiian sugar dynasty from a major Victorian scandal.

According to the book *Beautiful Stranger: The Ghost of Kate Morgan and the Hotel Del Coronado*, penned by Christine Donovan, who painstakingly went through the many records and made a chronological record about the weeks surrounding the mysterious woman's death, initially there was a great deal of confusion regarding the true identity of the dead woman.

Speculation about who the woman could be began as soon as the luggage-less Beautiful Stranger checked into the hotel . . . unescorted. In the end, there was a discrepancy found regarding the sum of $1,600 she supposedly had with her, instead of the $16 it became. Her employer stated she had a good deal of money with her and planned to deposit it in a national bank, and was also eager to sign some documents.

No one alive seems to know Kate Morgan better than Donovan, who painstakingly captured all of the hard-fact data surrounding Morgan's stay at the hotel. "According to the coroner's inquest, Kate Morgan's death was ruled a suicide, but we don't know for sure if it was deliberate or accidental or even if Kate might have been murdered," says Donovan, who is also director of heritage programs at The Del, where she oversees The Del's archives and is the official hotel historian. "I don't think her husband was part of it. It was kind of unfortunate she had his name; it seemed to be her only connection to him. If she was murdered, I don't think he did it. From what I understand, he was far away and a nice guy. I think there are too many questions that people who speculate raise. There are so many unknowns, and I don't think it helps for me to step in and have a theory. I think people like the idea she was murdered . . . it makes a much better story. Speculating on how she died [murder or suicide?] doesn't serve the purpose of history."

Long lines of people went to view the body at the San Diego funeral home where The Beautiful Stranger lay in her coffin waiting for someone to claim her. The body was finally claimed by Kate Morgan's grandfather, thousands of miles away, based on a line sketch. The body was buried in Mount Hope Cemetery (see Mount Hope Cemetery chapter).

"I do believe in the paranormal," says Donovan. "My job gives me exposure to people researching the paranormal. I've talked with people whom I respect that can go to the beyond. One San Diego medium who has investigated the Hotel Del pretty regularly asked Kate what she thought of me. The response she got back was that she likes me okay, but my head is too filled with facts about her. I have to say that's pretty accurate. I've had paranormal experiences before, but I haven't had anything like that happen with Kate. A shop employee related to the MSNBC writer that one day when she was opening up her store, all of the books on a shelf were put in spine first, which she though was strange. Then, a few days later, I entered my office one morning, and the few books I have were turned inward, spine first. They were all in backwards."

I stayed at the hotel during New Year's Eve 2011, hoping the spirits would be in full swing. Jeff and I took a walk on the beach before midnight. It was a foggy night, and we found a quiet place to sit on the beach for me to do some EVP sessions. I began shooting photos. Nothing was responding to the short-burst EVP sessions I was doing, but when I asked the question, "Is there anyone out there?" we did get an unintelligible response from what sounded like a female voice.

We did find the area we believe was the site where the body was found. Using the K-II meter, we got several yes/no conversations going. When we asked if the spirit was Kate, there was no response at all. With our questions, we narrowed the spirits' identities to an early construction worker who claimed he'd fallen off the roof in the general area, and another who had passed away in a boating accident off the shore in 1979. No Kate Morgan, but an interesting gathering just the same. While we sat on the beach in a quiet area, two eerie figures looked like they were running toward us. When they were about thirty feet away, I shouted toward them so they would know we were sitting there. A bright orb suddenly appeared between us and the figures. The orb disappeared, and then the two specters also vanished. I managed to get a picture of them before they dissipated and while the orb was between us.

Early the next morning, my husband went for a walk to find some coffee for us while I slept in. I awoke to feel someone sitting on the foot of the bed and poked them with my foot. I thought it was Jeff and jokingly said, "Good morning." When no one responded, I opened my eyes and got out from under the covers. No one was in the room but me.

Before I went to the spa for a massage, I ran a bath, put in some sea salts, and watched the water rise before I went into the bedroom to talk with Jeff about our afternoon plans. I returned to the bathroom—the lever on the stopper had been pulled, and the tub was empty.

The night before, the heat had gone out. I called the desk and it was fixed temporarily, but without anyone having entered our room. We left for the evening and the heat went out again, but no one was able to fix it. We called the desk for more blankets.

Was the heater on the fritz, or a victim of paranormal activity? Your guess is as good as mine. Despite the mechanical issues, we had a lovely stay at the elegant coastal hotel.

There is at least one person who has seen a manifestation of the spirit of a woman near the Hotel del Coronado property— a spirit that sounds a lot like The Beautiful Stranger.

"Many years ago when I was pregnant with my son, I lived for a brief period of time in San Diego," says Kala Ambrose, psychic medium and author of *Ghosthunting North Carolina* (Clerisy Press). "This beautiful area was a very relaxing and nurturing space to be, and I spent most of my time outdoors enjoying nature, especially the beaches. One day I decided to spend time at the Hotel Del beach, and headed over. I was there in the early morning hours and the beach was fairly empty. As I relaxed on the beach, I noticed a woman walking up the beach toward me.

"What immediately caught my eye was that she appeared to be wearing a light gray dress and matching hat," says Ambrose, host of the Internet radio show *Explore Your Spirit with Kala*. "As she moved closer, I could see that she was wearing a dress that we would refer to as period or vintage clothing these days. She stood still for a moment and appeared to be looking out at the horizon. At this point, I realized that she was a ghost, as I could partially see through her dress. I should say that I've seen ghosts and communicated with the spirit world since I was a child, so it's not uncommon for me to see spirits wherever I am.

"I sat calmly watching her as she scanned the horizon, at one point putting her hand up above her eyes, as we do when looking to shield our eyes from the sun to look at something far away. After a few moments of gazing out at the water, she seemed to resign herself to the fact that what she was searching for was not there. At this point, she turned and began to walk back from the direction she had come and as she did, she noticed me and stopped. She smiled at me and I smiled back at her, and she looked down at my very pregnant belly and smiled again. I cradled my belly as pregnant mothers often do when someone notices their condition. She looked at me for another moment, and though the exchange was very brief, it was a very nice and warm encounter. With this, she turned and walked back in the direction she had come from until she disappeared from my sight.

"I remained on the beach for a while longer until the hunger pangs of being a pregnant woman stirred me to pack up and head off to an early lunch," says Ambrose. "I went on with my day. The next morning I was out running errands and was driving along a road near the Hotel Del. To my shock and surprise, as I was driving I saw this same woman on the side of the road waving to me in an urgent and frenzied manner. She was not calm and serene like the day before; she seemed to be panicked and was urging me to come to her. Seeing a right turn near where she was standing, I made the turn off the road I was on to follow her. Now off the main road, I looked up to see where the woman had gone. She was now standing a few feet away and smiling at me, touching her belly and nodding to me.

"I was trying to discern what she was attempting to communicate to me. I heard the terrifying sound of two cars crashing into each other from the main road I had just been driving on. As the reality of the situation sunk in, I was so grateful that she had appeared and led me to turn off the main road to follow her; otherwise I would have been in the accident, and in my pregnant condition, I can't bear to think of what could have happened. As for ghosts inside the Hotel Del? I've only toured the hotel and never stayed overnight as a guest. I can't report seeing any ghosts while inside the hotel, nor can I confirm that the gray lady ghost was attached to the hotel, as I saw her on the beach and on the road, rather than inside the property. I am deeply appreciative to her for appearing to me on that day, saving me and my son from harm."

CHAPTER 20

Santa Catalina Island
SANTA CATALINA ISLAND

Santa Catalina Island has the feeling of a vortex—the island has a reputation of playing host to UFOs, ghosts, and Native American spirit energy. You never feel quite alone on the island. Avalon Bay, shown here, is the main harbor where people come in on the water shuttles from the mainland.

ONE OF THE FIRST THINGS that came to my mind when I first heard about the island of Santa Catalina was the song "26 Miles (Santa Catalina)," which my parents enjoyed on their hi-fi and I enjoyed dancing to when I was a kid. It sounded like a wildly romantic island—and only twenty-six miles from the mainland! Later I sailed through the Channel Islands with friends; twenty years ago we first anchored the three-masted

wooden schooner we'd sailed from Marina del Rey to dock off
what I now know as Two Harbors. This is where actress Natalie Wood met her fate after mysteriously going overboard and
drowning. We'd never gone ashore, but instead we went whale
watching and anchored through while sailing to Mexico—always
just watching from afar, enjoying cocktails, and barbecue from
lounge chairs on deck. Even at a distance, especially at night, I
sensed something very mysterious about the secluded island.

More recently, I finally visited Catalina's pristine shores
with my husband, Jeff, and our youngest daughter via ferry. We
stayed at the Glenmore Hotel, built in the late 1880s by work
crews that had just finished the Hotel del Coronado (see Hotel
del Coronado chapter). It was easy to see why the people I came
in contact with would never think of living elsewhere. Before I
came to Catalina, Rob Wlodarski told me the island was a vortex
for all kinds of paranormal activity. Rob and his wife, Anne,
penned the books *Haunted Catalina* and *Haunted Catalina II*
(G-Host Publishing).

"I am an archaeologist and historian and have worked on
Catalina with the UCLA Archaeological Survey, The Island Company, and Catalina Conservancy for almost forty years," Rob says.
"I began collecting ghost stories when I worked on the island,
interviewing people who shared their unusual experiences. After
visiting every part of the island and having hundreds of stories
in hand, Anne and I decided to write our first book about the
spirits of the island. Later we added new stories that stretch from
Emerald Bay and Toyon to Isthmus, Little Harbor, and Avalon.
Being an archaeologist, I soon realized that all of the activity recorded throughout the island was centered in areas where
Native American cemeteries had been desecrated since the 1870s.
Almost one thousand burials had been excavated and removed by
nonscientific personnel and sold and shipped across the United
States to various museums. I believed this triggered much of the

paranormal activity on the island. The fact that numerous Native American cemeteries have been desecrated, and that it is an island surrounded by a massive energy conductor—salt water—makes it a perfect laboratory for paranormal activity. Since numerous UFO sightings have also occurred, this location is also a haven for those interested in ET contact."

Our hotel, the Glenmore in Avalon, is believed to be haunted—at least according to the Internet. One can also stay on the other side of the island at Two Harbors. The island is privately owned by the Catalina Island Conservancy (see **catalina conservancy.org**), which maintains and regulates 88 percent of the island and has very strict environmental laws. Much of the island is closed to people in order to maintain the island's wildlife habitats. The challenge of transportation does not end once one gets off the ferry. There are a few cabs, no car rentals, and everywhere you go, you go by foot unless you rent golf carts with top speeds of fifteen miles per hour—still the preferred vehicle for many island residents.

We asked a few people where the Glenmore was, and we rolled our overnight suitcase to the center of town to the quaint yellow structure with the tower-room suite that's hard to miss. Built in 1891, this hotel (and the island in general) was soon to become one of Hollywood's hideaways for the rich and famous; Charlie Chaplin, Gloria Swanson, Clark Gable, Amelia Earhart, and Laurel and Hardy stayed at the Glenmore. We checked into the hotel and left to explore Avalon. I left my recorder on in hopes of catching some EVPs, and I did catch some voices while we were out. Although there was much ambient noise from outside the room and the hotel (music from the bar next door and patrons spilling out into the streets into the wee hours), these other voices sounded much louder, like they were in the room. A man said, "Is she gone?" (no response), and about forty-five minutes later, a woman said, "Get ready. . . ." (no response). And about twenty minutes later a man said, "Shot a turkey. Look." (no response).

After lunch we spent time walking around the island. Then I met Chuck Liddell for an interview in the lobby and invited him to dinner with us at the only Chinese restaurant on the island; and with food that good, there only needs to be one. Liddell has lot of stories to tell; he's the island's historian, and he's also very much the island's Norm from TV's *Cheers*—everywhere he goes, everyone knows him and thinks of him fondly. People were eager to share their news with him and give him hugs and handshakes. It seemed like it took twenty minutes to get from the hotel lobby to our seats for dinner. We had a great time listening to his stories. He invited us on a tour, but we'd already arranged for a tour that evening through Ghost Tours of Catalina Island, but I arranged to go with him on a private late-night tour after the ghost tour ended around 9 p.m.

That evening, we'd been told by the guide on the ghost tour that not only was our hotel haunted, but just about every other building we passed was also haunted—or at least it was the scene of some gory death. I spent most of the tour with my hands over my five-year-old's ears; this tour is graphic, and I really don't recommend it for anyone under twelve and those not used to hearing vivid stories of tragedy, violence, and murder. The stories also seemed to be greatly exaggerated from the stories I'd heard from people who'd been witness to the original events, though the tour is a good place to start if you're looking for local color.

Liddell came to pick me up in his vehicle, one of only a few on the island; he has two for his tours—an open-air Jeep and a large, closed vehicle that seats seven passengers. We drove his private vintage VW bus and toured the island's backroads under a bright moon. The bays were beautiful, and we saw lots of feral cats and foxes running into the darkness as our lights warned them off the road. We found the local teen hangout on the side of one of the narrow roads; at least twenty young people had piled into cars to meet there. It was like a modern-day scene from *Rebel Without a Cause*. I think scarier than any ghost story was the thought of those kids on the winding, narrow roads after 11 p.m. We saw several roadside *descansos* on our way, memorializing the sites of the deaths of some of the island's teens and reminding everyone of the cost of driving unsafely on the island's roads.

I felt safe driving with Liddell, who knows the backroads of Catalina like the back of his hand; he was born on the island.

"My grandfather was sent here by the Wrigleys after they'd purchased the island in 1919," said Liddell. "He built all the homes on Descanso Street in 1920. My father and mother wanted to come over, but because of the war there were no visitors allowed on the island from 1941 to 1945, only the military and the people who lived here prior to the war could remain on the island. The military prepared for the Japanese to attack, take over Catalina, and blow up the oil refineries on the mainland. So they had to wait for the war to end, and they moved here to retire—my father was only forty-three. Then Mr. Wrigley found out my dad was a 1923 mechanical engineer graduate of Caltech, made him an offer he couldn't refuse, and he remained Catalina's chief engineer until 1960.

"Right from the very beginning, my dad was in charge of all of the Wrigley holdings on Catalina. Literally from the start, we would drive around in the company car—a 1937 woody—to make sure the roads were in good repair. We went to all points of the island, year-round. I just took it for granted everyone did this, but they actually didn't have the access; it was just something I'd always taken part in."

Due to much of the island now being a wildlife sanctuary, many of those places are only in Liddell's memories, as very few have access to them. He's had a lot of wonderful experiences on the island, including many that remain unexplained.

People have lived on the island for more than seven thousand years, so it's hard to imagine a place such as this without spirits. The Pemu'nga Native Americans who called Catalina home were friendly to outsiders. Finally, after being abused by all the visitors who came to lay claim to the island, the final blow was dealt by Russian-hired Aleut Indians, armed with seal guns to slaughter otters for their pelts. They killed the native Catalina men, raped the women, and destroyed the Pemu'nga culture. The few Pemu'nga who survived the slaughter and European diseases were removed to San Gabriel Mission, where they were made slaves.

When the Wrigley family purchased the island, and after they'd managed it for decades, they formed a conservancy to keep much of the island the way it had been for thousands of years. They also realized they had to sustain the residents. They built tourist attractions, hotels, homes, and a ferry line that flourished into an industry of a million or so people visiting each year—keeping the majority of the three thousand residents on the island in business and busy. One of the buildings left from the Wrigley family reign is the Catalina Casino, built in 1929. Thousands of years before the Casino was built, the island's natives called what's now Avalon Bay, the safest of the island's coves, their home. I've been told that the Native Americans built one of their communities there, and many were born and died right there in the sheltered cove.

Liddell, having gone to the Casino since he was a small child with his father to check on the building, is now one of the tour leaders giving the history of the location. Unlike many who are spooked by the building, Liddell finds it one of the most peaceful places he can possibly be after a night of giving tours; when he relaxes in the dark theater, he experiences nothing but good energy.

"About ten years ago, my godson spoke to an apparition," said Liddell. "His job was to follow around behind the tour of forty to fifty people and make sure no one strayed behind, and at the end of the tour he'd tell me everyone had vacated the building and we'd get ready for the next tour. After one tour he hadn't come back to check in, and I got a call from my good friend, his grandmother, who said he'd come home really upset. She wanted me to talk with him. So I got on the phone and he explained that he'd gone up to a man and asked him politely to join the group, but the man looked at him like he was looking right through him.

"He described the man in great detail—dark socks, leather sandals, Hawaiian shirt, a woven palm frond hat, and a camera around his neck. Right then that struck me as odd. He would have seemed out of place in this time, but seemed more like he was from the 1950s," said Liddell. "The man, who was three feet away from him, turned and walked into the open women's lounge door and goes into the bathroom. He assumed the man had to go so bad he just went through into the closest bathroom, so he gives him about five minutes. Then he called in and no one answered Finally he goes in to look for the man—and checked all of the stalls, but there was no one inside. All of a sudden he got a horrible feeling he'd just talked to a ghost. He was really shook up, so I asked him if the ghost had done anything to hurt him, he said, 'No.' So, I just said, 'Welcome to the club.'"

Liddell also has experiences of his own, one of them being the day he went into the Casino and saw a man in a three-piece brown suit walk right through a wall. "I had two thoughts when I saw him originally—What's he doing here? The building wasn't open. And—who wears a three-piece suit like that during the summer?

"I have a theory about the ghosts I see," said Liddell, who broke his silence about the paranormal events he was witnessing on the cable TV station that broadcasts on the island. For three years, Liddell's interviews were seen several times a day. It was then that other people began stepping up and thanking him for being honest, and telling their own stories to Rob Wlodarski.

"As a Christian, there are references to ghosts in the Bible; I believe they're either demonic, or just energy: you cannot destroy energy—it just continues on in different forms. The conversation we're having will go on for an eternity . . . if it hasn't already. It will just be on another time band. When people see spirits, they see, for instance, a lady going into that room or this wall or by that window—if spirits are independent, you'd think they'd have more creativity than repeating the same action over and over. When people do see them, they always say, 'It's like they are looking right through you.' So it's as though they can't see us. Before they built the casino there wouldn't have been a wall where the guy in the three-piece suit went through. I think somehow, once in a while, we can break out of the present and go into another time band. How many times do we dream something and it comes true two weeks later? All we're doing is occupying another band."

After the tour with Liddell, and feeling the incredible energy of the island up on the backroads, I knew I was in store for some wild dreams. I curled up in bed with my already sleeping husband and fell into a deep slumber. A few hours later I was awakened from dreams of flying above the island like a soaring bird by a rhythmic sensation that seemed to resonate within my body. Everyone else was still asleep when I got up to investigate and tried to follow the distant sound. I opened the window wider and heard drums wafting down from the mountains. Being quiet not to wake anyone, I put on some street clothes and went quietly outside, where I stood in the center of the empty street with the early-morning wind on me and listened. The drumming sounded like it was coming from several different directions but traveled down from the mountain areas. Sound travels strangely on the island. The night around me seemed so surreal and alive; I walked the quiet street down to the beach to watch the waves that seemed to drown out the ethereal drums until I got tired enough to go back to sleep.

CHAPTER 21

Summerland
SUMMERLAND

The shore of Summerland has incredible energy, and it's hardly traveled. While other beaches (that aren't even haunted and have terrible parking) are packed to the highway with people, this one is the hidden gem on the California coast. Dolphins play right off the shore, and the surf is nearly always calm.

TV SHOWS WITH HOSTS THAT CAN, or try, to communicate, hunt, or tell stories about the dead are all the rage. Would it surprise you to find out that today's trends in ghost-hunting are a reflection of what was happening in the United

States in the mid-1800s—and that the movement was even more contagious than it is today?

In 1848, when two girls known as the Fox Sisters began communicating with the dead, their techniques (spirits rapping in response to questions and using mediumship to speak with the dead) spread like wildfire; just about every home in America had a parlor where "home circles" (séances) were held—even Thomas Edison's parents were members of a Spiritualist church and hosted séances in their home on a regular basis. It was during this time that one of America's oldest religions—Spiritualism (a religion that believes everyone has the ability to communicate with dead) was born.

During the Civil War, Spiritualism helped ease the mental anguish for people who didn't know where their soldier friends or family members were, or if they'd even made it through the last battle or city burning. Misidentifying the wounded and dead, a common occurrence, didn't make matters any easier. The people of the country were in mourning and wanted a way to contact their dearly beloved . . . *directly*.

Pockets of Spiritualist communities began sprouting up throughout America in the 1870s. It was during this era that Spiritualist Henry Lafayette Williams and his wife, Katie, founded the city of Summerland, California, in 1885. Summerland's hillsides were filling in with both resident Spiritualist homes and tents accommodating visitors during its summer season of lectures, classes, and séances. The town, situated between Santa Barbara and Carpinteria, was fairly isolated until 1887, when a train connected the coastal communities with the rest of the country.

There are several existing Spiritualist camps in which members live year-round. One such place is Lily Dale, New York, the subject of my next book and a city highlighted recently in the HBO documentary *No One Dies in Lily Dale*. The community of mediums living in the gate-enclosed city of more than two hundred Victorian buildings on Cassadaga Lake still thrives today, with more than thirty-thousand visitors a year.

In nearly a decade of doing research for my book about Lily Dale, I've become one of America's foremost collectors of Victorian Spiritualist artifacts (photos, books, and so on), but in all my collecting I'd never come across Summerland's relics, nor had I even heard of Summerland.

My first visit to Summerland was happenstance. I was looking for a summer rental that was both kid- and dog-friendly. Santa Barbara was too pricey, and my eye caught an online rental in a small town called Summerland. I thought it was a catchy name for a summer resort town, not a reference to the name given to the afterlife by the founder of Spiritualism, Andrew Jackson Davis.

The first night we got there—about 11 p.m.—we were exhausted and fell into our beds and drifted off. About two hours later, when we were all well into dreamland, I heard a knock on the door. Everyone else seemed to sleep through it except for Bulova, who was sitting at the door growling when I went into the living room.

I signaled him to stand down, as anyone outside the thin Victorian door would have already heard him and been alerted to his presence. I opened the door . . . to no one. Bulova went outside and searched, and when he was done he came back, sat and put a paw on my foot, letting me know his search was finished without incident. At that point, I would have thought I was dreaming . . . except he'd heard the knock too. Then again, out of all of our dogs, he's the only one who can see spirits—and hear them too. I looked at the clock. It was 1:30. A tug on my nightgown made me jump out of my skin; my youngest daughter, Sydney, was up and about.

"Momma, there's a boy in my room. He wants to know what he can take with him."

Remembering I'd left the girls' window open because it was stuffy when we opened up the rental, I panicked and burst into the room, my heart pounding in my throat. I flicked on the light and signaled Bulova into the bedroom where he searched under the bed and behind the dresser and the closet. Nothing. My eldest didn't awake, as she had awakened the earliest the morning before and was tired enough to sleep through anything—*ahhhhh, to be a teenager again!* I closed and locked the windows and closed the door behind us. I made mugs of warm soy milk in the microwave for both of us, and we sat at the dining room table.

"What about this boy?" I asked.

"He wasn't really a *boy*-boy; he was a spirit," she said, sipping on the mug and not at all disturbed by the visitation. She's been raised a Spiritualist, and she sees them all the time without much incident.

"Did he knock on the door?"

"Yeah, but he was scared of Bulova. He came in and shook the bed and pulled Miller out from under me." Miller is her long body-pillow dog that keeps her from rolling out of bed.

"Why does he want to *take* something?"

"He said it was for his house."

"Does he live here?"

"He said he lives in a big yellow house down the road."

I thought how odd it was for a ghost to want *stuff*.

"*Okay* . . . did he have something in mind he wanted to take?"

"I'm not sure. He played with my shoes [they light up when she walks] and made it all sparkly in the room. He's *funny*. I think he likes them."

"Why do you think he woke you up?"

"Maybe he's just lonely. Maybe there aren't any more ghost kids . . . maybe they all went on without him. I'm sleepy. Can I take Bulova back to bed?"

I tucked her back in with Bulova's long body spanning the bottom of the queen bed, and they were both back asleep in no time.

The next day, my family walked to lunch while I stayed at home and tried to take a little nap. Unable to sleep, I opened the drawer in the TV stand for something to read and found a curious, photocopied book. The stack of photocopied papers was folded in half and stapled at the fold. Many of the first and last pages were missing—I didn't know the title of the book or the author. It was about the town's history and the Spiritualists who once lived there! The booklet also told the story of The Big Yellow House, where the city founders lived. I assumed the house was the one my daughter's little spirit friend had spoken of the night before. Even the house I was in was part of the original Summerland village of Spiritualists.

People had come from all parts of the country to live in Summerland. Katie Lafayette Williams's death in 1888 was a blow to her husband, as Henry loved her deeply, and their dream of building the Spiritualist community was just coming to fruition. One-tenth of the lots they'd divided their property into had been sold.

Powerful men with assets don't stay single long, and Henry was no exception. He married again in 1889, when his young motherless son chose a wife for him and even proposed to her for his father. In 1890, Henry, who'd once held high positions in the United States government, hit oil after noticing the crude bubbling up from the sand on his beach. The rest is history, as both the smell of the crude oil wafting into the city and the unsightly rigs marring the once pristine beach made the city an unpopular destination. Although I know of no known records that state this, but because of the guidelines from Spiritualist camps throughout the rest of the country, I imagine Lyceum (see Andrew Jackson Davis's free book *The Children's Progressive*

Lyceum at **archive.org**) was taught there. Lyceum is a school that teaches children to be aware of the world and the world of spirits around them. I can only imagine what happened when the demographic changed, and the school's population was flooded with the children of oil riggers, whose parents probably weren't that agreeable to the subject matter.

For whatever reason, Spiritualists began to leave, and much of the original town was wiped out when the railway and highway came through, destroying many of the original Summerland buildings. Only the most devout Spiritualists seemed to stay, or visit, especially since there were so many other Spiritualist camps to choose from, including a large one called Harmony Grove in San Diego. One by one, the original founding family members died, and many of the remainder became Christian Scientists.

I quickly finished the book, and when my daughter came home I told her Summerland used to be a place like Lily Dale (where I take her every year during the open season for the children's program). We spent the rest of the day at Mission Santa Barbara, but we'd passed by The Big Yellow House. It literally had a sign identifying it as such. The next morning, the two of us walked down the street to the house. It looked like it had been closed a long time. There was a FOR SALE sign on the fence. I took pictures and my daughter walked over to a door that looked like it went down to the cellar.

"He's down here." She'd grabbed the doorknob and tried it. Locked. "Feel it, Momma."

I felt the doorknob, and even on that cold, overcast day, the doorknob felt like it was eighty-five degrees. Cellars are usually cool, not warm. I also felt a slight vibration from the metal of the old knob.

"That *is* odd," I said.

"He wants us to come in," she said, pointing to the barred windows.

"Can you *see* him?"

"Naw, he's inside—all the way back. I think he's afraid of the dog," she said, making me aware for the first time of a fenced little dog nearby that was yapping nonstop.

"I can appreciate that," I said.

That was the end of my daughter's connection with the spirit boy who lived there, though we've been back many times since. She was three when she had that experience, and the memory has all but gone. She brings shells up from the beach and little tchotchkes to leave at the basement door, though she's not sure why. For some reason, kids are like that with paranormal experiences—they fade as they get older.

On one of our annual trips, I went down to the beach when my family was asleep and I was restless. Summerland certainly has a vibrational energy that keeps one up at night. There are lots of spirits in town . . . everywhere. Summerland Beach is lovely in the moonlight, and Bulova and I descended the steep walkway leading to the beach below. Earlier in the day, Bulova, wrapped in his life jacket, dogpaddled out to swim with the dolphins playing in the surf. I finally had to swim out to tow him back in, otherwise he'd probably still be out there. He was still pretty wound-up after getting bounced around.

As we walked, I thought about the oil rigs the founders had put in place on the beach to make their fortunes. I wondered if Summerland would still be a Spiritualist community if greed hadn't consumed them—and if highway construction hadn't wiped out half the early town, including its original church.

I sat down and threw a stick for Bulova to chase; he went off to fetch it and got sidetracked by a pile of seaweed. Just then, I saw two shadow spirits in period clothing walking arm in arm in the surf. They seemed to float my way. The woman held a parasol above her head. They looked stunning in the moonlight.

"Hello," I said, as they passed within fifteen feet of me. They didn't respond. Bulova saw them, but instead of growling he wagged his tail. "Go to them," I encouraged Bulova, and he took a playful running leap at them, as though he knew what would happen.

The figures simply dissipated when his leaping body touched their images; it seemed as though the particles holding them together just burst outward into the universe. I assumed they were residual energy, as neither had looked toward me when I called out to them. It was an interesting science experiment. I wondered if the image had been so clear because of the abundance of negative ions feeding the residual memory energy.

Those aren't the only spirits I've seen meandering the streets and beach of Summerland. Although I can't put a finger directly upon it, the city has managed to keep some of that residual energy that you only seem to find at Spiritualist camps that remain in tact after a century of change around them. Despite the buildup other coastal towns have experienced, the little city has seemed to avoid sprawl and keep its small-city charm with its one main street. The energy is certainly different in Summerland . . . after all these years, it seems to have retained something very special from its past.

When I left Summerland the first year, I made an effort to find the author of the book I'd found in the drawer of our rental and ask him some questions. I did many hours of research to find Rod Lathim, author of *The Spirit of the Big Yellow House*, who was fifteen years old when he'd first written the book. His sister worked at The Big Yellow House, a chain of restaurants owned by Great American Restaurants that purchased large Victorian houses and opened restaurants all over California. The company went belly-up in 1983, and Summerland's Big Yellow House was one of the casualties of the failed business.

"My family were big fans of the restaurant," said Lathim, explaining how he got involved. "My sister worked there as a hostess. We were friends with the owners, who one day sat at our table. I began telling them ideas about how to make their wine cellar store downstairs—that was doing miserably—a success. They asked me if I would take it over and do whatever needed to be done to make it profitable. I was fifteen at the time but looked and acted twenty. I said 'Sure,' and in no time my parents had taken me to wineries in Northern California, and I learned everything there was about wine. I went to gift trade shows, and I had the store filled with *good* wines, antiques, and tchotchkes—and it was clearing a profit! I learned how to run a business there.

"I also learned I wasn't alone in the cellar," Lathim said about the experiences he'd been having while spending time there. "I'd never had any experience with ghosts before, but this kid-ghost was very specific in his personality, and I named him Hector. People would be in the store shopping, or just visiting, and Hector would come in. The air around the place would change; the pressure would become very heavy and it felt like being in an air vacuum. Then he'd go running by and I could feel a breeze as he did, and the air pressure would change back to normal. I'd see little sparkles—like the old *Star Trek* when they were being beamed somewhere. People visiting the store would also notice, and they'd look at me a little spooked and ask, 'Did you feel that?'"

Lathim was always curious about the plastered-over area at the end of the hall where Hector's energy hung out when he wasn't zooming around the store hiding things and playing pranks.

"I had to find out more about Hector and about the city. People always asked me about the house, and I didn't know too much. My sister Kim and I started to do research. My grandparents—my family goes back five generations in Santa Barbara—

were the ones to tell me Spiritualists used to live in the house and the town, so I went to The Church of the Comforter—which was the original Spiritualist church that used to be in Summerland, but relocated to Santa Barbara, to learn the history and about Spiritualists. I wrote a booklet to sell at the store."

And that was the book, or the copy of the book, I'd found in the house we rent every year. It's grown and expanded into a heftier book full of history and images of early Summerland. Lathim found a wealth of information about Summerland at the Carpinteria Valley Historical Society.

"I'll never forget when Thelma Morgan Clark, one of the granddaughters of the family, came in, visiting from Pasadena," Lathim said. "Before she left, I asked her if I could ask one question, and before I could, she put her hand on my shoulder and said, 'Are you going to ask about the boy? He was here when we were here; he was welcome—and they were all welcome. That's why they *all* came here.'"

This confirmed his experiences and answered a lot of questions for Lathim, whose first thought was, "I'm not crazy!" Lathim tells many of his stories in the updated edition of his book, which will soon be available on Kindle. He's also now in negotiations with Hollywood about his screenplay relating to other similar experiences he's had since that time.

The house now has a new owner, who is aware of its history and who told Lathim he's had nights at the house that have made his hair stand up. The house has been remodeled and is waiting for a tenant, which may include plans for a new restaurant in 2012.

"My hope is that the rich history of this special house will be honored and preserved with dignity," said Lathim, who interviewed the last living relative to have lived in the home and has been researching the city's icon since 1975.

Spotlight On:
Negative Ions

You've heard the stories that begin "It was a dark and stormy night," right? Apparently there's a reason that rain and lightning—not the night—are believed to be scientifically responsible for the increase in paranormal activity. One of the theories about ghosts appearing during storms at or near locations with bodies of water, is that ghosts feed off negative ions.

In a single cubic centimeter of inland office air there are about one hundred negative ions—at the beach you'll find more than five thousand negative ions in that same amount of space. Normal outdoor fair-weather ion concentrations are between two hundred and eight hundred negative ions per cubic centimeter.

The natural movement of the churning ocean and wind create negative ions and provide an electrical power source of sorts. Negative ions are made through a process similar to how static electricity is produced through friction. When an event such as water passing through air occurs, the friction detaches an electron from a neutral molecule (atom) and becomes a positive ion, and the molecule gaining the electron becomes a negative ion. This is why an abundance of negatively charged ions are found near the ocean. Thunderstorms also create negative ions via the friction caused by clouds heavy with moisture moving through the atmosphere.

When humans experience high counts of negative ions, they yield biochemical reactions that increase the level of the neurotransmitter serotonin (which seems to dispel normal levels of the blues and calm stress). If you believe the theory of negative ions increasing paranormal activity, you can see why it's easier to make contact in an environment filled with a natural electrical feed rather than entities having to find and suck energy off batteries one by one.

A comparison of the environmental factors of paranormal activity gathered on successful investigations versus less productive ones, seems to give credence to the theory of negative ions. I own a battery-operated negative-ion pet brush that creates trillions of negative ions per second. It's mobile and soundless, but you'll have to be willing to brush your hair at an investigation. Mini negative-ion generators are also available with a USB plug, and there are bracelets that are said to create negative ions using light and natural minerals (but I have found nothing in these products that would actually cause them to do so), and even a mobile wall unit that plugs in and is only a few inches in size. If you use an EM Pump and a negative-ion generator, the negative-ion generator naturally negates most EMF.

Just to test this theory, I invite you all to start keeping a journal of the paranormal activity you do (and don't) get and start writing down things like weather temperature and barometric pressure. There are also small devices to count negative ions. Add them to your ghosthunting tool kit and see what kinds of trends you find.

Orange and Los Angeles Counties

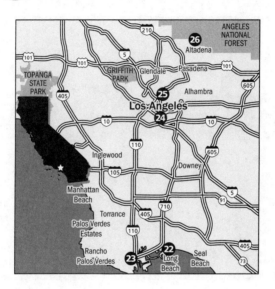

Altadena
   Cobb Estate and White City Resort **(26)**

Long Beach
   Queen Mary **(22)**

Los Angeles
   Heritage Square Museum: Hale and Octagon Houses **(25)**
   Linda Vista Hospital **(24)**

San Pedro
   Warner Grand Theatre **(23)**

CHAPTER 22

Queen Mary
LONG BEACH

The *Queen Mary* is docked in Long Beach. It's believed that she is home to six hundred ghosts! This ship seems to be an amazing vortex—the salt water surrounding her seems to be a conductor for paranormal activity.

THE RMS *QUEEN MARY* is one of the most popular paranormal-investigation locations in the country. Ghost sightings on old ships are not unusual, but what's extraordinary about the *Queen Mary* is the breadth of passenger experiences—the celebrations . . . and the horrific deaths—that set her apart from any other former ocean liner. Somehow, someway, this nearly eighty-year-old ship has become a soul cage for the men, women, and children who spent their last minutes aboard this grande dame of the sea.

My first experience on the *Queen Mary* was via Dave Schrader's Darkness Radio Conference. Now, for those of you who've never been to investigations held at conference venues, they're usually pretty much a wash. Newbies with equipment they don't know how to use, running all over the place with overwhelming aftershave and perfume and the noisiest clothes and jewelry you've ever heard, whisper to each other—as not to disturb anyone—and accidentally become your EVPs. This said, I was impressed with the conference and investigations. This is where I met paranormal investigator Gian Temperilli, coauthor and editor of *Heaven Can You Hear Me?*, which was written with the late psychic paranormal researcher Peter James of the Fox TV series *Sightings.*

When he was still in grammar school in Rochester, New York, James befriended three spirit children who'd died in a fire that had taken place at that address some thirty-five years earlier. Somehow, he empathetically connected to them and was introduced to many other spirits through his "special friends." Thus began his fascination with communicating with the dead. James passed away in 2007, but not before making the *Queen Mary* his second home via his research and tours. I imagine him still onboard, where he claimed to have found more than six hundred spirits.

"There are about five *vortices* on the ship—the main one I've discovered in the dressing room by the pool area," said James in a talk given aboard the *Queen Mary* (the talk is now on YouTube). "By the way, every home, every ship, every hospital has a heart. On this ship the first-class pool is where the main one is. It's an energy center—a portal to the other side. It's where they energize themselves—the entrance to and from . . . the vortex is ten to twenty degrees colder that the surrounding area," James said.

Before the investigation the evening of the conference I attended, I'd purchased Temperilli's book, which he'd written with James's research (with the permission of James's family). I was fascinated with what Temperilli told me about the ship. Now, the conference investigation had structure and meaning for me and wasn't the campy event I thought it was going to be. "Jackie," who is said to haunt the pool, was not some ghost invented by Disney when the company owned the ship and turned it into one of its ghost amusement rides, but an actual spirit with history and documentation of contact.

Jackie was the one spirit in particular that James connected with, and the one who became dearest to his research. Jackie is the spirit of a child who'd reached out to him through his mediumship abilities.

That night, during the event, a whole room of people heard— audibly and in real time—a little girl's voice humming. I also listened to her at the pool as people called out to her . . . and got responses—some barely audible, others detected in Class-A EVPs.

On videos of Peter James talking about Jackie, my heart really went out to the lost spirit. She sounded so frightened; she screamed and wailed. As a mother with a child about the same age—Peter believes Jackie was four when she had her fatal accident on the ship—I find it just heartbreaking when I hear her little voice. Like any other child that age, she also gets mad and is rather moody: She throws tantrums. She calls out for her mom and dad. She says she's stuck. She asks for candy. The thought of her being down there with what James called "something very forceful" makes me cringe.

As I watch the MySpace video titled "Queen Mary Investigation," I'm amazed to see how James conducted his work. I never met him, but I feel so grateful that the videos of his talks are posted. To see James via video calling out to Jackie, trying desperately to connect with her as he asks her to hold his hand, is otherworldly in itself. You hear her tiny voice screaming and crying as he pleads, "Talk with me, darling, let me help you. You don't have to cry like that, sweetheart. Show me where you are. I'm here with love; just take my hand."

Jackie does seem to have her moments when she, just as any other child her age, digs in her heels and doesn't agree to anything. This is apparent in a YouTube video titled "Jackie the Queen Mary Talking Ghost Child Speaks [to] Bob Davis and Brian Clune of PLPI." In the video, Bob Davis, founder of Planet Paranormal Investigations and Queen Mary Shadows, suggests to Jackie that she call him "Uncle Bob," and she doesn't like that one bit. She screams, *"You're not my uncle!"*

"I think she didn't understand why I said, 'Call me Uncle Bob,'" recalls Davis. "She doesn't usually talk to me that way; in fact, that was the only time she spoke in that tone. I took no offense from it, because if you listen to the Peter James audio, she gets angry at him too and says, 'Go away, Papa,' and Peter says, 'I am not going away until you know I am here with love and light for you.' Jackie has many moods, and that was just one of them. The reason I asked her to 'come see Uncle Bob' was because many kids call me Uncle Bob, and I thought she would be made more comfortable to know she too could call me Uncle Bob like the other kids I love so much. I did explain that to her, and she has never been snippy with me again. In fact, I often hear her and Sarah [another *Queen Mary* child ghost] playing hide-and-seek and laughing, and then little footsteps running around. I have a very long history on the ship going back to the 1980s, so the spirits know me well—I take no offense, and I feel they understand that I really care about them.

"As far as analyzing the voices [comparing the Jackie voice on Davis's video with the voice recorded on James's], we did have two separate professionals do voice-print analysis, and they both came out very high as being a match," says Davis. "Jackie was so loud and clear for seventeen minutes. As time went on, I became more drained until I finally told her I had to stop talking for a while and take a break. It took me weeks to recover my strength after that happened. It was unlike any other paranormal experience I have ever had before, or since, but she still talks fairly often to me, and I am very grateful for that."

In watching more Peter James videos, talking with his friends, and reading *Heaven Can You Hear Me?*, I think James's greatest asset in his mediumship work was his willingness to communicate. "My contention is there are no unnatural or supernatural phenomena," said James on video. "It's our lack of understanding and knowledge about what is natural—and ghost activity is very natural, just like death is a very natural part of life. And the dimensional afterworld is filled with ghosts and spirits . . . *naturally*. The experiences I've had regarding the mysteries of life after death have lead me to believe—with some compelling evidence—that we live in a parallel world with the coexistence of ghosts and spirits. Parallel and as close to an arm's reach—this is truly where the continuity of life exists . . . and there is life after life."

Another girl to whom James made a difference is paranormal investigator Sophia Temperilli, Gian's teenage daughter and host of *The Ghost Host Sophia Temperilli Radio Show* on **live paranormal.com.** She is a true believer since meeting James.

"On Peter James's final tour, our group all ate at Sir Winston's restaurant after Peter's greeting and introduction about ghosts," says Sophia. "While in the restaurant, I saw a figure by the window in front of where everyone was sitting. At that point Peter said, 'If everyone looks over there, Captain Jones is by the window.' When I saw the spirit, it was just the light of his face, and he had no eyes. They were just dark sockets.

"Peter James let me call out to Jackie in the infamous first-class swimming pool later on the tour," Sophia continues. "No

Author Gian Temperilli and his daughter, Sophia Temperilli, enjoying time together onboard the *Queen Mary*

one in the group heard anything. But when we played my dad's video the next day, there was a little child's voice that said, 'Hi' back to me after I called out to her. Also, when Peter was seen on camera, he pointed to our group at one point and whispered, 'Listen.' When he said that, a little girl's voice said a distant-sounding sentence over his voice saying, 'Listen.'

"My family gets invited to the ship by paranormal-research teams, psychics, authors, and asked to attend events—all because my dad coauthored his book. Peter James thought I looked like Jackie, so the *Queen Mary* director let us take special pictures of me playing her for the book. Now, because of the images, I sign copies of Peter James's book with my dad and get to call out to Jackie for ship events.

"When my family and I met with psychic Mike Loop, members of LA Paranormal, and four other fans of Peter James, we had a great paranormal investigation session outside the forward firehouse. Nothing happened at first, but at one point, Mike Loop looked up and said, 'Peter, is that you?' All at once, my K-II and Mel Meters, EMF detectors, Ghost Radar app, and dowsing rods began to move and sensors spiked. The Ovilus right then said, 'Himself.' It was Peter James!

"In December, 2011, Orange County Soul Searchers invited our family to investigate the *Queen Mary* with them [see YouTube: "Queen Mary Ghosts and Spirits Infirmary 12-28-11 Peter James"]. We had a session in the ship's infirmary that was much the same as Mike Loop's. Almost immediately after we got in and set up, all the sensors began to light up! The K-II meters, my Ghost Radar app, EMFs, Mel Meter, and dowsing rods began to come alive. Ghost Radar said 'German' more than once. The names Bill, Alice—from Greece—and Andy were identified. Each time these names and the countries they were from showed up, there were audible tap replies, K-II sensor hits, Mel Meter spikes, and everything when we asked them to verify.

"So do I believe in ghosts aboard the *Queen Mary*? The answer is—*yes!* Another time that proved to me ghosts exist aboard the *Queen Mary* happened in December of 2008. Chip Coffey [A&E's *Psychic Kids*], Richard Felix [A&E's *Haunting Evidence*], and Dave Schrader had me call out to Jackie in the first-class pool area.

"Chip Coffey had an assistant use the Ovilus device. At one point during the tour of the pool area and group session, I asked if Jackie knew where Peter James was, and the Ovilus's reply was, 'Peter, Peter, upper, stairs, top, safe, delayed.' It did this several times in a variation. Peter was there with us."

So what other tragedies befell passengers and staff riding on the ship? "When in dry dock under construction, two workers were accidentally sealed in the hull, unable to escape," says Gian Temperilli of the ship's darker history. "In 1942, the *Queen Mary* cut through her escort ship during wartime use, killing 338 sailors. Fireman/cleaner John Pedder was crushed in a watertight door during a fire drill in 1966. Second Class Officer William Stark accidentally drank tetrachloride that was kept in a gin bottle and died slowly and painfully in 1949. Peter James communicated often with a worker named John Henry in the boiler rooms, who was crushed in a work-related accident.

"A plaque in the *Queen Mary* infirmary lists many other tragic, unidentified, unexplained tragedies and details of worker, sailor, and passenger deaths," Gian says. "Of these, some were stowaways and deaths during childbirth. During a Middle East crossing in 1942, the *Queen Mary* carried more than fourteen thousand servicemen through the Red Sea region, with temperatures reaching over 120 degrees in some areas of the ship. The bodies of the sailors that perished from heat prostration were stacked in the infirmary room. Peter James could empathically receive sensations of the tragic souls' losses quite often in that room. Personally, it is the greatest honor to have coauthored a book with a legend who will eternally remain a memory aboard the *Queen Mary*. The tours that Peter James founded continue to be his legacy; and hosted events cannot be conducted today without questions in his regard. I am comforted to know that Peter James's memory is still quite alive."

Continual ghost tours and paranormal team investigations occur on a weekly basis aboard the *Queen Mary*, with many people having their favorite investigation spots on the ship—and their favorite spirits. Class-A EVPs, videos, and photos are collected constantly. Paranormal investigator Sharon Coyle, former Southern California resident and founder of Journey Paranormal Society, now has her choice of phenomena at the Rolling Hills Asylum, a monolithic haunted property in upstate New

York she purchased two years ago, but she still has fond memories about the spirits she left behind on the *Queen Mary*.

"I saw a shadow at the end of the galley/walkway near Door 13 and asked the spirit of John Pedder if I could take a photo of him. I took the picture and got a photo of whom I believe to be him standing there with a gray work jumpsuit on. John is my favorite spirit on the *Queen Mary*, though most people favor Jackie in the pool; John always was willing to communicate with me. For some reason, we had a connection. I've gotten EVPs from John in the engine room, including the complete sentence, 'Hi, Sharon, thank you for coming.'"

I recently attended a memorial service and fundraiser to help pay off the debt incurred by Donn Shy's family (Shy was a fixture in the SoCal paranormal community) during her fight against cancer in 2011. We were all hoping to hear from her during the late-night investigation. We felt her in spirit but unfortunately didn't get any evidence from her (not that we know of, anyway). Although we didn't get too much that evening in the way of EVPs, here's a response from an earlier *Queen Mary* investigation.

"My friend Donn Shy held a paranormal conference on the *Queen Mary* called *Queen-Con* in 2010," says Geoffrey Gould, cohost of *Paranormal View* on **para-x-radio.com,** "and I picked up this EVP while we were investigating the infamous first-class pool area. After going through hours of raw footage, I caught a Class-A EVP [see YouTube: "Queen Mary EVP May 01 2010"] where a female investigator asked ghost-girl Jackie if she could see the lights. A whispered reply can be heard: 'On this side. . . .'"

Peaches Veatch, founder and lead investigator for California Paranormal Private Investigations, has had some extraordinary experiences on the ship, including one where she captured evidence that was confirmed by a forensics expert. "I was on a tour and we'd been told not to use our camera's flash since it would disorient people," says Veatch. "I forgot that I didn't have the flash on, and when I took this photo, I had a bit of camera shake. When I finished with the photo, I realized that it was blurry and probably a horrible photo. It wasn't until a few days later that I put it on the computer and looked at it more closely. I saw that it was blurry and was about to discard it, until I noticed a few things. I saw the streak of light through the middle and then my friends' silhouettes standing in front of me when I took the photo. But then I noticed the outline of a face. A friend of mine, Tony Howard, is a retired mortician and an expert in facial reconstruction. He also has some forensic software he uses to enhance photos. He told me he didn't believe in ghosts—I told him I had a photo to prove their existence. He said to send the photo to him to check out. A few days later, he got back to me and told me that the photo had not been tampered with (i.e., no Photoshop, etc.) and that there was genuinely something in my photo. He gave a description of her—a woman forty to sixty years of age, and she was looking straight at me! I get goose bumps every time I think of that last part."

The ship has many such stories. The paranormal community seems to harvest incredible evidence of paranormal activity aboard the majestic steel queen. As I close this chapter thinking about the connection Peter James still has with the living, I can't help but think he's continuing his work on the *Queen Mary*, learning the ropes of whatever parallel universe he's in and teaching those he is now among how to communicate better with the spirits on this side—namely, us. I also believe in my heart that he is now the protector of the spirit children who run around the pool playing tag and calling out to us, and that they have indeed embraced him and taken his hands and released their fear and trauma and learned to embrace the joy of their life beyond death.

CHAPTER 23

Warner Grand Theatre
SAN PEDRO

THE WARNER GRAND THEATRE in San Pedro is a gem of a building to investigate. It has history, charm, and architectural allure—and it's an incredibly active paranormal location. I first encountered the building when my family attended a

Lee Stewart

birthday party there to celebrate writer Ray Bradbury's birthday
a few years back. Watching *Something Wicked This Way Comes*
with Bradbury was an amazing experience, especially in such a
magical venue. I'd never seen the movie, and it was a wonderful
first-time event at the theater because afterward we got to hear
Bradbury's story regarding its production. Although I sensed
something about the building, I didn't realize the venue was so
completely haunted until much later.

The Warner Grand kept coming up in conversation, and
everyone I spoke to about the location had a ghost story attached
to their visits to the grande dame. When I went there again, it
was with psychic medium and paranormal investigator Kathryn
Wilson, and Lee Sweet, who manages the theater for the City
of Los Angeles Department of Cultural Affairs. The building
is an amazing feat of architectural wonderment and a beautiful example of how ornate theaters once were; it was a different
time when movies were works of art that needed a most mag-
nificent frame.

The theater, built in 1930 by Jack Warner, Jr. (of Warner Bros. fame) was the first sound-equipped theater in the South Bay. Warner dubbed the theater "The Castle of Your Dreams," and so it was. Double features entertained the working-class masses as they flocked to the theater and were transported to a different frame of mind from their hard lives as cannery workers; the mundane became extraordinary for as long as the projector reels continued to roll.

The Warner brothers built only three sound-equipped theaters because they cost a great deal of money, and construction started just as the Depression hit; everyone was cutting back, but people still managed to find the money to buy a ticket. Profits were low because of the initial costs of the theaters—nine-hundred thousand dollars for the Warner Grand alone.

The gorgeous building was the work of the dynamic duo of architect B. Marcus Priteca and artist Anthony Heinsbergen, the dream team that created Hollywood's Pantages and the iconic Los Angeles City Hall. The fine detail and workmanship in the Art Deco theater are purely inspirational. The fact that the building still survives is a testament to politics and how much the city of San Pedro loved the memories created within her walls. Her two siblings had different fates—the Warner Theatre in Beverly Hills was demolished and became a parking lot, and the Huntington Park Theatre, closed for many years, is now extensively altered and divided.

The 501(c)(3) Grand Vision Foundation was incorporated as a charitable corporation to preserve and promote the Warner Grand Theatre, and shortly thereafter the building was given historical status by the City of Los Angeles and the State of California to go along with its inclusion on the National Register of Historic Places.

When I visited the Warner Grand the second time, I wandered her halls and stairwells in search of life . . . life *beyond*

The Warner Grand Theatre is a grande dame of the American heyday of cinema architecture. Built by Jack Warner of Warner Bros. Studios, the theater was beloved in the community. Paranormal investigators hear voices in the seats when the theater is empty.

life. I wanted so badly to find the army of souls that had been described to me.

"The main areas that are active are the lobby, theater, dressing rooms, and lower-level restrooms," said Kathryn Wilson. "I was leading a Meetup group investigation for 3AM Paranormal there—it's always great to work with eager enthusiasts. We started off in the theater, did an EVP and ITC session. We'd been told to listen for whispering spirits, waiting for a show we could not see. The host for the evening, Plankey, a hospitable young man, told us of an experience he had. While sitting with a small group of friends, he witnessed a man come out of the second-story balcony door and walk to the upper lobby. He quickly got up to confront the intruder. When he got to the area, no one was there, but he continued to look for the man and could not locate him anywhere.

"After that," continued Wilson, "we went down to the dressing-room area where we heard close-range audible voices and footsteps. We were convinced a man and a woman were on the stairs, but when we looked . . . no one was there. The most action for the evening was down in the lower restroom area. We all experienced seeing shadow people movement in the main room and what appeared to be a person peeking out of the women's restroom. After checking all present for movement and light sources, we determined the shadow figures were not being made by any of the investigators. While we were down there, Joe Mendoza [cofounder and paranormal investigator of 3AM Paranormal] joined us and conducted an ITC session where he asked if there was a vortex in the theater. We heard positive responses for the location of the vortex being in the women's restroom. When Joe asked if the vortex was in the second stall, the ITC device replied, 'Third.' You never know where activity will be centered in any given building, this is not the first time that I've found the greatest activity located in restroom areas. Perhaps it has to do with running water being a conductor to spirit energy."

Sharon Coyle, a former Southern California resident now living in upstate New York, remembers her visit to the Grand vividly. "There's definitely lots of great activity there," says Coyle, founder of Journey Paranormal Society. "The place is really amazing, especially the orchestra pit." Coyle now has her choice of constant phenomena at the monolithic paranormal property Rolling Hills Asylum she purchased two years ago. She's had some interesting company, including the Booth Brothers shooting *Haunted Boy* and *Ghost Adventurers* and *Paranormal Challenge* filming crews. There are unmarked graves for more than seventeen hundred patients and staff at Rolling Hills, many of whose spirits now call the manse and grounds home.

"I've felt children there," says Coyle of the Warner Grand. "And a guy in the projector booth who's not very accommodating.

On the right side of the stage there was a really heavy smell of oranges. One guy with us started to get pain in his back, he lifted up his shirt and there were big scratch marks that were still red. He'd been videotaping with us, and his hands were visible. Normally, I'm very skeptical of scratches—if you can touch it, you can scratch it—*this* I believed.

"We got a lot of EVPs downstairs in the smoking area and downstairs bathrooms," continues Coyle. "The hair on my arms stood up when I was down there, but I never felt threatened. I'm the type of investigator who wants to learn why we experience activity—that's how I approach investigation. I go in with a nonjudgmental attitude. I've captured and seen a lot of movement—scurrying and walking at the Warner Grand. There's this long, narrow bank of mirrors in the dressing room. My team and I cleaned the mirrors in the dressing room of the basement, and as an experiment we sprayed them with Pam vegetable spray with flour. We were hoping a spirit would try to write on or touch the mirror and that it would show up. Nothing like that showed, but when I took a series of three photos—I was surprised to see the images of the large, green anime-type head in the photos. It was rather sweet-looking, with long, fluttery eyelashes. What was it and why was it here? Perhaps it was actually a former actor, a spirit of an actor dressed in costume. Whatever it was, I was surprised and intrigued, especially since earlier in the evening, as we were all walking into the theater, a medium accompanying the team, actually made reference of a large, round, green head floating above the theater. Coincidence or something else?

"I was speaking with the people who have a shop across the street from the Warner, and both of them saw people huddled under the marquee during a rainstorm. They were in period clothing. At the time, the theater was closed and the streets were empty. The man who witnessed this is originally from the islands, I think, and he was very familiar with unexplained things. He also worked on cruise ships for years and traveled around the world, experiencing many things, which made him believable to me. I was amazed and intrigued by his descriptions and only wished I had been able to see the gathering of spirits. Why was he able to see these visions? Was it extrasensory perception or something more scientific, such as the bending of dimensions due to climatic changes that allowed him to see these images? Was it residual energies or were the images, in fact, spirits continuing on in a parallel dimension?"

Joe and Rebecca Mendoza are a husband-and-wife team and founders of 3AM Paranormal, an investigation group that transforms would-be investigators into the real thing through their Meetup training group. They also go out on their own to work private investigations. Both are highly sensitive, as just about everyone who does this for long enough becomes.

"The longer you do this kind of thing, the more you pick up on it," says Joe Mendoza of how they can go into a paranormal-saturated area such as the Warner Grand and audibly hear and sense those who are no longer of this world.

"My first impression is that it was a beautiful building—even the end caps of every row of seats has an elaborate wooden carving," says Joe of the architecture and design of the structure. "I was really surprised because it's so large, it was a little overwhelming about where to begin. I'm glad we did get a little guidance going in; we were told by our friend Vickie to check out the bathroom downstairs. This visit was one of our Meetup training sessions—we set up, and, although a lot of those people were new to investigation, it didn't take long for them to start noticing the bathrooms downstairs. There seems to be activity in that entire area downstairs . . . a lot of things moving around. I kept getting the sense that something was coming down the stairs. I tried to get as many people as possible to sit against the back wall, and I could see a black mass moving—others seemed short and quick. They were blocking out the lights on the equipment. We use the term *bailing* for this; it takes about ten to fifteen minutes for your eyes to adjust and your pupils to widen to take in more light. When that happens, you can see more in the darkness. Sometimes I wonder: Is it because I'm a believer and more willing to connect with the spirits that I'm seeing them? Sometimes you wonder if what you're seeing is really there. That's when it's great to have others around you who can confirm you're seeing the same thing. Downstairs, everyone was seeing this dark mass move around.

"I had one of those 'ah-ha!' moments at the Warner Grand," Joe says. "I got tired of standing, so I decided to take a break and walked back—maybe six rows from the back row of the theater and tuned off all my equipment and just sat there. Then I heard my name called: 'Joe. Joe.' It was really clear. And I thought, *Oh my god this place is haunted!*"

"All we had to do was sit there quietly and we heard whispers," says Rebecca of the activity their group was picking up in the theater. "Quiet voices—like theater voices, and little taps. A few of us got touched on our arms. The downstairs bathroom is really haunted, and we got a lot of EVPs in there. After doing the main session, I went to use the bathroom, and there was another woman from our group using the bathroom, and she was still on the toilet when I left. I was halfway up the long stairs to the main level and I heard, 'What did you get?' from right behind me, and I thought it was her, and I said, 'Oh we—' because I just had an intense experience in the theater I was going to tell her about. I turned around and no one was there. Now, normally, I can tell a spirit voice from a human, but I couldn't differentiate the two—they're pretty strong there."

"It doesn't make sense that there are thirty different ghosts at the Warner Grand that have such a strong connection to that building that they never wanted to leave," says Joe about the number of spirits that seem to have an interest in the venue. "Maybe it's one of those portals—or a vortex. Maybe there's some kind of time slip there."

Rebecca believes that the spirits she's detected are not tormented. "Most of the EVPs I've gotten there have been really happy voices. In some darker places we go we get, 'Help me, help me.' It's not like that there."

"There was one that sounded like *me*—we get that all the time," Joe said about a verbal doppelgänger. "I've had my own voice say hello to me. The one that really got me was one we kept asking its name, and he said sarcastically, 'Casper.' That really messed with me for a few days."

"I've been here eleven years," says Lee Sweet regarding his overseer position. Sweet schedules the after-hours paranormal investigations events and has been hearing for years about what investigators have been finding. "I haven't seen anything, but who am I to disbelieve it? Yes, I do believe it's occupied. My concept of it after having talked to a bunch of these folks about this and what they've seen is that they live on one plane and we live here—and we're right next to each other and walking through each other. I have no background in physics, but that's my best concept of it all. I don't think they come and go. I don't have any evidence for them to emerge other than they're just going about their business. Remember the *Superman* comics? The character Bizarro—it's kind of like that. We hopefully don't get in their way, and they certainly haven't gotten into mine. I'm kind of hoping I'll see one because I have myself convinced it won't bother me if I do because I've been so immersed in all of this. It'll be like, 'Hi, it's nice to see you! How are you?' Yeah, maybe—or I'll turn around and run down the street screaming like my hair's on fire. Whatever happens, I just think it'll be real interesting."

CHAPTER 24

Linda Vista Hospital
LOS ANGELES

Although Linda Vista Hospital is no longer operating, the historic landmark's sign still reminds the community of the part the property played in its history. The building is one of America's most active locations for paranormal activity.

IMAGINE IF YOUR PARANORMAL-investigation group were based in a huge, empty hospital compound known worldwide for its paranormal activity. And imagine that hospital as an island in a sea of thousands of people—many raised in a religion that doesn't really allow for dabbling in the paranormal. Your mission? To protect the historic hospital from further damage occurring from age, vandals, and careless, uncaring movie crews—while trying to create awareness through the Boyle Heights Paranormal Project (BHPP), which is trying to save the hospital's history while continuing its research within the wildly active vortex that is the heart of the historic location.

Sounds like a fantastic paranormal-based, postapocalyptic video game, right? It's not. It's real—and the scenario is being played out even as I write this chapter. The hospital compound is Linda Vista Hospital, in the historic East Los Angeles district of Boyle Heights. Welcome to the reality of BHPP, one of the most successful paranormal-research groups in the county. Its mission? To preserve the buildings and to educate the public about the rich history that happened within the gates of the Linda Vista Hospital and the Boyle Heights neighborhood.

And when they can find time, BHPP members clean up the compound, which is sporadically trashed by movie-production crews, *and* collect thousands of hours of video and audio footage for review at a later date. Because of a recent change of ownership, the group's future is somewhat uncertain for BHPP's place inside the Linda Vista Hospital property, but I've been told that for the next few years its doors will be open to the public (by appointment only).

Richard Standing Bear Berni, cofounder of the group, along with his son Jeremy Berni, created BHPP to save what history was left in Boyle Heights, a place four generations of their family have called home. BHPP collects the oral histories of the neighborhood's collective memory regarding the people, cultural traditions, and everyday happenings of those who worked and died within the Linda Vista structures and the neighborhood around the hospital. It's a huge undertaking—especially when you consider that much of its research also focuses on interviewing the dead who still inhabit the building. Believe me, it's a unique experience.

"Growing up in Boyle Heights and going to the hospital was like running out to the supermarket—it was just a place to go hang out. My aunt worked here as a receptionist. My Uncle Carlos, a railroad employee, passed away here in 1959," said Richard Standing Bear Berni as he sat in the office off the entrance of the main building. I had paused before going inside the office, peering into the dimming light of the long entrance hall. I paused because I saw someone . . . *something* . . . shift into the darkness as I walked in. I'd been in the building before during an investigation, and it had been a wildly active experience—somehow it felt like my return had been announced to those spirits I'd communicated with before.

At BHPP's central hub, we absently watched monitors displaying live video feeds coming from the many security cameras located throughout the hospital. I watched as shadow people crossed the halls. It was like a scene from *13 Ghosts*. Throughout the few hours I was there, what I call my "ghost sonar"—a high-pitched frequency like a dog whistle that sometimes rings in my ears when spirits come into my space—kept going off. On playback, I actually make a verbal reference to a spirit I'm hearing come in, and I can, for the first time, actually hear the high-pitched noise captured on my digital recording: a frequency that I've only heard in my head for all of these years. For me, that was amazing affirmation. In the office, I heard the frequency buzz, and I mentally acknowledged a spirit's entrance. At that same moment, Richard's eyes went to the door where I'd heard the spirit enter.

I asked him, "Do you hear it, too?" He shook his head and told me about the heat waves he saw when one spirit entered his space. We both acknowledged the spirit in our presence.

I was not surprised to find a spirit with us. Both Berni and my ancestors grew up on neighboring reservations in Arizona, with belief systems in which the living and spirits walk beside each other. We both honor those traditions, but we find it necessary to gather proof for everyone else to see. For some reason, that proof is just a little easier to get at Linda Vista.

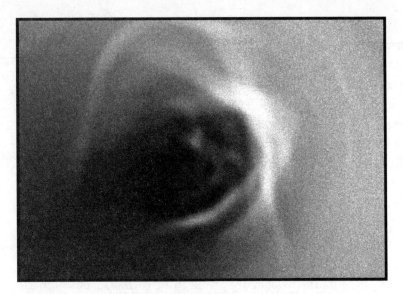

This is the spirit that manifested itself when I took a photo into the darkening hall of the main Linda Vista Hospital building. Taken with my with my D-300s Nikon, the photo incorporates a technique I devised—I set the ISO at 3200 and gave the camera a quarter-twist while I took the picture. I believe that these parallel-universe beings travel at a much faster speed than we do, and the reason traditional photography hasn't reaped more than a handful of phenomenal spirit images is because we're thinking the same way as we've thought for more than a hundred years about capturing photographs—people shoot cameras like they're taking a portrait. If this field is to continue to grow toward understanding what it is *exactly* that inhabits the Other Side, we need to find better ways of documenting its existence.

As I reviewed the recording of my visit there, I heard Richard talking about the work his group is doing. Then there was a whispered "Thank you"—words from the netherworld coming directly into the recorder's microphone and right over our conversation. When I was in the office, the spirit left, and the high-pitched noise in my ears and on my recorder went silent.

"The hospital was just part of the community—part of the family," Berni said as we continued to monitor the shadows on the video screens. "We would go fishing across the street at Hollenbeck Park. It—*the hospital*—was always was looming over the park."

The hospital opened in 1904 as the Santa Fe Railroad Hospital, a state-of-the-art amputation center, one of the first in the country. It served the blue-collar community surrounding the hospital, most of whom were Santa Fe employees and their families. The building was designed in a Moorish/Art Deco–style architecture that allowed the building to remain relatively comfortable without air-conditioning in the warm climate. In 1924, the building was razed after railroad workers began using alternative medical-insurance systems.

Eventually, a new hospital was built on the grounds in its current Mission Revival style, which the architect felt better represented the community it was meant to serve. Times were tough, and many patients defaulted on their hospital bills; in an effort to cut costs, staff and services were reduced, and the hospital was blamed for an increase in the death rate. Many say the increase in the hospital's mortality stats was due to the rising crime rate in the deteriorating neighborhood; stabbing and shooting victims were coming in more frequently. In 1991, the hospital closed its doors, and a decade or so later, thanks to BHPP, the hospital became a research center for paranormal activity.

"I had a friend who briefly was a security guard for a Clint Eastwood movie that was being filmed here," said Berni. "I came in a few times with him and decided it was a pretty cool place. Later, I decided to get really involved with the local history, and I brought the newly formed BHPP into Linda Vista and asked the owner if he needed help taking care of the place. I offered help from the group that were preservation type of things—sweeping, mopping, trash pickup, and he said, 'No, we have everything covered.' So I just gave him a detailed account about who we were, where we come from, and our goal as a paranormal group that focuses on historical research and documentation of the oral history of the East Side of Los Angeles. After listening to all of this, we talked and eventually he dropped his guard, and about three months later I get this call from him asking, 'Hey, does that offer still stand?'"

Berni walks these halls in darkness from memory. To Berni, a firefighter who worked at Ground Zero, the spirits here are nothing compared to the horrors he'd seen. He doesn't need a flashlight to *see* or to ward off what lives in the dark corners of the hospital. He seems to have an understanding with the spirits.

As I conducted the interview, we simultaneously acknowledged the nuances in light and energy that shifted in the room as another spirit walked in and remained by the window, as if to listen in on our conversation. We continued talking, forgetting it was there until it shifted again and dissipated.

"People crossed over here and were also born into the world here—I think there is a doorway that has been created here," Berni said of the constant paranormal activity. "Clearly something is here; I can see that by the constant shadow traffic in the halls and in the office. I'm not afraid in this place; there's more to fear driving on a highway than some shadow people that have an interest in what you're doing.

"The Santa Fe Community Hospital [what it was called before Linda Vista] has amazing history. The people that populated and surrounded this hospital were Russian, Mexican, Yugoslav, Jewish, Japanese—they had to live east of the river; that's the way it was back then. They formed a community; I believe they were getting good medicine here—creating a good vibe.

We took a break and walked out to the parking area where we met a young couple, Dianna and Vance, who'd driven from Riverside. Berni told me that they weren't here to do an investigation, but rather to experience something about this place, perhaps to review some evidence.

"They're young; they should be out on a date, but instead they're here," Berni said. That's the kind of people who come here. I think that's what draws the project together. In 2010 we suspended investigations and concentrated only on community outreach—not just the paranormal community but everyone. Sometimes we'd get ten or fifteen professionally dressed people coming in on a flashlight tour [not all of the parts of the building have electricity], and they'd just come in to hear the history. They'd leave here realizing this place has an amazing history. When it belonged to the Santa Fe Railway, they used to have cattle, crops, chickens, a dairy . . . it was a community."

In March 2011, BHPP held the First Annual Paranormal Pow-Wow, an event my team and I attended. It was so different from any paranormal event I'd ever attended. It wasn't a conference where the bright and shiny paranormal celebrities came to hawk their latest projects; it was a good lineup of people you don't normally find at conferences, and money was raised for the upkeep of Linda Vista Hospital.

Throughout the decades, the community has heard many paranormal stories from former patients and employees. Many steered clear of the property, walking away from its looming shadow to avoid what lived in the darkness. Others were dying to get into the place—so much so that they used to break in, and this activity generated even more stories of ghosts that spread like wildfire. A generation was born into the community that had known the hospital only when it seemed an abandoned haunted curiosity. Vandalism escalated.

Taking a break from the interview, we drove to dinner at an excellent, packed Chinese restaurant just down the road. We passed by houses with elderly Hispanic women set up in their driveways, serving dinner outside their homes to bring in a little extra income. They remind me of my now-passed entrepreneurial Grandma Mary, who used to make vats of tamales to feed the neighborhood in San Jose. Although I'm a vegetarian now, I still help my mother make tamales for Christmas to feel close to my grandmother and our old traditions. For me, the East Los Angeles neighborhood is a comforting place to be.

Jeremy Berni, Richard's son, is growing into his father's shoes. The young man is now a licensed armed security guard who watches over Linda Vista Hospital; people trespass and arrests are made. But they continue to come, as if drawn by some magnetic force. My mind wanders to horror movies when I'm in the place (perhaps it's because many where filmed here), but I can't help but think of John Carpenter's *Prince of Darkness* every time I step foot on the grounds: a movie premise that centers around paranormal researchers gathering evidence in a looming Los Angeles church, mysteriously cut off from all communication while surrounded by zombielike creatures who won't let the researchers out or let help inside. I tried to push the movie from my mind as Jeremy told me about his experiences at the hospital while making his rounds in what seems to be a center of paranormal activity in the hospital: the boiler room.

"I was downstairs after a big investigation and doing a walk-through," said Jeremy of his duties. "I saw a gurney roll across the hallway and heard it crash and overturn around the corner. I ran around the corner and its wheels were still turning. I checked around; there was no way anyone could have done that and gotten away so quickly."

Jeremy survived his childhood thanks to a sense of self-preservation that taught him immediately what to do when he heard gunshots outside of his home. He continues to survive because of those street-smart senses he developed to protect himself.

"If something has so much energy it can throw a gurney—what else can it do?" asked Jeremy. "I've never *seen* any spirits here, but I seen stuff thrown. I don't know if it's because I'm a bigger guy so they feel the need to prove something to me—the need to get rough and throw stuff around when I'm walking around—though they have not ever touched me. One night I heard footsteps down the hall, so I went to see if we had trespassers. I saw a chair—I didn't see it get lifted—go through the air and hit a wall and fall. So I ran over to see if someone had broken in. No one was there."

The hospital, slated to be converted to apartments for senior citizens, earned a place on the National Register of Historic Places in 2006. The new owner, a multihousing developer, plans to keep the facade in place and gut the weathered interior. So what will happen to BHPP's relationship with the historic buildings and the relationships between its team and the spirits who've grown accustomed to each other? No one knows.

"We'll still be here as long as the new ownership allows us to be," said Richard of the group's future at the location. "They've said, for now, as long as everyone is safe and no one gets hurt, we can stay until the building is restructured. Will we get to come back? I don't know. We are hoping that we'll get to open up a coffee house on the second floor—a place to put all the pictures of the old hospitals up on the walls so people can see what this place once was. We want to open up the history we've gathered and the evidence we have to researchers to have access to. We've done a lot of volunteer work for a long time here and in the community, and I hope that earns us a place to continue our work. In the meantime, we've been preparing for an exit and gathering thousands of hours of research on video so we'll have something substantial if one day we do have to leave, although we do hope to find a way to phase into the new life of the Linda Vista Senior Community."

CHAPTER 25

Heritage Square Museum: Hale and Octagon Houses

LOS ANGELES

The Octagon House at Heritage Park is quite an amazing place; it seems to be loaded with poltergeist activity, and we saw quite a few people leave the house because they were uncomfortable with the energy and what was going on inside.

I RECENTLY ATTENDED A FUNDRAISER to help pay off the medical bills for the family of Donn Shy, an amazing woman in the paranormal community who lost her battle with cancer. One of the many things I love about our community is its ability to quickly band together and help out when needed. The fundraiser was held at Los Angeles's Heritage Square Museum, a community of Victorian-era buildings saved from demolition and moved to their present location, where they were lovingly restored in an effort to educate people about what life was like in Los Angeles during the 1800s.

The event, sponsored by Haunted Orange, an Orange County paranormal organization, re-created what was going on inside Victorian homes across the country in the 1850s—when Spiritualism swept the United States and Europe, and "home circle" séances were regularly practiced (think Ouija-board séances in the 1970s, but without the board) to communicate with the dead. The event was a great success, with people coming from all over California to celebrate Donn's life and fill the Victorians with laughter and paranormal activity until past midnight. The group of about seventy people broke up into smaller groups of about a dozen to explore the homes in dark séancelike settings. I was especially attracted to the Hale House and Gilbert Longfellow's Octagon House.

I have a great passion for octagon homes and have explored many on the East Coast that have survived from the boom that Orson Squire Fowler started in 1849. I'd come across Fowler's name as one of the foremost phrenologists of his time in my research on the subject of Spiritualism. Fowler was a classmate and close friend of Henry Ward Beecher, a noteworthy advocate of both Spiritualism and phrenology. Octagon houses were quite popular in early Spiritualist camps. Fowler, the Buckminster Fuller (designer of the geodesic dome) of his time, believed that life would improve vastly inside an eight-sided home. He spoke endlessly of the bountiful health benefits one could expect living in such a structure. He, like Fuller, began a movement for the home of the future. Personally, living inside of a geodesic dome, I've not found it energy-saving or beneficial, especially when it comes to having to find contractors who know the math involved in working on such a structure; I can only imagine what a pain living inside of an eight-sided home must be.

Fowler was on the speaking circuit for decades, examining the heads of statesmen and celebrities and telling them what their future held, and what their talents would be best served doing. On the podium, he spoke about sex, love, children's rights, memory, the Suffragette movement, marriage, intellect, fashion, animal magnetism, temperance, vegetarianism, medicine, and spirituality. Like many intellectuals of the era, he wrote numerous booklets (Beecher published some of them) and sold them at his talks.

For as much criticism as he faced, he was certainly right about one thing: wood is an objectionable home-building material. He pointed out that the next five hundred years would come as fast as the last, and there were better materials to construct homes with, such as gravel and stone (cement) because of the need for the earth's surface to grow food, not walls. Orson built his first octagon home—a sixty-room mansion—in Fishkill, New York, the same year Spiritualism was getting a foothold upstate in Rochester. The design promoted fresh air by positioning the windows toward each other, allowing maximum light to save on energy costs (primarily lamp fuel). It was the feng shui design of its day. Some believed that the corners were angled so wide that bad energy—otherwise known as evil spirits—could not get stuck in such a house.

Before the big octagon craze, Thomas Jefferson built a brick octagon home near Lynchburg, Virginia, at his Poplar Forest retreat in 1806. George Washington had built a sixteen-sided threshing barn on his Mount Vernon estate. Eventually, Fowler's own house was dubbed "Fowler's Folly" and was destroyed, but he'd inspired the construction and sold the designs (home

design was patented and plans were sold—if you built one without buying the plans, it was legally considered patent infringe-
ment) for one thousand octagons (only a handful were actually
made from cement due to the initial cost). Today, about half of
these homes on the East Coast are said to survive. An octagon
house built before 1897 still stands in the Spiritualist camp of
Lily Dale, New York, and serves as the community's Mediums
League gathering hall.

Gilbert Longfellow, the owner of the Octagon House in Heritage Square, was a lumberman, orange grower, and landholder,
and passionate about the octagon. He'd built his first, a two-story
octagon (still in existence), in 1869 in Maine. With several of his
own family members dead from what he suspected was tubercu-
losis (so much for the health benefits of the octagon), he moved
his three surviving daughters and his son to Pasadena, California,
where the weather was more conducive to good health. In 1893,
he built his octagon, which was eventually moved to the Heritage
Square Museum. He was first forced to move it one mile north of
its original location when the California Institute of Technology
was established on his property. By 1973, the home was owned
by Longfellow's grandson—and slated for demolition. The Cultural Heritage Foundation of Southern California, which runs
the Heritage Square Museum, agreed to save the home and move
it to its current location if he would sell the home for one dollar.
He did, and the home was moved in 1986. Hopefully, the third
time's the charm. The home is believed to be the last surviving,
unaltered example of octagonal architecture in California.

Our tour guide/host in the octagon was going to be Rob
Hansen, a paranormal investigator with Haunted Orange, but
just as we got there he was switched with Ernie Alonzo, another
Haunted Orange investigator, and Ramiro Ramirez, the group's
lead investigator. Paranormal investigator Ashley Hansen, Rob
Hansen's daughter, had also been in the Octagon House with

Ashley Hansen shows her purse handle, which snapped when all kinds of para-normal activity broke out in the Octagon House the evening of the fundraiser for Donn Shy.

her father earlier when a poltergeist-like event occurred (before they were switched over to the Palms Depot building).

"My dad and I had just finished the first group tour of the night at the Octagon House," said Hansen. "We walked to the area just before the stairs and right into an extremely cold spot. It seemed as if the spirit had been hiding in the little alcove beneath the stairs. It was a dramatic temperature change of at least five to ten degrees, and it gave me chills all over. Usually I do not think too much about cold spots, but then my dad got, as he describes, punched or kicked in the butt. It was enough to make him jump and say, *Whoooa!* Shortly thereafter, I felt a forceful tug on my arm, though it didn't hurt. Then I heard my purse hit the floor. I looked down quizzically at my wristlet, wondering how it had come off my arm. When I picked it up, I noticed the strap had completely broken off. It was a brand-new purse; it was the first time I had used it. I only had my phone and some mints in it, so it was not the weight that had broken it. Clearly, the spirit was not entirely thrilled to have us in the house."

On the heels of that incident, my group, Roadside Paranormal, led by myself and lead investigators/case managers Leo Aréchiga and Anne Marie, entered the home. The Octagon House, with all of its claims to good health and energy, had a very dank and dark feel to it. *Repressive* is the word. The bathroom had a really negative energy, as though someone had been very sick there for a long time and perhaps passed in the house . . . maybe in the bathtub—a place popular for suicides. We had some time to tour the house on our own, though we were asked not to go upstairs. This seemed unfortunate, because there seemed to be a lot of *something* going on up there. The circular stairs leading up to the cupola were definitely ominous. We gathered in a front room to the right of the house and listened to the introduction regarding the house. Ramiro Ramirez (from cable network MUN2's *From Beyond*) began the tour with a talk about the building and ITC (instrumental transcommunication). At that time, Ramirez entered the room to the left of the front entrance, and the group heard a loud slam and a yell. Ramirez came into the room telling us that an unseen force had slammed against the wall next to him. We were told to continue the tour with extreme caution due to the escalation of physical activity in the home. If there was one atom of good energy in this building, I certainly didn't feel it, and I was relieved to be outside in the fresh air once the effort was over.

Psychic medium and paranormal investigator Kathryn Wilson (the medium from A&E's *Storage Wars*) was the evening's hostess at Hale House, built in 1885. The house's architecture is described as Queen Anne, Eastlake, Carpenter, and Gothic. The

Psychic medium Kathryn Wilson in front of the Hale House after the evening's activities.

last woman to live there was Bessie Hale, who purchased it in 1901 with her husband, but even this wonderful home couldn't make the couple happy, and they separated a few years later. Bessie, deciding she preferred the company of strangers, opened a boardinghouse, and the home became a well-established business. She passed away in 1967 at age ninety-seven.

Hale's niece inherited the home and couldn't wait to sell the property—the plan was to tear down the *grande dame* and build a petrol station on the property. Like the Octagon, the home was saved from the wrecking ball at the eleventh hour by the Heritage Square folks at the cost of $1. However, it cost $10,300 to move her, $3,000 to lift the wires as she passed through town during a midnight event (the crowed roared when the fireplace

The Hale House is the crown jewel of the Heritage Park Museum. It's an amazingly active location with paranormal phenomena that you can both see and hear in real time.

remained intact), and $300,000 to restore the house to her original glory, as somewhere along the way it had been "bombed" as a movie set. Originally built at the cost of $4,000 (a small fortune back in the day), the Hale House had been moved from the Highland Park neighborhood, but like the Octagon House, the house had been moved a total of three times as well. The restoration work on the home is beautiful.

Now, this is one of those houses that had a lot of living within her walls, and there seemed to be many spirits in the house, including an adolescent girl. We had several sessions with the PX, and it was alive with characters coming through to speak with us. Wilson picked up on a schoolteacher who lived at the house; in my recent research of the house, I did find the house had some association with the old Page School for Girls, which stood directly across from the home when it was a boardinghouse. Perhaps this is where the single schoolteachers lived. Wilson also felt that the husband Bessie Hale thought she'd gotten rid of is still in the house with her, and that Mrs. Hale had blocked her from psychically probing any further into her business, as she felt quite ashamed about a matter. The PX was sitting on a table and saying "cards," "frog," and "rabbit"— toy items actually on the table as one of the home's displays. Both Wilson and I picked up the message that we should sing to raise the vibration in the house, and oddly enough we were both thinking "Row, Row, Row Your Boat." After we sang a few rounds, several people in the group looked up at once into the back parlor, where we'd all seen a mist go by. We also heard audible disembodied voices in the back room and saw shadow people racing around. Both of us felt that the house had been used for séances in the past. Throughout the event, we were hearing noises in the kitchen, as though someone was working away making a meal, but there was no one there.

In the upstairs bedroom, we'd heard audible breaths that came from the area of the bed where no one was standing or sitting; I picked up some of these on my digital recorder. Back downstairs, we continued to hear walking upstairs after every-one had already come down.

Is the Hale House haunted? I'd say there are so many ghosts in the home now that Mrs. Hale had to open an ethereal board-inghouse to store all the dead who've decided to make this place their home . . . again.

"Hale House is alive with spirit activity," said Wilson of the Heritage Square's gem. "Shadow figures, mists, footsteps, voices, and movement can be seen and heard. The frustrations of life, suffered by Mr. and Mrs. Hale, seem to have carried over into the afterlife. The very walls vibrate with their struggle, shortcomings, alcoholism, and resentment, as well as social dis-course, celebration, and daily life from decades past."

CHAPTER 26

Cobb Estate and White City Resort

ALTADENA

The Echo Mountain Promontory with the world-famous White City after a snowfall in 1896. The White City layout is as such: the Echo Chalet, Echo Mountain House, Incline Powerhouse, dormitories, and car barn. Behind the car barn is the inflatable reservoir for the storage of hydrogen gas. *Photo courtesy of the Mike Manning Collection for use in the public domain by Wikipedia.*

WHEN I FIRST HEARD ABOUT THE COBB ESTATE, it sounded fascinating. What I found even more exciting was an eerie abandoned resort known as White City, set atop Echo Mountain. The trailhead there begins on the Cobb property and takes you to the world-famous "City in the Clouds." For guests at the resort, the property could be accessed only by the Mount Lowe Railway, owned by the same entity as White City. The railway made a harrowing journey up the mountain in rickety cable cars on cliff-hanging rails all the way up Echo Mountain. Today, the railroad's path is a dangerous hiking trail from which hikers have fallen to their deaths. The walk from the Cobb property to the ruins of White City is about three-and-a-half hours, probably much less if you're in fit condition and you can climb like a goat.

Roadside Paranormal lead investigator Anne Marie and I decided to stop by on our way back to San Diego from the James Dean crash site (see James Dean chapter). Many people have felt as though they were being watched at the Cobb Estate—and there's good reason for that. Apparently, several large hiking groups meet there on Sunday afternoons. Personally, I prefer working in silence, or near-silence, and with a limited number of people around, as too many people may contaminate evidence. But we made do.

It was late afternoon and a good opportunity to stretch our legs. Anne Marie and I toured the Cobb Estate grounds, where a multitude of crows were swooping down around us. We picked up some EMF spikes around the area, but the K-II was pretty flat. The area is fairly well attended, and it's difficult to get uncontaminated evidence. We wanted to get through the basic area before it got any later, and we had to hit another location that day.

I'd seen several ghosthunting videos regarding the Cobb Estate and the White City resort. It seems teams are apprehensive of the location due to the amount of human traffic at night wandering around the estate area. The place is covered with gang tags. At night you'll find young people blasting boom boxes, drinking, and, yes, fornicating. You may hear moaning at this location, but chances are it's from earthbound youth higher than a kite and having sex somewhere on the foundation where the estate once stood. During the day—and night—you'll smell reefer and hear hysterical laughter wafting in from all directions, which explains why people drop five hundred feet off of cliffs during broad daylight and need to be medevacked out.

And then there's the skeletal remains found on the Cobb estate in 2011. A big to-do was made of finding the remains, which were less than six months old. The Los Angeles County Sheriff's Department's Altadena Station lieutenant in charge of the case reported that the body was discovered "on the fire road inside the Cobb Estate, which leads towards a seasonal waterfall and is often used by hikers. The remains were found near a water tank structure near the end of the road." I've since called the LACS Altadena Station and left messages to find out what happened but have heard no response. If I were a detective and someone was calling me about an unsolved crime, I'd probably call back . . . but that's just me. Now that I've called, either my message went into the circular file, or maybe I'm now a "person of interest" for the staff to investigate next time someone's on vacation here in San Diego. Bodies and skeletal remains are unearthed on a regular schedule in the Angeles National Forest; like most bodies, they fall into the cold-case files pretty quickly if someone isn't looking for them. Throw all that into the mix, and you have the makings of a pretty good B movie . . . and we haven't even gotten to the beginning of this story.

Andrew Thompson, cofounder with Stacy Ann Raposa of the Los Angeles Paranormal Network, along with cohost (of the team's Internet show) Joey Harrison, went to the Cobb Estate and filmed their investigation in the difficult environment. The team's initial effort was thwarted by a battery that went unexpectedly dead. The second time, they came prepared with an extra charged battery and got some good results.

"Our Sony IR camera went dead about forty minutes into filming, though it was supposed to last ninety, so we went back

This is what I believe to be the entrance to the now-completely-gone Cobb Estate, which the Marx Brothers once purchased in hopes of turning it into a cemetery.

again," says Thompson. "We had some interesting experiences with our electronic equipment at the site. We had general feelings of being watched, and when we explored there was some uneasiness, more so with Joey Harrison—our self-proclaimed 'scaredy cat.' Personally, I'm a skeptic with an open mind. I like to record some evidence to feel there is something else with us. I left him alone with Stacy filming, and at one point in the video there's a disembodied breath. There are cold spots in a canyon pass—that could be a natural weather phenomenon. There's significant changes in temperature further in where the body was found—it wasn't really cold air passing through; there was no wind blowing. There are also high EMF fields near the water tank. The high EMF readings were consistent in that area. At one point, there was an unexplained mist that we captured. We only captured it one time in the five or six hours we recorded; it could have been something atmospheric, but it only showed up once. I knocked 'shave and a haircut,' and I got the 'two bits' response. The response sounded otherworldly. Video doesn't do it justice. It seems if someone human would have responded, they would have had to knock on a tree, but it sounds metallic. How can you do that out in the woods?"

You can catch both of Los Angeles Paranormal Investigation Network's investigations in the YouTube video "The Cobb Estate/Haunted Forest Investigation."

The YouTube video "The Enchanted Forest—Trail to the Mansion and Tunnel" will show you where the body was found as well as one of the mining tunnels, one of many that run through the mountain. As the guy who made the video said, the trail is not safe—go at your own risk! On this same movie at the 3:00 mark, the unaware filmmaker seems to have captured the EVP *"Get out!"*

I doubt if retired lumber magnate Charles H. Cobb, a member in good standing of the Scottish Rite Temple who built the estate as a family dwelling in 1918, and his wife, Carrie, could have foreseen the odd activity occurring today on the very foundation of what used to be their home. Not many family photos can be found, which leads me to believe the Cobbs were *very* private about their home life and weren't up all night throwing extravagant soirées, though they had the means to do so. Perhaps this is the reason for all of the paranormal activity that seems to be captured on the foundation of the once stately home. If you were a spirit of means and your beautiful family home was gone to its foundation and teens were using it to further advance their carnal knowledge in addition to doing drugs there, wouldn't you be outraged—even in death? I don't know about you, but I'd be hanging out and scaring the crap out of everyone.

After Carrie passed away, only a few years before him, he had the Scottish Rite Cathedral built in her honor. The estate became a retreat for the Sisters of St. Joseph. What about the rumors of a nun being raped and hung from a tree? I assure you, there is no truth to that rumor. After Cobb passed in 1939, he willed the 107-acre property and the home to the Scottish Rite Cathedral in Pasadena.

What's even stranger is what happened next. Hollywood's iconic Marx Brothers purchased the home in 1956 for well over $400,000, but I couldn't find evidence of them ever having lived in it. I assume they purchased it purely as an investment, hoping to turn the grounds into a cemetery and the home into a mortuary. It would have been a good investment, as the only stocks that never crash (though they did dip in the seventies when the popularity of cremation made an impact) are death-related stocks: private cemeteries, casket-makers, and embalming-supply companies (the makeup, plugs, tubes, needles and sculpting, prodding, and plying tools). Perhaps death was on their minds—during that time two of the brothers passed away, and the last three were either in or headed toward their late seventies and eighties. In 1998, the legacy of the Marx Brothers ended with Zeppo, the good-looking brother who married Las Vegas showgirl Barbara Blakely, who then left him to marry Frank Sinatra. With no family plot in the Cobb Cemetery, and as a sign of the times, Zeppo was cremated and his ashes spread over the Pacific Ocean.

Over the years, the Marx estate sought the proper licensing to convert the Altadena property to a cemetery, but the zoning was never approved. The Marx Brothers' estate finally put the land up for auction in 1971. Local preservationist groups rallied together to raise money to save the park, and with the help of the John Muir High School Conservation Club, the cause raised $175,000 and the property was turned into a park. The Angeles National Forest now has control over the property.

From what I understand, though this is unconfirmed, the home was demolished because of vagrancy, trespassing, and petty crimes resulting in more than one hundred arrests and many citations on the estate over the years. I imagine after having been vacant for such a long time, the home had all kinds of structural damage.

An even stranger tale is that of Echo Mountain's White City. The access to the haunting mountain peak originates on the Cobb property. The city is a ghost town—complete with ghosts. The ruins are now strewn with immovable giant cogs, giving an eerie feeling of a cemetery for once-great mechanical feats. Who on earth would decide to build a resort on a steep mountain and believe someone would come? It was the ingenious vision of Thaddeus Lowe, the original poster boy for steampunk. A character ripped straight out of a Jules Verne novel, Lowe had performed aerial reconnaissance on Confederate troops for the Union Army. In 1861, President Lincoln himself appointed Lowe chief aeronaut of the Union Army Balloon Corps. Lowe and his men floated silently over the Rebel forces in the night and early-morning hours and reported back to Union commanders about enemy troop size and locations. Though Lowe was innovative in his tactics, there was a great deal of jealousy regarding his pay scale and the favoritism Lincoln had shown him, as the two had gotten along famously. Not long after the president's death, and others had been found to replace him, the inventor was forced to resign in 1863.

This dismissal seemed to light a fire under him. As a civilian, he invented the "water gas" process, by which hydrogen gas could be created via charcoal and steam. His patents on this process and ice-making machines made him a wealthy man. When civil engineer David Macpherson came to him with the drawings for White City, he was beside himself. He could not wait to get started on building it. In his unbridled enthusiasm, he decided to include access for astronomers, meteorologists, volcanologists, botanists, and zoologists to study. His city, once built, was featured in *Scientific American* as the cover story and highlighted the state-of-the-art observatory. Scientists came from all over the world at his invitation; this was no ordinary resort—Lowe had built a scientific platform in the clouds to further knowledge, or at least that's how he'd convinced others to see him. He could do no wrong.

Construction on the Mount Lowe Railway began in 1891, and the line opened in 1893. It began on Lake Avenue and went to the "Mountain Division," where there was a twelve-bedroom Victorian hotel called the Rubio Pavilion. There, people transferred to a funicular train that scaled the steep 40 percent grade straight up to White City. There they'd find Echo Chalet, a forty-room staff dormitory, as well as a car barn and an inflatable reservoir for the storage of hydrogen gas. And then they could make themselves comfortable at the seventy-room Echo Mountain House, a beautiful Victorian structure four stories high, with a southern exposure more than four hundred feet long. Visitors enjoyed a restaurant, state-of-the-art observatory, bowling alley, casino, dance hall, souvenir shop, Western Union office, billiards room, and barbershop. The world's largest searchlight was brought up from the World's Fair, and people on Catalina [see Santa Catalina Island chapter] said they could read their newspapers by it.

Famous astronomer Dr. Lewis Swift became director of the Mount Lowe Observatory; he'd discovered more than ninety-five new nebulae from the mountain-high vantage point.

The resort was an instant success, but it was in a location where not many went to vacation; there were many stops and starts and a harrowing incline where the funicular train took people around the bends in a cliff-hanging, heart-stopping kind of way. Unfortunately, Lowe had expanded too quickly, burned through his money, and gotten an incredibly high-interest loan that he couldn't pay off immediately. In 1899, the company and all of Lowe's assets, including his twenty-four-thousand-square-foot Pasadena home, went into receivership. He moved in with

SAM MERRILL TRAIL

CASTLE CANYON TRAIL JCT   3 1/2 MI. ↑

ECHO MOUNTAIN   2 1/2 MI. ↑

ECHO MOUNTAIN IS   TO DIRECT CONNECTED
WITH THE MT. LOWE RAILWAY.

DONSOR: SHAMBLIN FAMILY

The dangerous trails are clearly marked. (A few notable incidents: a body
found in the last year that detectives are keeping hush-hush, rattlesnake
bites, and people falling off mountains.) I highly recommend going
during the day. Use extreme care, and make sure you're fit for hiking.

his daughter's family in Pasadena, where he died at the age of
eighty. A flood and fire took out the entire complex; you can still
see the remnants of charred trees along the trail.

I visited White City with after-death specialist Paul Hoffman, who'd taken the trail a number of times. We took minimal
camping gear in case we got stuck up on the mountain after
dark. It took roughly three hours. The ascent was dangerous.
We made it only because Hoffman knew what to anticipate. On
our way up, a man and his friends rushed down the trail; apparently one of them had been bitten by a rattlesnake. They shouted
back at us that they'd tossed it off the cliff. We were hesitant to
keep going, but we moved on. There was no way we'd be able to
get back down safely at night.

We set up our base camp on the platform where the Echo
Mountain House hotel had once been. When Lowe had first

seen the property, he'd been intrigued by the feeling that the high altitude gave him; he was a thin-air junky from his days as a balloon spy. He wanted everyone to feel it in their lungs and their minds and had even convinced himself that it was quite medicinal. In reality, high altitudes are more likely to cause heart attacks; I remember this from a study done about tourists between the ages of twenty and fifty who visit Colorado and the disproportionate number that drop dead.

We ate and set up our battery-operated lamps, rolled out our sleeping mats, and made ourselves comfortable. It was very cold, but we'd both worn thermal underwear and brought down coats. Some curious coyotes prowled around our camp; one even barked at us before backing off and running down the other side of the mountain. Around 10 p.m., I took out Frank's Box #55, built by Frank Sumption himself, and began our ITC (instrumental transcommunication) session

Paul asked if it there was anyone with us. It immediately answered through the combined oscillating signals, "Yes, we are." When we asked how many, it answered, "thirty-seven." We thought about the numbers involved. I'd read that there had been three million visitors to White City and Echo Mountain; there had to have been a number of deaths at the resort. Even after White City was defunct, there were probably a fair number of deadly hiking accidents and perhaps even suicides. But what had gone on before the city in the clouds had been built? Who had lived in the Angeles National Forest before that time? I'd been doing research on my iPad and found a notice from the forest office notifying five Indian nations and seventy individuals of the discovery of two skeletons. Many Native American tribes had lived in the forest, much of it preserved the same way it had been for centuries. I imagine that many of them hid there as bounty hunters pursued the Native Americans for the price on their heads (literally) that the government was paying for the heads and scalps of Native American men, women, and children.

As if Indians were still there, we caught the scent of a campfire. It was a bright moon and the lighting was beautiful, so we walked around using the binoculars but couldn't find a smoke source for the smell. We continued to ask the box questions for about forty-five minutes but got no response.

Paul said to the box, *"Ma kti'ka, Paul"* ("My name is Paul"). *"Ka sch ha, Sally"* ("Her name is Sally"). *"Suk' a pti?"* ("What is your name?").

The box answered, *"Pa kice"* ("You're welcome"). *"Yila' a kiskon"* ("All my people").

Although this wasn't the first time I'd heard it speak another language, I was blown away by the response of Frank's Box. Paul had worked with a company programming Samala, or what is also called Chumash (from what I understand), and had learned the language while inputting it into the program. He knows at least seven languages; nothing surprises me about him anymore. Nothing surprises me coming out of Frank's Box either, as it has sometimes spoken complete sentences.

I speak to many investigators regarding their evidence and the clear words they get—but cannot comprehend. With no way to interpret if an entity is speaking a foreign language, they are completely bypassing good evidence. I wish there was a clearance site where everyone could dump these kinds of EVPs and people from all over the world could review them. I got my first EVP when I was a cub reporter interviewing one of the directors of Amnesty International—the EVP was clear as day. We were talking—no one else in the room—and a rich, deep voice spoke into the recorder (you could still hear us in the background) and said something cryptic in what sounded like an African language. I played it back for the gentleman I interviewed, and he said it sounded very eerie and he never wanted to hear it again. It was completely bone-chilling stuff. I didn't even know what an EVP was in the 1980s. But, that's my point—my first EVP was in a foreign language, and I never knew what it meant. Frustrating for both parties, I'm sure.

At one point during the night's ITC session, the temperature got very warm, going from a windy (winds at 30 miles per hour) 35-degree night to 65 degrees with no wind. At that point, both Paul and I looked at each other.

"You feeling *that?*" he asked.

"Yeah, temp just went up twenty degrees in the last five minutes," I said checking my Mel Meter.

"Yeah, but do you feel *that?*" he said, looking around in back of him and all around us.

"What is *that?*" I asked, now feeling something that sent shivers up my spine.

"It feels like sweat-lodge energy. Like there's a bunch of people all around us . . . like there's something *tribal* going down."

Indeed, that's exactly how it felt. The Native American sweat lodges I'd participated in on the East Coast felt exactly that way. Once the chanting begins, there's a different vibration. It was literally like we had a steam pit between us. Although the temperature never went above 65 degrees, we were both sweating. Paul was always going to meditation and Native American retreats in New Mexico and Arizona; he knew more about this than I did. We took off our jackets and Paul began to chant. I didn't know the words, so I kind of hummed along. Paul pointed to his ear for me to listen. I stopped humming, and I heard the drums in the distance. I couldn't believe what I was hearing. I also heard what sounded like others vaguely chanting. I went to turn on my recorder, but the batteries were dead. I swapped them out with fresh ones, and then my flash card said it was full—I'd replaced both earlier in the day. I tried another card, and my new batteries were dead. One equipment failure after the next. I tried to use my D300s, and *that* flash card read full—I had double-checked my cards earlier to make sure there was nothing on them. I tried to erase the cards, but as soon as I did, my Nikon battery (which usually lasts weeks on one charge and was fresh off the charger that morning) died. I pulled out my cell phone and thought better of it; if something were to happen, I'd want the ability to call for help. When I got home to download the cards, there was nothing on them.

Echo Mountain did not get its name without reason. We couldn't tell where the sounds were coming from, but it sounded like they were coming down a long tube right in between us. It was possible that someone in the valley below had a campsite and had a drum, but the drumming sounded like it was around us *and* coming from between us. It was difficult to pinpoint the sound. We were hearing all of this while Frank's Box continued to oscillate, except no sounds were coming from the box; it was completely dead. I suspected the batteries. The temperature continued to rise (our own temperatures, not the air temperature actually around us). All at once, a huge white owl came out of nowhere and *screeched,* scaring the hell out of both of us, and then everything was quiet—*except* Frank's Box, which had come back on. About a minute later, one of our lamps died, and we got very jumpy. The temperature dropped and we were both freezing again. We put our jackets back on, and just when things had calmed down and my heart rate was back to normal, I nearly jumped out of my skin when the utterance "Yawe'n!" came out of Frank's Box.

I looked at Paul. "They say, 'Go sleep!'" he said.

I turned out the lamp but kept Frank's Box on in case they wanted to tell us a goodnight story. Paul said it was best to turn it off so we wouldn't annoy them. I reluctantly turned it off because I would rather hear an oscillating radio than anything else I might hear . . . or think I heard. It was going to be a long night. Paul went immediately to sleep. I, on the other hand, was restless until about 1 a.m. and then fell into a deep sleep. At 2 a.m., both Paul and I bolted upright when we heard a woman's scream and what sounded like a thud no more than thirty feet away from us. We grabbed the one lamp that worked and used our powerful LED hand flashlights and frantically searched the area, calling out to anyone who could hear us. We looked for at least an hour for anyone who could have been injured.

"What did you hear?" Paul finally asked.

"A woman screaming like she was falling and then a thud."

"That's what I heard as well."

"There's nothing she could have been falling from here that we didn't already check. Is this where you heard the thud come from?"

"Somewhere over here," I answered, still sweeping the area with my flashlight.

"There's no one here," he said. "Sounds like residual energy."

"I think maybe she had jumped at one time," I said, trying to get a bead on where the roof of the lodge would have been.

We tried to get back to sleep, but neither of us could. In the morning, trashed for the day, we headed down the hill at daybreak. About halfway down the hill, I hit a slippery spot, lost my balance, and sprained my ankle, also pulling something in my knee. Paul grabbed a folding walking stick out of his bag for me to help keep my balance, as some areas of the path were too awkward for two. He took my pack and we moved on. When we were just about at the bottom, a group of four guys came up, packing camping equipment. They noticed I'd been hurt.

"Rattlesnake?" one of them asked with concern.

I shook my head, "Just landed wrong."

He asked me if I needed ibuprofen. I eagerly nodded my head, since my ankle had swollen up to three times its normal size, as had my knee. I'd been in such a hurry to get off the mountain, I'd not let the pain slow me down. One of them had one of those crack-it-and-chill injury ice packs. He cracked and activated it, then taped it around my ankle with duct tape that would hurt coming off, but it felt really good at that moment. I commented that they must have been former Boy Scouts.

"Eagle Scouts," his blond friend corrected.

He started to tape another pack to my knee. I thanked him and told him to keep it. We'd be at a store for ice in a few minutes, and they might need it.

They all looked like they'd walked out of a *GQ* photo shoot—only in LA. They commented how tired we looked. Ibuprofen Guy crooked his head and asked, "Screaming woman?"

We were shocked they knew. Our looks registered with them.

"Yeah, she's woken us up a couple of times as well. Scares the f——— out of us every time," he said, the rest of the guys laughed a little nervously. "We've got one of those night cameras we're setting up tonight." I gave him my card in case they came up with anything, but I never heard back.

Paul asked if they'd had any other experiences. Two of them turned around and showed they had little bongos tied to their packs. Ibuprofen Guy said, "If you can't beat 'em, join 'em."

Spotlight On: Poltergeists

The word *poltergeist* comes from the German words *poltern* (to make noise) and *geist* (ghost), and the term itself literally means "noisy ghost." We've seen poltergeist activity featured for the last three years in the blockbuster *Paranormal Activity* movies (filmed in Rancho Peñasquitos/San Diego). You see it all the time in films, but rarely in real life. You also see it happen in almost every episode of paranormal reality TV, where someone will say something to provoke the resident spirits, and suddenly, out of nowhere, a rock or brick is thrown at the back of the host's head.

But is poltergeist activity real? Personally, I've seen things fall off mantels and shelves on investigations and in my home, and even a book fly so hard out of a bookcase (backwards) and hit the wall so hard it cracked the binding and put a dent in the drywall. Those instances were few and far between over the years, and only twice was there someone around to witness it. More often, poltergeist activity is poking, tugging of hair, and touching, and in one case in the Julian Jail chapter, the witness was pushed off her bike. It takes a lot of energy to manifest a physical action, so know the minute things start to happen—you're messing with some pretty serious stuff. Seriously, I would avoid provoking.

"It seems to always start with unexplained noises and objects moving on their own; poltergeist phenomena are one of the most inexplicable and disturbing paranormal events you are ever likely to witness," says Melissa Martin-Ellis, a paranormal investigator, photographer, and author of *101 Ways to Find a Ghost* and *The Everything Ghost Hunting Book*.

"Although similar to other hauntings, at least initially, these events are usually as short-lived as they are intense," continues Martin-Ellis. "Although I've had several poltergeist encounters of my own and have developed my own theories and protocols, I like to check in occasionally with fellow investigators and see what the latest news is. I recently compared notes with fellow New England paranormal investigator Andy Laird, and I found there were similarities in our poltergeist experiences—and ways to be prepared to capture the paranormal behavior.

"For instance, poltergeists often draw more media attention than other, subtler forms of paranormal activity. The phenomena can involve rather spectacular shenanigans and are very popular subjects for investigation. Everyone wants to find one of these cases, but they're extremely rare. If you hear reports of a possible poltergeist incident, move quickly," suggests Martin-Ellis. "Most are over within a couple of weeks. If you're lucky enough to learn of one that needs investigating, grab your camera, your recorder, your trifield meter, ratchet up your nerve, and get to the site ASAP!

"If activity in a publicly accessible place turns up, you can be sure that those experiencing the phenomena usually suspect a trick, maybe even a hoax. Investigators sometimes call the person that the case revolves around the 'agent.' The agent is the one person who seems to always be there when activity is at its liveliest. This is not to say that the agent is perpetrating a hoax. But they can be the focal point of the activity and the investigation, and one theory has it that they are somehow inadvertently feeding energy to whatever entity is causing the ruckus."

Martin-Ellis suggests that before you investigate, obtain written permission to be on-site to videotape and photograph, and try to interview witnesses separately. "It's very important not to let witnesses cross-contaminate and influence each other's accounts of incidents they've witnessed, and to be sure to record the interviews."

Bring your arsenal of equipment, and be ready for anything. Martin-Ellis suggests a trifield meter, preferably a trifield natural EM meter, which is helpful for tracking energy spikes. Readings can go from negative to positive and quickly back again, particularly when activity is at its height.

"I recommend sharpening your observation skills and bringing an experienced person along on this type of investigation," says Martin-Ellis. "These cases can be so lively they're exhausting and can be dangerous psychologically and even physically. Investigators are sometimes attacked—pinched, punched, bitten, and/or slapped. Don't be afraid to walk away at any point if you sense things are getting too intense; this is serious business."

Santa Barbara, Ventura, and San Luis Obispo Counties

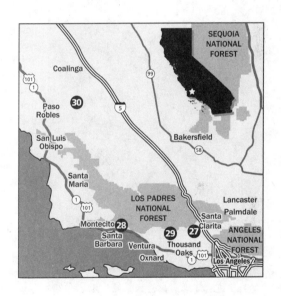

Cholame
  James Dean Memorial Junction **(30)**

Piru
  Rancho Camulos **(27)**

Santa Barbara
  Mission Park Jail **(28)**

Santa Paula
  Glen Tavern Inn **(29)**

CHAPTER 27

Rancho Camulos
PIRU

The rose garden outside of the Rancho Camulos chapel: the inspiration for the fictional Ramona's wedding place in Helen Hunt Jackson's book *Ramona*. People from all over the world have visited this location because they became so wrapped up in reading the romantic tragedy. This pathway is where I saw the dark figure walking toward the chapel.

I WAS DRIVING BACK FROM SUMMERLAND to San Diego when it started to rain. Realizing how close I was to Rancho Camulos, a place I'd always wanted to visit because of its reported paranormal activity, I decided to visit. When I arrived,

I didn't see anyone, so I walked to the back of the property loudly announcing, "Hello, is anyone here?"

That's when I saw someone in the rose garden about sixty feet away, walking toward the chapel. I hollered, "Hey, wait up a sec!" but they kept on moving so quickly it looked like they were on roller skates; an unlikely possibility. The figure was that of an adult-size human. That's when Jim McGowan, historian and manager of the education program, came out of the school-house building.

"Can I help you?" he asked from the door.

"Sorry," I answered. "I was calling to the person who was walking over there." I pointed toward the chapel. The person was gone.

"There's no one here but me," he said, looking both confused and curious. He came out to meet me and found no one wandering about. He was getting ready to lock up and was taking care of some last-minute business. I caught him just in time, any other day he'd already be gone.

That was my first ghostly encounter at Rancho Camulos; and it happened nearly immediately. We walked back into the schoolhouse, and while we were discussing the location's history, I continued to see the energy of two girls around eleven and six years old, one in pigtails. They wore pastel period dresses. They danced playfully away from me in my peripheral vision, as though they were including me in on a game. Like all children are apt to do, they were trying to distract me from the business at hand.

"This is one of the many places that capitalized on the *Ramona* mania that unfolded in the 1880s," said McGowan, speaking of the book *Ramona*, Helen Hunt Jackson's bestselling novel of 1884, which flooded California with tourists from other states in search of the ranch where the book took place. It's a romantic and sad story about a Scottish–Native American woman who grew up an orphan on a ranch and fell in love with a Native American ranch hand. Like *Romeo and Juliet*, the story ends in tragedy.

"She—Helen Hunt Jackson, not Ramona . . . there was no *real* Ramona; she's a fictional character—did stop here to research the setting," said McGowan. "If you pay close attention while reading the book, you'll see that this is where she set the story."

Legendary filmmaker D. W. Griffith shot the silent film *Ramona* in 1910 at Rancho Camulos, with actress Mary Pickford playing Ramona. In doing research for this chapter, I watched the film at the Internet Archive (**archive.org**), and I saw at 07:29 (if you stop and play it frame-by-frame) a large, dark shadow pass over Pickford from the right to the left. She wears an odd expression of surprise or confusion, as though she's seen or sensed something. Pickford, one of the industry's earliest film directors, admitted in an autobiography to being somewhat of a medium herself and foreseeing the death of her brother. Pickford was close friends with Amelia Earhart, who gave mediumship readings to friend Mae West (who raised money for the Healing Temple at the Spiritualist camp Lily Dale, in New York State).

Had Griffith seen the shadow on the set while he was filming, the persnickety perfectionist would have insisted on shooting the scene again. Perhaps the shadow was captured only after the film was developed. So was it a stage snafu, or one of Rancho Camulos's shadow people making an early cameo in a silent film?

"The land is still owned privately—and it's still a working ranch," says McGowan. "After the earthquake hit, the historic buildings needed restoration, so they built a nonprofit around that effort, and I run the outreach program, the museum, and manage the docents. We have a lot of paranormal interest and people contacting me to come in and do investigations. All the money raised from anything the museum does, goes directly back into restoring the area and running the program."

The property was originally the site of a Tataviam Indian village known as Kamulus. After the founding of the area's mission, San Fernando Rey de España, Native Americans were rounded up and delivered to the location to work on building the mission. The Tataviams were among the California tribes displaced from their land, their religions, and their ancestors.

The original 48,612-acre Rancho San Francisco land grant was assigned to Antonio del Valle, majordomo and administrator of Mission San Fernando; 1,800 acres were willed to his son Ygnacio in 1841. Today, this land is Rancho Camulos.

Ygnacio's ranch grew until it was self-sustaining with more than 200 residents. It offered safety to its Native American and Mexican workers and their families. A cemetery was added to the property to accommodate the small settlement. By the time Ygnacio died in 1880, the ranch house had increased to twenty rooms, and the family business expanded to include a winery, barn, chapel, and employee housing.

The *rancho* became popular with the public after the success of the book *Ramona*, and the Southern Pacific line began featuring it in its advertisements. By 1888, offering hospitality to strangers who were coming by the trainload had become so expensive for the family that Reginaldo del Valle (Ygnacio's son) asked his mother to stop being so hospitable. Untrustworthy houseguests were helping themselves to the family's belongings, stealing them as souvenirs. Others helped themselves to the fruit in the orchards, packing it away to take home. With the failing health of the del Valles' matriarch and infighting among the family, the successful venture came to an end with the ranch's sale in 1924 to August A. Rübel, a native of Switzerland.

Rübel managed the ranch so you'd hardly notice a change in ownership, as he kept the employees and didn't make any

drastic changes. He even built a school for his children, complete with a stage for them to perform, and employed a teacher.
Life was good for the Rübel family.

During World War II, Rübel volunteered for active duty and
served in Tunisia where he met his fate in 1943 while driving an
ambulance that hit a land mine. His wife, Mary, married Edwin
Burger, who had no interest in participating in the business of
running a ranch, though he enjoyed its proceeds. Upon Mary's
death in 1968, Burger closed the ranch entirely, and the buildings and grounds were left abandoned for decades. Rübel's heirs
made a power play for the property after the 1994 Northridge
earthquake, which devastated the property's historic buildings.
They were successful in reclaiming the ranch and lobbied to
have Rancho Camulos listed on the National Register of Historic
Places. Today, the buildings are slowly being restored thanks to
donations from the community, the decedents of both the Rübel
and the del Valle families, and fees garnered by paranormal
investigation teams that spend time at the location.

"Fifteen years later," says McGowan, "the nonprofit museum
is a historic site, and all money goes right back into maintaining
the program and restoring the buildings."

Paranormal investigator Gerald S. Reynolds has been
involved with several investigations on the property. "Late one
evening, I made my way with other paranormal investigators
into an attic area of the main adobe," says Reynolds. "This attic
area had been a bedroom for servants and family children. We
collected an EVP—a personal favorite for me. While the others
were conducting the EVP session, I placed my video camera on
a stationery tripod pointed away from the group and toward the
western end of this room. An anomalous ribbon of light—not
seen by any of us at this time—was recorded. It moves eerily
from left to right in front of my camera's lens. As it reaches a
point directly in front of the camera, a Class-A EVP is heard.

The voice sounds female and asks, 'Gee, what happened?' The ribbon of light then continues on its way and appears to leave the area."

Rob Wlodarski and his wife, Anne, are regulars at Rancho Camulos and have harvested incredible amounts of evidence from the location. They also created G-Host Publishing and founded the International Paranormal Research Organization. Rob is a frequent guest on *Coast to Coast Radio* and has administered more than fifteen hundred archaeological and historical projects for federal, state, county, and city agencies as well as private companies.

"Over 160 years of history involving two families, and it is the oldest still operating rancho in California," says Rob of the location. "At Rancho Camulos, home to *Ramona*, the spirits are plentiful, and there is never a dull moment when investigators come to open the doors to its past." And that statement from Rob is apparent in even a very small sample of transcribed data from one of his and Anne's recent investigations at Rancho Camulos. What you are about to read is an abbreviated transcript of recordings made at Rancho Camulos. The words marked with quotation marks are being said by the team; the words in italics are EVPs captured on the master recorder. There is also a running narrative by the team to show what is going on around the group. This transcript is a much shorter version of the original. Reynolds was also a member of the investigation that evening. This is fascinating evidence because it kind of gives me the impression of a group much like their own on the Other Side trying to communicate with them. As you read it, you'll probably snicker because you can picture your own group making such comments as the EVP group does. In this way, and by looking closely at what the "ghost team" must be hearing/feeling, one can begin to see the paradigm of a parallel universe such as our own unfold and the ability of both sides to communicate.

Paranormal Investigation of Rancho Camulos
Report prepared by: International Paranormal Research
    Organization (IPRO) and Jerry Reynolds
Date of Investigation: Saturday, January 14, 2012
Time of Investigation: 4 p.m.–9:30 p.m.
Case No. IPRO01142012

BG and RW arrive at Rancho Camulos before the rest of the group. We unload and begin the set up in the schoolhouse and await the rest of the group. The group sets up trigger objects, motion sensor detectors, and other equipment to aid in monitoring any activity in and around the room during the séance.

[Tape is rolling and recording.]

004 A female says, *Yes* and *I got nowhere* as the group is setting up the séance table in Room 5.

005 A male says, *Stop.*

It is now 5:31 p.m. We take numerous photographs of the objects in place.

014 A female says, *What did she think?*

We place KII meters, two candles, a quartz crystal, analog and digital tape recorders, sage, feather, bell, and other items on the table.

019 A male says, *I'm hanging out with Robert.*

023 A male says in a drawn-out sentence, *It's you who prefers mercy.*

025 A male says, *At last.*

027 A male says, *Bleeds through fella?* Followed by another male who says, *I like him.*

029 A male says, *What's that?* Followed by a loud EVP bump.

045 As RW leaves to turn his car lights off, a female says, *Thatta way* . . . followed by a child calling, *Out!*

060 A female says, *They're a team.*

072 A young girl says, *They heard me.*

089 A female says, *Listen, let's donate.*

099 A male, in a raspy voice says, *Tear it down.*

105 A young female says, *Oh . . . hide robbery.* A male follows with, *Quickly.* Followed by another male who says, *Quiet.* Followed by a female who says something like, *James Hendrick.* Followed by a male who says, *From del Valles.*

113 A female quietly says, *Hopefully now he'll be down soon.* Followed by a male who says, *I'll wait.* Then a young female says, *Thank you.*

123 A very loud ethereal exhale.

RW comes back after turning off the light in his car. We set up two targets; building blocks and toys.

135 A male says, *Odd actor.* Followed by all KII meters spiking.

137 A wheezy female voice says, *Call me.*

143 A male says, *I brought it myself.*

We all begin sitting around the séance table.

147 A strong female voice says, *I'm pissed at you.*

149 A young child calls out something unintelligible in the background.

151 A male says, *Get him.* Followed by another male who says, *Do you want that?*

153 RW remarks about taking a nap and a male says, *Soothing.* Preceded by a loud EVP bump, followed by another male who says, *Yes.* RW says, "There is somebody here." Followed by a male who says something like, *Ask those.* Followed by a female who says, *Sorry I'm a little late.*

170 A male says, *Don't!*

171 A female, young, says, *No high regard.*

175 A very loud, grumbling man yells out, *Quiet!*

Followed by another male who says, *Quit that*. Another male says, *He'll hit you*.

176 A Munchkin-like female voice says, *With us, now*.

Several members begin smelling tobacco in the room near where LJ and CD are sitting; fresh, not burning tobacco.

201 RW asks, "Does anyone hear a child?" A female says, *Talk*. Followed by a male who says, *Contact*. Then another male says, *Probably* (sounds British?).

207 A loud EVP, male. Can't make out what he says, he blurts out something over DH talking; something like, *Start*.

211 A male, raspy voice, says, *We'll keep back*.

LJ and CD say to RW that his mom is right by him protecting him. The KII meters go off again.

240 A loud male groan: *Ahhhhhhhhhh*.

RW has Vici read the opening prayer! It is 5:55 p.m. The group around the table: RW, DH, CD, LJ, BD, CB, AH, JR, HW, JD, VR.

Our spirit guides: Howard Bonner, Dutch Reynolds, Hank Wlodarski, Guenther Davidson.

302 A young girl says, *Who's this?*

305 What sounds like an owl.

311 A female says, *We want to know who you are*.

We set up a flashlight to communicate.

353 RW says, "Saturday night at the del Valles'," and then there are two loud knocks.

359 A very loud snap!

363 RW asks if they can spike the candle and a voice says, *Yes!* Followed by a male saying, *There*. RW says, "Did you hear that?"

It is 6:10 p.m. DH on his digital playback got someone saying, *Children*.

A member asks, "Is the little girl [here] we heard skipping on the outside porch?" The flashlight goes on for an affirmation.

381 RW asks, "Can you tell us your name?" A young child says, *I . . . know you . . .* RW then says, "I hear something, and I am cold!" The ambient temperature in the room is 60 degrees.

391 RW asks, "Is this Tillie [a seven-year-old girl we have reached numerous times here]? If it is, turn the flashlight off." The light turns off. A child can be heard in the background, but what she is saying is inaudible.

397 RW asks, "Are any other children with you [Tillie]?" A female child says, *Hello.*

DH says "Tillie is here but we have another spirit in the room." The flashlight turns on. RW says, "If this is Tillie's father, then turn off the flashlight." A male says, *Is this enough?*

411 A young girl says, *I'm no ghost.*

This is the kind of evidence that inspires a new look at how evidence is collected and how we view and treat the entities we've contacted. I mean, if the little girl doesn't think she's a ghost—maybe she isn't. Though maybe she is and she just doesn't realize it. Screaming at her isn't going to help the situation, right? This investigation certainly opens our minds if we allow it to. This team treats each other and the spirits they're contacting with a great deal of respect, and I hope their example and results give you pause if you're applying "provoking" techniques to contact spirits.

CHAPTER 28

Glen Tavern Inn
SANTA PAULA

The mysterious turn-of-the-century Glen Tavern Inn is quite a different place after dark, when the spirits seem to wander the halls in search of guests to communicate with.

THE 1911 FRENCH TUDOR/Craftsman–style Glen Tavern Inn is not especially dark or looming. It's actually quite a quaint, cozy building. The first time I was there a wedding was taking place in the lobby, and I assure you there was nothing dark or sinister looking about the event—just a happy couple surrounded by loving friends and family. But at night, when everyone retires to their rooms, it's quite a different story.

The hotel was built in the heyday of Santa Paula's history, when the town was booming as home to Union Oil. The hotel was built by an investment group of individuals who thought building an inn across from the train station would be a good investment—*ca-ching!* It was, until it wasn't. The oil went away, so did the train station . . . and so did the people.

Luckily, the hotel had charm and a solid foundation—two things a grand Victorian-era building needed to survive. The hotel passed through the hands of several owners until the current owners bought it, restoring it to its original grandeur.

When you visit Santa Paula, you'll immediately recognize the small city from movies such as *Carrie* and *Amityville 4: The Evil Escapes* (filmed just outside of town) and dozens more. A favorite of filmmakers since the silent era, the community is on I-126, less than an hour from Los Angeles, Santa Barbara, and Santa Clarita. The city has a population of nearly thirty thousand and is built where Chumash Indians originally lived ten thousand years ago. It's known for its Christmas steam train and airport classic-car shows—and for its paranormal activity at the Glen Tavern Inn, a regular haunt for many paranormal investigators.

At times over the last century, the hotel has had a shady past—as most secluded establishments near Hollywood that served alcohol during Prohibition once did—especially when you take into account that the third floor of the hotel was used as a brothel and gambling establishment. It was also playland to the elite of Tinseltown, such as John Wayne, Carole Lombard, Marilyn Monroe, and Steve McQueen.

"The old hotel has seen a great deal of life in her century of being open," says Richard Senate, paranormal investigator and author of *Ghosts of the California Missions,* who had a rather chilling experience at the inn.

"Ghosts have a habit of causing a distinct coldness in haunted places. This is well known and can be traced back to the earliest records of ghosthunters in the nineteenth century. I was investigating Room 307 one night, and I had set up twelve old-style mercury thermometers all over the room. Each one was given a number, and they were plotted on a map. Every half hour I would go to the room and read each one. Rather than write the numbers down I logged the data on a tape recorder, giving the time at each reading. I was the only one with the key—and no one accompanied me in this rather drab and unexciting experiment. The readings were a bust—as the thermometers only varied four to five degrees difference. When I went to graph the data, I played back the tape and then logged in all the temperatures. In the middle of the ten-to-fifteen reading, there was a loud, gruff voice that clearly said, 'You will die!' I had heard nothing while I was there, and the voice wasn't me. Was it a threat from the spirit world or just a statement of fact? Yes, in time, I will die. It was one of the more bizarre things I have had happen in my thirty-three years as a ghosthunter."

I recently stayed at the hotel with Paranormal Practice case manager Linda Casebolt. It's a great place to do an investigation—with the exception of a large, loud birthday party group that had also booked the hotel—but we managed to work around the group by staying in the basement and up on the third floor with Bridget Odien, cofounder of the group Paranormal Practice. She is also the cocreator, with her husband, Larry Odien, of the EVP Field Processor (EFP) that's been featured on *Ghost Hunters, Ghost Adventurers, Destination Truth, Fact or Faked: Paranormal Files,* and *Ghost Hunters International.* It's an amazing tool that you plug your digital recorder into and set the baseline—the light readings tell you if you may have captured an EVP. You can also listen live to the recording through headphones. It allows you to interact in real time with any entities that may be trying to have a conversation with you (see **evpfield processor.com**).

Bridget was in the closet doing an EFP/EVP session while Larry Odien (cofounder of Paranormal Practice and known for his special-effects work on movies such as *Hellboy II: The Golden Army, Legion, Fantastic Four: Rise of the Silver Surfer,* and *Spider-Man 3*) was sitting in the bedroom with Casebolt, me, and Glenn Hetrick (one of the judges on the Syfy original series *Face Off* and special-effects makeup artist/designer for *The Hunger Games,* and Emmy Award recipient for *Buffy the Vampire Slayer, The X-Files,* and *Babylon 5*). Larry captured a Class-A EVP that answered, "We're here . . ." in response to his question, "Who's here?" I thought the voice sounded childlike. It wouldn't be the first time children have been heard at the Glen Tavern Inn. Using the EFP, Larry was able to see that he'd captured the EVP, and played it back for all of us immediately.

"Having previously experienced only a scant few occurrences in my life that I would deem legitimately supernatural—through no lack of trying—I admit that I was somewhat skeptical about our chances of capturing anything substantial during a purposeful hunt," Hetrick recalls. "However, mainly due to my belief in and study of the occult sciences, I held out hope that we might catch an ephemeral glance of some diaphanous form. Understand, I do not doubt the existence of that which we sought . . . quite the opposite actually, but the scarcity with which these types of things manifest in our physical realm in a substantial form caused me to doubt our luck.

"The technique of calling out or questioning to a possible entity and then recording a response was intriguing, and I very much was excited by this methodology," Hetrick says about his first EVP/EFP session. "Being cautious to disallow that excitement and expectation from causing me to hear what I wanted to hear, I can tell you this—I witnessed, with all of my senses, a response to Larry's question in that bedroom! The equipment registered a spike at a moment in which there was *absolute* silence to the normal ear, and upon playing the recording back, I was shocked and delighted to hear the unmistakable sound of

(Left–right) **Glenn Hetrick, Paranormal Practice's Linda Casebolt, and Bridget and Larry Odien in the Glen Tavern Inn restaurant area after-hours as we wrap up the investigation.**

some spectral voice. Seemingly sentient in its response, it manifested with a singular clarity and volume so as to have made it *impossible* for us to have missed in the room had it been audible in our natural range of perception. Most intriguing!"

Casebolt had her recorder going simultaneously with Larry's and captured what sounded like the spirit somehow swishing by her recorder right into Larry's.

"He was about six feet away from me with the same model digital recorder; both of us had EFP processors; we just each caught something different. It's a really rare thing to get a Class-A EVP; capturing two different EVPs simultaneously was interesting."

While at the Glen Tavern on an earlier investigation, Bridget caught another Class-A EVP with the EFP. "While investigating the Glen Tavern Inn in a room on the first floor," explains Bridget, "Larry was touched on the back while we were looking at our computer screen. Linda turned on her recorder while we were talking to see if we could pick up a voice, and we got an EVP that said, 'Welcome to my home.' Room 307 seems to have a lot of activity—we've collected some impressive EVPs in this room."

Both Bridget and Casebolt were staying at the hotel. Casebolt was sitting in the third-floor hallway waiting for Bridget and had set up lights that go off if they detect movement in the area around them.

"I caught a really faint EVP," said Casebolt. "I don't know what's up with those stairs, but something definitely is. And the lights continued to go off that whole time, though there was no light fluctuation from movement I could detect, and they've never done that before. It was outside Room 307; it was like someone— or something—was walking in and out of the bedroom and setting them off. I've been in Wolf Manor investigating alone—and that's pretty chilling, but it's got nothing on the Glen Tavern."

As far as spirit children being heard at the hotel, I'd looked out several times thinking I'd heard real children running down the hall late at night and was ready to give their parents some unwanted advice, but when I opened the door, saw nothing and closed the door.

"I was helping out the manager of the inn years ago, pitching in when the night manager was out," says medium Debbie Senate. "About two in the morning, I head the distinct sound of two children on the stairs running and making noise. I didn't want them waking people up, so I waited to confront them at the foot of the stairs. The sounds got closer and closer—but I saw no one. Then a cold breeze swept down the stairs, and I head the footsteps retreat into the lobby. Later, maybe twenty minutes after this, the sounds of two children were heard again running up the stairs. I am told others have heard this as well over the years at the Inn."

I arranged with management to have investigation time in both basements as well as various places throughout the hotel for myself and the members of Paranormal Practice. When we were in the basement, we captured several EVPs, including one when we were all goofing around and the guys were singing. We heard a real-time, audible whisper, and the recording captured, "Figaro." Was this a reference to *The Barber of Seville?* Though Figaro (the character) is normally calm, collected, and intelligent, he can be irrational when angered. There's a line in the opera that sums up Figaro as a person but perhaps is a glimpse at what the spirit in the basement was feeling as well: "I must force myself to laugh at everything lest I be obliged to weep."

CHAPTER 29

Mission Park Jail
SANTA BARBARA

Richard and Debbie Senate investigate the Mission Park Jail with the PX.

I FIND THE ENTIRE MISSION ERA in California a very depressing time in the history of the Native American tribes that flourished for thousands of years without Spanish or Mexican overlords—not to mention the whites who came in, supported by the United States government, which offered the bounty of fifty cents for a scalp and a dollar a head for men, women, and children of Native American descent. Native American slaves were still being auctioned in Los Angeles as late as the 1860s. Many find the missions comforting and beautiful. Personally, I hear and feel the oppression within their walls. Being inside one makes me agitated and nauseated.

Although I am Native American (Apache), I am also European (Welsh, Irish, and German) and also have ancestors directly from Spain (who married into the Mexican/Apache side of my family), so now I feel guilt by association. Nothing would make me happier than to see a wrecking ball taken to each one of the missions in California and to amend fourth-grade textbooks to reflect the truth about California's history. If we don't learn from our mistakes, how will we ever learn at all? In many of the chapters in this book, much paranormal contact was made with Native Americans who occupied the land well before the spirits I had originally been looking for.

In California, kids make models of missions in grammar school, but what they should do is take those kids out for a day of making and laying adobe bricks under the hot summer sun, as Native Americans did day in, day out—with no hope for change, their loved ones dying all around them, and their old ways and freedom lost. That's what textbooks can't convey. That said, I'm writing about one building in the mission system that is no longer the property of any of the religious organizations still housed in some of the missions. This building is known as the Mission Park Jail. We went during the day, because at night the area is rather dodgy and frequented by the homeless and partying teens.

Near the jail in Mission Park, there's a plaque with the folliwing inscription:

THE CITY OF SANTA BARBARA
MISSION HISTORICAL PARK

Santa Barbara Mission was founded December 4, 1786. Portions of five units of its extensive water works built by Indian labor are preserved in this park—a filter house, Spanish grist mill, sections of aqueducts, and two reservoirs. The larger reservoir, built in 1806, is used today as part of the city water system. Ruins of the pottery kiln and tanning vats are here. Also, the fountain and lavadero *are nearby in front of the old mission. A dam, built in 1807, is located in the Santa Barbra Botanic Garden, one and one-half miles up Mission Canyon.*

REGISTERED HISTORICAL LANDMARK NO. 309
PLAQUE PLACED BY CALIFORNIA STATE PARK COMMISSION
APRIL 21, 1957

Could they not have known the mission was actually in used as a jail when the plaque was placed, or did they think having the ruins of a jail would attract the wrong type of attention when they were trying to book weddings at the rose garden area? I really don't know. The history of this little building is sketchy at best, as I'd not been able to find in writing that it had been used as a jail.

I recently went on an investigation at the location with Richard Senate, author of *The Illustrated Guide to the Ghosts of Ventura County* (**phantombookshop.com**) and his wife, paranormal investigator and medium Debbie Senate. These two have a wealth of inside stories to tell you about any haunted location in California, but especially those in Ventura County.

We took the PX (a device that converts EMFs to algorithms that in turn form either phonetic sounds or words) out to the jail ruins to have an ITC session with it. I was amazed by the great responses we were getting with the device in phonetic mode. Normally it stumbles around for words as it puts them together phonetically, but it was hitting spot-on and frankly, I thought, delivering some interesting communication. Debbie was holding the PX, and it seemed to respond wonderfully to her energy; I've never heard it speak in the phonetic mode so clearly:

PX's first response immediately when turned on:

PX: *Find* [not audible] *and you will be happy.*
PX: *Dog. Dog. Dog.* [A dog walked by.]
Debbie: "Are you babbling?"
PX: [In response] *No.*
PX: *Outside Jesus. In the earth buried.*
Debbie: [Repeats the last words.]
PX: *All magic amulet buried.*
Debbie: "Are you ready to talk with us?"
PX: *Ready, talk badly are we. Talk to us. Ready. Fine.*
Debbie: "Do you think we should leave?"
Richard: "Will you appear to us?"
PX: *Robert did not do her. Dog pound. Listen.*
           [We again see a dog being walked nearby.]
PX: *Officer around.*
           [On our way to the location, there was a casualty accident on the nearby 101.]
PX: *Highway ambulance.*
PX: *Irreverent. Cold. Bikes.* [A bike passes by.]
PX: *Suffer recourse.*

[The PX makes a sound I've never heard it make before—a noise like static or tuning in a transistor radio.]

PX :   *God blesser. Current vacant. Access is short.*
Richard: "What happens when access is over?"
PX: *Pain.*

Richard: "So they have a short time to talk with us and
then they hurt?"

PX: *Bereavement. Uncle. Disavowed. Go home.
Change.*

I credit Debbie's mediumship abilities with somehow boosting the amplitude in the device and giving a clearer channel to the entity/entities around. Clearly, they had some things to say.

"All the missions are haunted," said Richard. "One of the chief reasons so many of the missions are haunted was because the natives died like flies. There were diseases they had no immunities for, and they died in huge numbers. There was also a lot of hopelessness. Every day was the same, and their lives were controlled by a bell. There was a huge death rate. Native Americans lost a lot of freedom at the missions. There was a battle fought here, too. Spain used to own California. Then Mexico owned it and charged taxes, and the natives were unhappy about it. There was an uprising at three of the missions, including this one, and they killed Spanish people, and they were killed as well. Eventually, the rebellion was put down, but I think that's why they're still here. We think of the mission as a church. It's more than that; it has a chapel, but it's like a business and agriculture center—food, cattle, and materials of industry. Each mission has some weird supernatural happenings. The Franciscan brothers were a very mysterious organization. Over the years, many buildings of stone still remain and seem to have retained psychic memories and impressions.

"This was the *mayordomo*'s [caretaker's] house and then the jail," said Richard of the location. "That would happen all the time—buildings would be repurposed to whatever it was they needed at the time. The buildings at the missions tend to be very haunted. We never failed to get EVPs, ghost pictures, and people feeling pushed and touched."

Debbie mentioned that she doesn't feel comfortable at the missions; I'm with her. Having attended Catholic school early on in Hawaii in my childhood, I have an issue with being in most churches—ancient or modern. And from the time I was a child and my dad took us to all the missions, I've always been creeped out by them.

"We get pictures of dark shadows," said Richard. "We were taking pictures with a team. and a woman was literally pushed against the wall. Another time when we were dowsing, we got a picture of a big orb sitting on top of the dowsing rods. The picture of the day was a dark, angelic figure floating in the air— *it was all black.* Doing EVP work we got, 'John artist flair.' Our friend John was with us—he was wearing a French beret and paisley neck scarf; he's a flamboyant-looking fellow. He didn't take his hat off in the church, and we did EVPs and we got some French phrase, and we went by a French pastry shop in Ventura and they translated the phrase: 'Take your hat off,' it said. I did some research into the mission, and during its later years the Spanish group of priests were replaced by a group of French ones. We caught some other EVPs, 'Covet each day, John,' and, 'Keep Christ in your heart.' Of course—they were priests—it makes sense that we'd get religious messages."

Many missions still exist from the days when the Spaniards populated vast areas of the American South and Southwest. I'm sure that each one of those missions has a history of hauntings. Many are owned by the state governments in which they're located and are open to tourists. If you go on a weekday during off-season, you'll pretty much have the place to yourself, although you may want to call in advance to see if they have any school tours scheduled. Be prepared to remove your hat in church, and make sure to bring someone who can speak Spanish, or get ready to find someone who can translate your EVPs.

CHAPTER 30

James Dean Memorial Junction
CHOLAME VALLEY

This area sure looks a whole lot less dangerous when headlights aren't rushing right at you in the night. Many people pull over here; make sure you and your vehicle can be seen.

JAMES DEAN MADE ONLY THREE MOVIES in which he starred. *Three movies* and a handful of TV shows. Only one of his films—*East of Eden*—had been released by the time of his death. He died on September 30, 1955—more than fifty-five years ago. He's been dead more years than I've been alive, and I'd never seen any of his movies until I started thinking about writing this chapter. I'd seen his iconic face on a million pieces of merchandise, but I'd had no special interest in him. So what was I doing in Cholame Valley—essentially the middle of nowhere—beside a cow pasture in the middle of the night?

I was at the place where James Dean died, the scene of the car crash in which his body was crushed in the car that looked as though some giant had stomped on it, like squashing a soda-pop can with the heel of your boot. What paranormal investigator could resist such an opportunity?

There's been much conjecture about what happened the ill-fated day that Dean's race car, nicknamed "The Little Bastard," took him headlong into death as it impacted with a car whose owner was told to make his own way home (his own car had been totaled, he'd been injured, and lived some fifty miles away) by the officer in charge at the scene. I think that action is the key to what has become the most baffling car accident in history.

According to author Warren Newton Beath, a Dean expert and author of the quintessential 1986 book *The Death of James Dean* (a must-download book if you're going to be investigating the site), there is something quite mysterious about both the life and death of James Dean.

At the height of his short life (but long-lived success), after being warned by several people that he would die over the weekend, twenty-four-year-old Dean raced the long highway to his death. Did he know that he would never make it to his destination (an auto race in Salinas that he planned to win)? In a split second, instead of becoming an obsolete reference in Hollywood history, he became a demigod of the silver screen. How? His movies were great, he was a good-looking guy . . . and he died under tragic circumstances shrouded in mystery, as later did his close friends and costars of *Rebel Without a Cause* Natalie Wood (who accidentally drowned, though some insist she was murdered; see Santa Catalina Island chapter) and Sal Mineo (whose stabbing remains unsolved).

Many claim that the spirit of James Dean still lives on, searching for justice—no one was ever charged with the tragic accident. In all of my research for this story, one of the most disturbing things I found about the case was film footage. Not long before his death, Gig Young interviewed Dean during the final days of filming *Giant* (a film that he never lived to see) for a public-service announcement/movie promotion. Smiling that coy James Dean smile and dressed as his character Jett Rink, he delivered a message that in hindsight is downright eerie.

"I used to fly around quite a bit and took unnecessary chances on the highways," Dean said into the camera (see YouTube). "I started racing; now I drive on the highways extra-cautious, because no one knows what they're doing half the time; you don't know what this guy's going to do . . . or that one. I just find myself very cautious on the highway. I don't have the need to speed on the highway. People say racing is dangerous, but I'll take my chances on the track any day rather than the highway." His last words on the PSA: "Take it easy driving—the life you save might be mine." With those words, he walked through the frame and closed the set's door behind him.

The website snopes.com posted an encounter written by the future Sir (and Obi-Wan Kenobi) Alec Guinness. Dean, who'd just introduced himself to Guinness, took him to see his new Porsche 550 Spyder convertible, which had just been delivered; it still had a cellophane wrapper and red carnations all over it. "The sports car looked sinister to me," wrote Guinness. "I heard myself saying in a voice I could hardly recognize as my own, 'Please never get in it.' I looked at my watch. 'It's now ten o'clock, Friday the twenty-third of September, 1955. If you get in that car, you will be found dead in it by this time next week.' He [Dean] laughed [and replied to Guinness], "Oh shucks! Don't be so mean."

On Friday morning, September 30, 1955, Dean and his German friend and Porsche factory–trained mechanic, Rudolf Karl Weutherich, took off from Los Angeles in Dean's Porsche. They'd been preparing the car for the Laguna Seca racing weekend in Salinas.

Behind them drove stunt-car driver/producer/actor and close friend William "Bill" Hickman, who'd been training Dean on how to handle the car. He followed in a 1955 Ford Country Squire station wagon with photographer Sanford Roth, who was doing a photo spread on Dean for *Collier's* magazine. At one point during a stop, Hickman told Dean to slow down. Earlier in the day, Dean received a speeding ticket for going 65 in a 55-mile-an-hour zone south of Bakersfield.

"It was a nice machine—a beautiful car. Built strictly for speed," said Otie V. Hunter, a former (now-deceased) CHP officer in a National Geographic Channel special about Dean. "I clocked it going 70 in a 55. I didn't know who he was; I'd never heard of him. I told him to slow down a little bit because if he didn't slow down, he wouldn't make it to the race. Apparently, he didn't heed my warning too much."

The group pulled into Blackwell's Corner, a gas station, store, and lunch counter on Highways 33 and 46, for fifteen minutes. They met up with friends Lance Reventlow and Bruce Kessler, also headed to the races with their cars. Dean grabbed a Coke and an apple and sat at the back counter talking with his friends. They left, agreeing to meet sixty miles away for dinner in Paso Robles.

According to Beath, Roth asked Dean, "How do you like the Spyder now?" (It was essentially his first real drive with the car.)

Dean answered, "I want to keep this car for a long time—a real long time."

Hickman wanted to talk to him. He looked seriously into his eyes. "Be careful of the cars turning in front of you," he said. "The Spyder's hard to see, and it's getting near dark."

At about 5:15 p.m., the Porsche headed down the long Antelope Grade. At Routes 46 and 41 (now the James Dean Memorial Junction) in Cholame, a 1950 Ford Custom Deluxe Coupe drove at a high rate of speed heading east on Route 46 toward the junction. The time was nearly 5:45 p.m.

Testimony at the scene was sketchy at best—there was no forensic science team to send out back then, and most California Highway Patrol officers weren't especially trained in crime scene procedure. According to a report, Donald Turnupseed (see **tinyurl.com/donaldturnupseed**), a year younger than Dean and driver of the Ford, said at the scene as he stood watching Dean take his last breath in Hickman's arms, "I was going to turn. When I got to the intersection, I started to slow down. Just before I made my turn, I looked straight down 466 [now 46] but didn't see the car. I was already in my turn when I heard the tires and saw him. I tried to miss him, but I couldn't."

CHP Officer Ron Nelson asked, "How fast were you going?" Turnupseed responded, "About fifty-five miles per hour."

Beath wrote, "There was a small convulsive stiffening, and a rasping sigh from the lips. It was the air leaving Jimmy's lungs. His head fell over. Hickman knew he had just seen his friend die, but he could not believe it."

Weutherich, a member of the Nazi Party who was employed in the Luftwaffe, was injured but survived because he'd been thrown from the car, as neither he nor Dean had his seatbelt on. The two were transported next to each other in the same ambulance to the hospital. According to Beath's book, the money in Dean's wallet had been stolen and the ring Dean had given to Weutherich as a gift that day after he'd commented on it were both missing when they were checked at the hospital. The actor's glasses were also stolen at the scene.

At that exact moment, far from the scene, Maila Nurmi, (known professionally as Vampira), who'd become an unlikely close friend of Dean's, claimed to have had a paranormal experience at her home. According to Beath:

Maila and [friend] Jack Simmons had been in her house on Larrabee Avenue in Hollywood. As always, the curtains were drawn. At about 5.45 p.m., an unearthly light had infused her living room. Jack said, "It's creepy in here, let's go out." Maila found the light mesmerizing in its eerie beauty, but they left.

Fifteen minutes later, she returned. Tony Perkins had stopped by, and he was with her.

On one occasion, Jimmy had come to visit when she was not at home. He had climbed through her window to leave a strange calling card. He had taken one of his 8 by 10–inch publicity photos and cut out the eyes, nose, and an ear, then pinned the mutilated picture on the wall so she would know who had dropped by. It had amused her, and she had left it up.

Now, her phone rang. It was Randy at the Villa Capri. He told her the news. She told him he must be joking. At that moment, one of the pins holding Jimmy's partial face to the wall came loose. The picture swung back and forth like a pendulum.

According to several online sources—including one with a picture of the note—and Beath's book, before Dean left that fateful weekend, he asked a friend to take his cherished cat, Marcus, a gift from Elizabeth Taylor. The night before his fateful drive to Salinas for the Laguna Seca races, he left Marcus with actress friend Jeanette Miller, along with handwritten instructions for his care and feeding . . . and a reminder to take him to the vet's for his vaccinations the following week. It seems that he had no plans of coming home. I tried unsuccessfully to reach Jeanette Miller, still working in Hollywood, to find out more but received no return call.

Much of the evidence relative to the accident has disappeared. Even the car, on tour to promote highway safety, has vanished. Google "Curse of the Little Bastard" to find out the specifics. The first instance of the curse happened when driver George Barhuis, who was transporting the car, was killed later when he was thrown from the cab of his truck and crushed by the Porsche as it rolled off the bed. While on tour, the crushed vehicle was transported by truck and train and on several occasions injured people as it mysteriously fell off vehicles. Others were injured when it crashed from its staging while on exhibit. The mechanic who owned the garage to which the car was originally towed after the accident subsequently purchased it and parted out what was left of its engine, transmission, and tires. Of the three cars that received parts, one crashed, killing its owner; the next was totaled in a serious accident; and the third was involved in a wreck that the owner said was caused by the two donor tires from the Porsche blowing out simultaneously. Two garages that had housed the vehicle, including the one owned by the mechanic who'd purchased it, burned to the ground. The car's remnants, crushed like a soda can and last seen publicly in 1960, mysteriously disappeared midroute on a train.

Many believe Dean's death was a self-fulfilling prophecy— not an accident at all. Others point out that he'd been close to a Satanic organization before his death. Roadside Paranormal investigator and case manager Anne Marie and I went in search of the truth in this complicated case. There have been many sightings of both "The Little Bastard" and Dean on the highway where he was killed. Why would James Dean come back from the dead?

When Anne Marie and I drove to the site, it had been a cold day and it was an even colder night. We'd just barely missed rain; the mountains had snowcaps. We had the accident map on the iPad and were trying to figure out what corner we needed to set up on; the road had been shifted after several deaths at the intersection. It was about 11 p.m. when we drove up to park at the corner location closest to where the accident took place. We'd made a turn to come up on the right side of the road, and I was hit by the strangest brief feeling of vertigo. I momentarily felt as if I were free-falling. I took a breath and the feeling was gone, but my hands gripped the wheel even tighter.

By the time we pulled up on the right side of the road where Dean's car had ended up, I felt queasy, as though I'd just gotten off an amusement park ride. That was a new driving experience for me. Once I got out in the fresh air, I felt better. We were setting up at the back of the vehicle when we heard what sounded like people coming toward us from the field. It was dark, and our flashlights seemed to be consumed by the inklike night. In the end, the "people" turned out to be cows. It was eerie being there and left me feeling so vulnerable to the fast-moving traffic. Any car could have easily decided to pull over to offer us help, misjudged the dirt shoulder, and plowed right into us. We quickly set up our recorders, EMF readers, and K-II meters.

We compared all the data with our location and where Dean's car had ended up via the diagrams from **crashscenes.com,** a forensics company that examined all the facts and evidence and modeled the accident with computers. The company determined that Turnupseed had not seen Dean due to the color of his car and the sun's position at twilight, which had made Dean's low-profile car even less visible, as it was nearly the color of the asphalt on the road.

While we were at the site, the traffic was steady, with a punctuation of big rigs lighting us up and honking as they passed us at high speeds. The location made for what was easily the most dangerous investigation we'd ever conducted. Investigators had gone out before us and captured EVPs, but as we found out, because of the noise, the digital files we got were highly contaminated. I didn't expect to get much better results.

At one point I felt paranoid about being out there; the feeling came and went in waves. Then I was fine, although at one point I briefly felt a choking sensation, making it difficult to breathe. Anne Marie walked on the side of the road with a recorder and

K-II and went to the intersection. We got a few hits with the K-II, but it was unclear if it was equipment anomalies, or evidence.

After we'd gotten back into the Jeep, we took off our coats and I noticed a bruise on my arm. The bruise hadn't been there when we'd been driving, or I would have seen it just a few hours earlier when we stopped for dinner. I showed it to Anne Marie, and she also wondered where it had come from. By the time we got to the hotel, the bruise had gotten darker, and within the next two days it had developed into a mark that looked as though someone had grabbed me tightly. That was weird, because I'd not felt any pain when it happened. It took two weeks to go completely away.

During the investigation, the PX—a next-generation Ovilus manufactured by Digital Dowsing (**ghostshop.com**) that is triggered by EMFs and turns those signals into computer-generated speech frequencies, words, and phonetic sounds—kept picking up the words *highway, accident, help, drive, time,* and *dark.* On the phonetic mode, it continued to say *Help, help me,* which is also not uncommon for it to do. This seems to be a common algorithm inherent to either the device or the spirits we run into. When I asked how I could help, the box replied *Hi* or *high, drive, go.* Maybe whomever we were contacting was ready to drive away with us? Were these the words of astral hitchhiker James Dean looking for a ride out of there?

Later at home, on playback of the EVPs through Audacity, I kept hearing short words spoken by a voice barely audible in between traffic sounds. I thought the word was *say,* but that didn't make sense. I did a little research into the area and found that Salinan Indians had lived there. Not much is known about their language, but a Chumash language was developed to unite members of different tribes for survival in that area when they were taken and forced to live together at missions and reservations.

I noted and researched the words I could make out on my recorder—the words *to'w,* meaning "fire" in Chumash, and *se,*

Roadside Paranormal investigator Anne Marie points out the message at Blackwell's: *James Dean made his last stop at the corner on Sept. 30th 1955. The young actor died in a car crash a short time later while en route to Salinas for an auto race. Although he appeared in only three films, James Dean remains a legend.*

meaning "bones." *Qunt'taw*, meaning "lightning," caught my attention, as I'd been hit by lightning. Another word had a more significant meaning—the word *wastap*, meaning arm. Maybe it referred to my bruise?

There have been many incidents of the paranormal type having happened in the area. "Ghost lights" (a phenomenon described as large balls of light), fireballs in the sky, and UFO activity have all been experienced throughout the area. James Dean's ghost and the image of his Spyder speeding down the highway have also been sighted by travelers for years, including one sighting by a Hispanic man who didn't recognize the apparition as the American idol.

"The truck driver came in around midnight. He'd just passed through Shalam [near the memorial]," explained Gary Dethloff, manager of Blackwell's Corner in Lost Hills, the last place James Dean had stopped. "He came in and saw the cardboard stand-ups of James Dean we have . . . and he freaked out. He'd seen a reflection of the man in the cutouts in his windshield that looked like it was the reflection of someone sitting next to him. He didn't even know who James Dean was—*he had no idea*. He left in a hurry, telling me he was never going to drive this route again."

Blackwell's Corner has seen a lot of tragedy, and people often come in asking if they can use their paranormal equipment there; Dethloff doesn't mind. Dethloff says he's not a believer, but in the same breath he will mention some strange things that have gone on in and around the building.

"Back in the '40s," says Dethloff, "a little girl, she must have been around eleven, was using the outhouse at the farm near the building. Curious, she'd stolen a cigarette and lit it up in the outhouse—full of natural methane—and the gas ignited and blew her up. Also, right out in back, a homeless guy got tired of the world and stabbed himself in the heart. My brother-in-law and I hear what sounds like voices sometimes, but we have a lot of wind physically going through a large space in the ceiling above us."

Today, you can still order lunch from the place where James Dean ate his last meal and enjoyed a quick conversation with friends.

I wonder if, by the one-hundredth anniversary of Dean's death, we will have finally developed the equipment Thomas Edison once discussed in a *Scientific American* interview that speaks directly with the dead. If so, I wonder what James Dean would say in response to the question, "What do you think of all this mystery surrounding your death—and why didn't you listen to all the warnings that you were going to die?"

Spotlight On:
Mediums and Psychics

I have a disclaimer before I begin. There are no hard-and-fast rules about the difference between mediums and psychics, and everyone has different opinions on the subject. These are only my gleanings from my experiences over the years. Psychics or mediums? Or psychic mediums? Spiritualist mediums? There is no "better than *this*," "better than *that*" in this field—it's whatever works for the those involved. Sometimes experience counts just as much training. A clear head, intent, intuition, confidence, and experience (and in this case, it is quality versus quantity) are what count. I just want to make that clear before I continue on with the subject at hand.

Many of the paranormal reality shows you see on TV have a strict rule about mediums—*don't have them on the team*. The primary reasons are that their work cannot be immediately affirmed, and they are often thought of as the "wild card." Mediums get information, but not always what the team is expecting. There's a reason for that—mediums are open to the universe.

How does a medium know if what she's getting genuinely belongs to the location or if it's from a spirit who came with a team member and is just along for the ride? Many mediums can't tell the difference, and when they can, they have to decide to either tell someone about the message they're receiving or continue investigating. Often, a message is here and then it's gone; the medium has only a few seconds to touch in with the spirit and ask for any affirmation (names, dates, and so on) about the information she is receiving, so she can pass on the message as well as whom that message is from. Then the spirit is gone and the medium has no way to get the spirit back.

Sometimes a medium knows who the message is for, but it may be inappropriate to give the message because it may be too private or not the right time to divulge it. That's when some spirits decide to get in the medium's face. At that point, for a medium to keep a message to herself while continuing in an investigation is like listening for footsteps when someone is yelling in your face: sometimes it's better for the medium to deliver the message if she's going to be able to continue at all.

There are many signals going on around us at all times—all of them going from point A to point B due to charges of energy. There are sound frequencies, optic signals, naturally occurring EMFs, and cosmic communication signals. Since the mid-1800s, physicists have observed mediums under scientific conditions and during séances and investigations. Many of the world's greatest scientists have been curious about the afterlife—such as Edison, whose childhood home is close to Rochester, New York; the birthplace of Spiritualism is nearby in Hydesville, New York, (see **nsac.org /FoxProperty.php**), a small town that no longer exists by that name. Edison's parents and brother were Spiritualists who conducted weekly séances in their home. It's no wonder Edison had such a fascination for communicating with the dead.

Relying on his scientific theories, Edison believed that there was a way to speak with the dead, a way by which they could be recorded and studied. Edison was fanatic about recording every piece of music, every poetry reading, every person of worth giving a lecture. Some of the only footage we have of people such as Sir Arthur Conan Doyle, author of the Sherlock Holmes series and a Spiritualist leader in the United Kingdom, is due to Edison's persistence to get them on record. Edison was an early version of the Internet Archive. Fortunately, many of his recordings bubble to the surface each year in auctions when they are unearthed by professional estate-sales people as they pull them out of the trunks of the next dying generation.

Edison's talking-dead machine was only alluded to by Edison himself in a *Scientific American* article, and no schematics were ever located nor patents filed. His partner developed the vacuum tube in which his electricity would be captured and was working on a machine that would take pictures of the dead. Many early scientists tried to demystify mediumship and communication with the dead but failed, and in the end—even without the scientific proof of being able to take it back to their labs to poke and prod—became believers in an afterlife until their dying day.

Everything on earth is made of atoms. Our own bodies are made of them. Everything in the world has a unique structure of atoms, and our atmosphere is filled with both natural and synthetic radiation and lots of spectrums of sound, light, and vibration. There's a lot going on within our own bodies—not to mention the whole universe of subtle actions and reactions taking place around us. Imagine, on top of all this, that you could hear some people's thoughts, feel their emotions, hear the dead—as well as feel things like the emotions of animals, the moisture in the air, and even the water under the ground. This is what many mediums feel every day. Can you imagine taking all of this on a paranormal investigation and just focusing on the matter at hand? It's not an easy thing to do, especially if you're not a trained medium.

If you're going to bring a medium with your paranormal-investigative team—especially if you're going to a client site—make sure you've worked on enough public investigations with this medium to know how he works. I've seen so many teams bring on a "medium" who goes berserk and becomes "possessed," causing a lot of drama. Andrew Jackson Davis, the father of Spiritualism, was the first to write on the subject of mental illnesses facing mediums in the late 1800s because of what he was seeing around him. Also, don't be afraid to ask for references. Ask how long they've been doing what they're doing; ask about some of the clients/cases they've been involved with; test them (take them to an undisclosed site they don't know anything about, and ask them what they're picking up). Ask hard questions of people claiming to be mediums, including if they are on any antipsychotic drugs (check out their pupils for the ability to focus, their size, facial tics, manic behavior, and so on). Many so-called mediums are victims of mental illness and must take medication for it. Somehow, the paranormal seems to draw all kinds of people (especially if you have a Meetup group)—and not necessarily the kind you'd want on your team. Some of the "mediums" who've joined my Meetup group have been on heavy pain medications that I believe cause hallucinations. For this reason, people in my group who use "mediumship" or "psychic" skills need to sign a document stating that they are drug-free at the time of the investigation and have been for forty-eight hours, including the use of prescribed drugs (if not, they must list the drugs ahead of time so I can do a little research).

True sensitives are often bombarded by every thought, impact of energy, change in environment, smell, and sound. It's not an easy life, but mediums don't choose to be who they are; they are chosen because of their ability to tune into frequencies. Not all mediums get every signal coming in around them. Mediums are like radios that have different antennas, and they can't just twist a knob to adjust their pick-up. You can have four mediums at a location and they may all get different messages—even from different spirits. If they're good mediums, you'll get good information that will serve as independent affirmation for each message.

Carl Jung, the Swiss psychiatrist and the founder of analytical psychology, believed that we're all connected in our dreams; toward the end of his life, he began talking about his dreams of the undead— the ghosts of family members and friends. Jung was interested in Gnosticism, alchemy, Kabbalah, Hinduism, Buddhism, and Spiritualism. He believed that all these religions and philosophies held truths and were connected. He believed that at night the global population would meet in our dreams to share experiences and try to solve problems. For most people, these types of visions end when the alarm clock goes off. For others, they continue on. The universe touches these people all day long with messages from the spirits of dead.

In the *Star of India* chapter, San Diego Ghosts and Paranormal founder Dave Hanson makes a good point about bringing a medium along on an investigation: sometimes, instead of providing information about a location, the event becomes all about the medium.

This is exactly what happened at a SDGAP investigation aboard the *Star of India*. Hanson's recently departed mother gave a message to the medium who was working with them that night. His mother must have been resourceful in life, because she came through with flying colors for her ability to choose a medium who could help her get a message to her son. His information became the focal point of the investigation, as he was provided more information regarding why his mother was there. He now knows that she's often around checking in with him, but he doesn't have a medium around him 24/7.

I'm sure other members of the group were as surprised as Hanson was when his mother came through, and although she wasn't part of the investigation, she became part of the event. Hanson received affirmation of intelligence beyond death. So you never know why spirits are at a location unless you ask. Never assume they are the ghost of whomever is *supposed* to be haunting the location. Many investigators spend so much time asking, "Are you there?" instead of asking, "Who is there?" I imagine spirits have limited time and resources, and many just answer the questions you ask—and sometimes, as Hanson found, *it is all about you*. Despite the negative rap mediums get from the paranormal community, they are handy to have around and may even give you a whole different facet of information about a location or a spirit or imprint, some of which can be researched for confirmation.

I want to briefly clarify the differences between a psychic and a Spiritualist medium—some just say "medium" because they are not affiliated with a Spiritualist association or training. The line between psychics and mediums is quite blurred. A psychic is someone who gets her information from a person—she is essentially a mind-reader and is highly skilled at picking up vibrational clues for her work. She may also be able to pick up images at a crime scene or be able to touch something and get information about an object or location. She can "read" energy well. She also gets messages directly from spirits, which often come through flashes of emotions, visions, speech, or images. She is great at solving crimes.

A Spiritualist medium gets information from the guides she's been trained to communicate with; these guides acts as middlemen for their communication with other spirits. Spiritualists normally believe in a common god or power-that-be; the religion respects all icons of other religions and belief systems. Spiritualist mediums are trained to get information from outside the body (unless one is also a trained healer or medical intuitive); psychics work from the inside out, while mediums work from the outside in. One can also be a psychic medium.

Classically trained Spiritualist mediums (from whom many famous mediums got their start) are trained and mentored by older or more experienced mediums. Spiritualist churches and organizations also have a point system for classes and demonstrations ("serving on the platform") in which a medium gives people readings that are specific with names, dates, and details. Programs take several years to complete but are a great way to learn and meet like-minded people. As far as I know, there is no formal training for psychics, such as a certification program. Also, without formal instruction, and with much trial and error, mediums and psychics do learn what they're doing along the way—time is a great instructor. I believe anyone with an open mind and a good sense of intuition has the ability to be trained to use mediumship or psychic skills.

Resources

Old Town San Diego

Four Winds Trading Company, Old Town, San Diego • (619) 692-0466 • **4windsarts.com** • 2448-B San Diego Avenue, Old Town San Diego, CA 92110.

Creole Café, Old Town, San Diego • (619) 542-1698 • **neworleanscreolecafe** **.com** • 2476-A San Diego Avenue, San Diego, CA 92110.

El Campo Santo, Old Town, San Diego • **usgwarchives.org/ca/sandiego** **/elcampo.htm** • 2410 San Diego Avenue, San Diego, CA 92110. No posted hours.

The Whaley House, Old Town, San Diego • (619) 297-7511 • **whaleyhouse** **.org** • 2476 San Diego Avenue, San Diego, CA 92110. Victor Santana arranges events and private tours.

OTHER NEARBY PARANORMAL LOCATIONS

Captain Fitch's Mercantile, Old Town, San Diego • (619) 298-3944 • 2627 San Diego Avenue, San Diego, CA 92110. This is an amazing store in Old Town State Historic Park. Lots of nautical gifts, pirate *everything,* and an extensive collection of ghosthunting books—one of the largest I've seen! The building certainly has a long reputation for being haunted; many have reported the feeling of being touched here. From other team's previous investigations here, the northernmost part of the store seems to be where the paranormal activity here is centered.

D'O Thai Cottage, Old Town, San Diego • (619) 366-3771 • **dothaicottage** **.com** • 2414 San Diego Avenue, San Diego, CA 92110 • Contact Kan Timpruskanon. This extremely good Thai restaurant is next to the El Campo Santo graveyard—on what I believe to be more graves. Activity has always been reported at this location. Kan is open to having teams that wish to conduct investigations after-hours with your group dinner. He's new at this (at the time of this writing), so you might want to clarify what you'll be doing.

McConaughy House, Heritage Park, San Diego Old Town · (619) 291-5464 · **heritageparksd.com.** This two-story Stick/Eastlake structure is managed by the same folks who own Captain Fitch's, so expect quality—this store focuses on *everything* Victorian. The house itself was built in 1887 and named after the original owner, John McConaughy, entrepreneur and owner of the much-needed first scheduled horse-powered freight and passenger service in San Diego County. McConaughy's passenger stages and wagons ran between San Diego and Julian. It is the ghost of McConaughy's daughter, Mary, who is believed to haunt the building. There is a lot of activity going on in Heritage Park, which is not the original location for any of the buildings in the park. Although owned by the city, the buildings are managed by the Best Western Plus Hacienda Hotel down the street.

Robinson Rose House Visitor Information Center, Old Town San Diego State Historic Park · (619) 220-5422 · **parks.ca.gov/?page_id=663.** The park is on San Diego Avenue and Twiggs Street, inside Old Town San Diego State Historic Park. This building is rumored to have a shadow man who walks past the windows, and disembodied footfalls can be heard upstairs when no one is in that part of the building. Tugging of hair and touching is said to take place in the store, which sells period toys as well as many history and ghost books about the area. Stop in here first to get all of the information you'll need about Old Town. They also have regularly scheduled tours and activities.

SOHO/Whaley House Gift Shop, Old Town, San Diego · (619) 297-7511 · **sohosandiego.org/shop/shopwh.htm** · 2476 San Diego Avenue, San Diego, CA 92110 · In the Verna House, a building that's definitely known for paranormal activity. The store has many paranormal book titles, as well as vintage-style toys and gift items. If you're going on a Whaley House tour, you'll need to walk inside to buy your ticket. Receive substantial discounts with SOHO membership—and also check out the other historic locations of SOHO-owned buildings in the area.

Tours

Haunted San Diego Tours · (619) 255-6170 · **hauntedsandiegotours.com.** Historical tours with a haunted theme. This tour company grew out of Ghosts and Gravestones employees who were left when the company exited San Diego. This is a small, shuttle-based historic tour with a haunted theme. The guides wear costumes, and the bus goes by and stops at San Diego–based haunted locations. Stops include Old Town (the bus leaves from the Best Western Plus Hacienda Hotel), the Whaley House, Villa Montezuma (no inside access, as it is closed to the public right now), El Campo Santo, Horton Grand, and the William Heath Davis House. Pay by PayPal or credit card. A very entertaining tour for anyone who loves ghosts and local history told with dramatic flair.

San Diego Ghost Tours • (619) 972-3900 • **oldtownsmosthaunted.com**. San Diego's ghost tour is based on the personal experiences of company founder Michael Brown, who, after ghosthunting for six years, created a ghost tour in Old Town, San Diego. Brown was featured on *Ghost Adventurers* talking about historic Old Town (see the video on his page). The company's slogan is, *You've seen it on TV—now, come see it for yourself.* A great tour for out-of-the-area ghosthunters or people who've always lived here but never had a real tour of Old Town.

ANNUAL EVENTS

Día de los Muertos, Mission San Luis Rey, Oceanside • Check for dates in late October or early November • (760) 757-3651 • **sanluisrey.org** • 4050 Mission Avenue, Oceanside, CA 92057. Oceanside's annual celebration of Día de los Muertos is at Mission San Luis Rey, one of the state's original missions. Altars (*ofrendas*), food vendors, a carnival, children's activities, live music, and a flowing landscape of marigolds covering the mission to celebrate the lives of departed loved ones. This is a three-day event with a ton of people having a great time. A wonderful cultural experience for kids and people who've never heard of the celebration.

Día de los Muertos/All Saints Day, Old Town, San Diego • November 1 and 2 • (619) 297-7511 • **facebook.com/diadelosmuertosotsd**. Old Town's Día de los Muertos celebrates the history and heritage of California's first city. Decorations and ceremonies remember the dead. Old Town's cultures meld together with cultural events (children's activities available, but a fee may be applicable), live music, and festivities, ending with a candlelight procession of costumed skeletons and period-dressed citizens who walk from the Whaley House to one of California's oldest cemeteries, decorated with huge paper blooms hanging from the trees. More than forty altars belonging to local businesses make for a beautiful backdrop. Live music. Activities at Fiesta de Reyes in the state park will keep kids busy.

Downtown San Diego and Surrounding Area

Pioneer Park, San Diego • hiddensandiego.net/pioneer-park.php • 1501 Washington Place, San Diego, CA 92103 • No posted hours, free.

Mount Hope Cemetery, San Diego • sandiego.gov/park-and-recreation /general-info/mthope.shtml • 3751 Market Street, San Diego, CA 92102. A beautiful cemetery that the Whaley and the Horton families, Raymond Chandler, and other historical figures call home. Open 365 days, 8 a.m–4 p.m. Please respect people's right to privacy. Gated cemetery, security. Sometimes dodgy—located in a high-crime neighborhood where a man was recently murdered on the street.

Cabrillo Bridge, Balboa, San Diego • N32.731412°, W117.154185° • en.wikipedia.org/wiki/Cabrillo_Bridge • On El Prado at the Sixth Avenue Balboa Park entrance, San Diego, CA 92101 • No posted hours, dodgy area; free.

Proctor Valley Road, Chula Vista • Near Proctor Valley Road and 125, Chula Vista, CA 91914 • Under Highway 125 at Proctor Valley Road. It is connected to open space and is patrolled by rangers. Blind road curves are dangerous night *and* day. Highway 125 is a toll road both ways. The Mexican border is just an exit away—if you go too far, you will be stopped and detained if you don't have a passport. Go to YouTube and enter "Proctor Valley Road" for (really weird) videos. Border Patrol flies overhead at night with spotlights.

Northern and Eastern San Diego

The San Pasqual Battlefield, San Pasqual Valley • San Pasqual Valley Road (Highway 78) and Ysabel Creek Road, Escondido • San Pasqual/Escondido, CA (on Highway 78, surrounded by stone wall) • **sanpasqual.org.** No posted hours; free but very dangerous both night and day because of the way the pull-off is situated. You will also not be able to see the snake and gopher holes at night. Watch out for the aggressive heron on the property.

San Pasqual Cemetery, San Pasqual Valley • San Pasqual Valley Road (Highway 78) and Ysabel Creek Bridge • San Pasqual/Escondido, CA • **interment.net/data/us/ca/sandiego/pasqual/san_pasqual.htm.**

State Route 67 · Runs from Interstate 8 in El Cajon to Lakeside as the San Vicente Freeway. It then becomes a smaller roadway through Poway before becoming the main street running through Ramona and turning into State Route 78.

Los Peñasquitos Creek Arch Bridge, Poway · Cara Way and Scripps Poway Parkway, San Diego, CA 92131 · No posted hours; 24-hour cameras and security. Please respect people's right to privacy. Memorial garden.

OTHER NEARBY PARANORMAL LOCATIONS

San Pasqual Battlefield Museum, San Pasqual Valley · (760) 737-2201 · **parks.ca.gov/?page_id=655** · 15808 San Pasqual Valley Road, Escondido, CA 92027 · N33.1191°, W117.0201°. A great place to find out more about the San Pasqual area. The museum pays tribute to the soldiers who lost their lives in the battle between the U.S. and Californio forces on December 6, 1846, during the Mexican-American War. Visit the **San Diego Archeological Center** next door (16666 San Pasqual Valley Road, Escondido CA 92027; [760] 291-0370). The Center Museum has rotating exhibits and hands-on activities that explore 10,000 years of history of the San Diego region through the archaeological record. Learn about the lifeways of early Native American hunter-gatherers who lived in our region and the many groups and immigrants who have contributed to the region's archaeological record.

ANNUAL EVENTS

Renaissance Faire, Escondido · (805) 496-6036 · dates vary · **goldcoast festivals.com/EscoGenInfo.html** · Felicita County Park, 742 Clarence Lane, Escondido, CA 92029. There is something about this park that is enchanting and haunting simultaneously. I have captured many strange EVPs here, as well as well as strange mists on the creek running through the property. The large, forestlike park is on sacred Native American land—one of the largest and oldest Indian villages in the county. To this day, grinding holes and other artifacts reveal evidence of the centuries-old community of the Northern Diegueño Indians. Something about the reenactors and their historical activities and live music brings out the restless spirits.

The Anza-Borrego Desert and Surrounding Area

Warner Springs · **en.wikipedia.org/wiki/Oak_Grove_Butterfield_Stage _Station.** Warner Springs Ranch is closed until it reopens after bankruptcy proceedings. I have seen the Warner Springs Historic Museum, at 30950 Highway 79, Warner Springs, but have never been by when it's open. There is no phone number listed.

Julian Pioneer Museum, Julian · (760) 765-0227 · **julianca.com/historic _sites/index.htm** · 2811 Washington Street, Julian, CA 92036. The museum boasts the finest lace collection in California, a selection of 1896–1913 vintage clothing, historic photographs, household and mining equipment, Victorian-era pianos, an original Julian City buggy and sleigh, and an extensive exhibit of Native American artifacts. The original structure, built in the mid-1880s, served as a brewery for Peter Meyerhofer.

Julian Jail, Julian · Corner of C and Fourth Streets, Julian, CA 92036 · Usually not closed. Free, but a donation is suggested. Do not go into this building at night without being aware that someone could be camped out in the darkness of the corridor in the back of the cells. It seems the place is host to transients, as it does smell like human urine.

Blair Valley and Pictograph Trail, Anza-Borrego Desert • **desertusa .com/anza_borrego/du-abpblair.html.** Don't take a car out here unless you're planning on getting it aligned and the scratches buffed out afterward. Pump up your spare and get a full tank of petrol at the last stop you're at (you may want to check your POIs on your GPS to get a sense of where that may be before you pass them all), because there is nothing out here and you'd be lucky if AAA can even find you. The last stop may be Ramona depending on where you're coming from, or somewhere before you leave I-8. Bring plenty of water and ice in your cooler. There are no stores for miles around. **Stagecoach Trails RV Park and Resort (stagecoachtrails.com/tour.html)** is it for a while. Rattlesnakes are a constant worry out here; I suggest boots, a shade hat, sunscreen, and a fully charged cell phone. People with more experience than you have died out here.

Vallecito County Park, Anza-Borrego Desert · **sdcounty.ca.gov/parks/ Camping/vallecito.html** · 37349 Great South Stage Route 1849, Julian, CA 92036

• Seasonal hours. Investigation-friendly; no entrance fee. Campers need paid reservations. The stagecoach building is normally closed, although it is open from time to time. If there is a ranger at the campsite, you could ask him to open it up for you. If you're not the outdoor type, **Stagecoach Trails RV Park and Resort** (showers, pool, laundry, small store) is nearby; see **stagecoachtrails.com/tour.html.** Bring your citronella and Epi-Pen; lots of bees and mosquitoes. There are no restaurants or hotels out here; bring your camping gear and camp stove—and plenty of food and water. There are fire rings, so don't forget your wood—it gets cold at night.

Other Nearby Paranormal Locations

Amargosa Opera House and Hotel, Death Valley Junction • (760) 852-4441 • **amargosa-opera-house.com** • 608 Death Valley Junction, Death Valley Junction, CA 92328. A hidden haunted jewel—I've heard from so many teams regarding EVPs, digivids, photos, and poltergeist evidence captured at this location. Investigation-friendly. Built in 1923, for the past thirty-five years it has been owned by proprietor Marta Becket, who has lived and shared her art and dreams with those fortunate enough to find this wonderful and magical place. Located a few miles west of the California–Nevada border, near Death Valley National Park. There is a hotel and diner at the location. Dog-friendly! *Ghost Adventurers* visited the site and found activity.

Haven of Rest/Julian Cemetery, Julian • **juliancemetery.org** • **tinyurl.com /juliancemetery** • On Farmer Road; entrance on A Street. This is one of most peaceful and historic cemeteries I've seen locally—and very active (para-normally speaking, that is) during the day. They say there are only 375 graves here, but that seems like a very low count for such a large piece of land, and considering that the next cemetery is so far away. If you'd like good results, bring flowers for America Edison's grave. It's near the two parking spaces in the cemetery—you'll know it when you see it. She is the spokeswoman for the dead here. Posted hours.

Coastal Southern California

Hunter Steakhouse, Oceanside · (760) 433-2633 · **huntersteakhouse.com** · 1221 Vista Way, Oceanside CA 92054. Call for special group buffet rates for your talks or investigations.

***Star of India*, San Diego Harbor** · Maritime Museum of San Diego · (619) 234-9153 · **sdmaritime.org** · 1492 North Harbor Drive, San Diego, CA 92101. Reasonably priced day tours and special events. Contact Jim Davis for paranormal investigation events and conferences. Bring your kids and parents to this venue. Touring the organization's ships and submarines is a wonderful way to spend the day with your family. There are plenty of exhibits and things to do. Balboa Park museums and Old Town are a quick drive away.

Hotel del Coronado, Coronado · (800) 468-3533 · **hoteldel.com** · 1500 Orange Avenue, Coronado, CA 92118.

Santa Catalina Island · **visitcatalinaisland.com/avalon/transportation.php** · **catalinaconservancy.org** · For private tours: (310) 753-1854, **liddell@catalinas.net, catalinaislandman.com.**

Summerland · I highly recommend you read this book before you go: *The Spirit of the Big Yellow House* by Rod Lathim (**rodlathim.com**). The main street in Summerland is **Lillie Avenue;** park and see where it takes you. Rentals in Summerland are cheaper than its neighbor, Santa Barbara (make reservations four to six months out). **Summerland Beach** is where Lillie Avenue goes underneath the highway, and you can park at one of the cafes and easily walk over. At the other end of the street, you'll find the **Sacred Space** (see next page).

Other Nearby Paranormal Locations

Berkeley · Maritime Museum of San Diego, San Diego Harbor · (619) 234-9153 · **sdmaritime.org** · 1492 North Harbor Drive, San Diego, CA 92101. One ticket allows tour of the entire ship and submarine armada. Reasonably priced day tours and special events. Contact Jim Davis for paranormal investigation events and conferences. The *Berkeley* is an 1898 steam ferryboat known to be haunted. It was a destination point for *Ghost Hunters* and is a great place to do an investigation. Lots of stories about after-hours activity the staff has seen and heard. This boat was used in 1906 during the San Francisco earthquake aftermath to ferry the injured en masse to Oakland and help others escape the fires chasing them to the shore. Has an awesome gift store where you'll find nautical gifts and a huge selection of pirate and seafaring books. Great place for a wedding!

Carpinteria Historical Society, Carpinteria · (805) 684-3112 · 956 Maple Street, Carpinteria, CA 93013 · **carpinteriahistoricalmuseum.org.** If you're looking for information on Summerland's history, this is the best place to find it. Besides the great exhibits and information you'll find here, there are amazing documents and photographs about Summerland in the files (you can order copies for your research—just ask). Make sure to call for hours and to get an appointment to be able to access information not on exhibit. The CHS also hosts a wonderful holiday arts-and-crafts fair in November and the Museum Marketplace, where you can buy from local artisans and others; see **carpinteria historicalmuseum.org/events.htm.**

The Sacred Space, Summerland · (805) 565-5535 · **thesacredspace.com** · **facebook.com/thesacredspace.us** · 2594 Lillie Avenue, Summerland, CA 93067. Jack and Rose Herschorn have created a sacred space where you go to feel the energy. They've created a labyrinth of rooms—filled with amazing handmade items from all corners of the Earth—leading outside to a series of Zen gardens where you breathe in fresh sea air and take a load off, enjoy the vibration with some tea, and meditate about your upcoming investigation. I believe this property is one of Summerland's Native American energy vortices, and perhaps the reason that it was chosen in the first place to build a Spiritualist community upon. This is private property, so ask before using any equipment. At the back of the location is an outdoor seating area where the venue presents world-renowned speakers on the subjects of mind, body, and soul.

Orange and Los Angeles Counties

RMS *Queen Mary*, Long Beach · (877) 342-0738 · **queenmary.com** · 1126 Queens Highway, Long Beach, CA 90802. My Nikon D300s was stolen onboard. Never leave your equipment unattended at any location.

Warner Grand Theatre, San Pedro · (310) 548-2493 · **warnergrand.org** · 478 West Sixth Street, San Pedro, CA 90731 · Contact Lee Sweet at the theater's business office. Private investigations and mainstream public events and movies. If you're a big history buff, visit **grandvision.org.** One huge vortex of paranormal activity! Amazing investigation location. Also, if you're a movie buff, this is one of the last majestic theaters in the country—a building from another time when the movies were as grand as their frames. Conferences and other performing-arts events are held here frequently. Down the street is **Williams' Book Store,** founded in 1909 (**williamsbookstore.com**), where you will find an excellent selection of history books on California and San Pedro.

Linda Vista Hospital, Los Angeles • **boyleheightsparanormalproject.org** • 610 South St. Louis Street, Los Angeles, CA 90023 • **bhpp2009@gmail.com** • By appointment only. Be alert: Boyle Heights is a high-crime area. Read all about Boyle Heights' rich history before going out (**en.wikipedia.org/wiki /Boyle_Heights,_Los_Angeles**) and you'll add a lot to your experience of touring the neighborhood first. The restaurants out here are diverse (and good!), so make time before the experience to stop and eat. Go to **citysearch .com** and search "Boyle Heights restaurants"; this area is so culturally diverse that you'd be kicking yourself if you didn't eat dinner somewhere nearby before going on your investigation.

Heritage Square Museum, Los Angeles • (323) 225-2700, ext. 224 • **heritagesquare.org** • 3800 Homer Street, Los Angeles, CA 90031 • Hours vary; reasonable entry fee for daytime tour. The beautiful Victorian homes in this park have been restored with great care. A rare opportunity to see an octagon home from the turn of the nineteenth century. The docents have a great deal of information about the era in which these homes were built, and about the original owners. Make sure to stop by the gift shop!

White City Resort/Echo Mountain, Angeles National Forest • **tinyurl .com/cobbestatetoechomountain** • Search YouTube for detailed video directions. Free. Hiking boots recommended; consider this your rattlesnake warning. Bring water—lots of it—and snacks. For $50 at REI, you can pick up a great hiking beacon. Fully charge your cell phone. I highly recommend a handheld hiking GPS with topo maps. People die all the time in the Los Angeles National Forest because they simply fall off a cliff, break their legs, and can't make it back up to the trail and are overcome by heat and dehydration. Make sure someone who cares knows where you are. Better yet, never go hiking alone; women are raped and murdered on trails. Don't be the next ghost investigated in this series because you didn't use common sense.

Cobb Estate Ruins, Altadena • East Loma Alta Drive at Lake Avenue, Altadena, CA 91001 • Free/walk-in. Parking is a bear because there is none avail-

able on the property. The only parking is in the quaint residential area outside
the park, which fills up quickly in the morning due to Meetup groups gathering
there. Get there early, or arrive in the afternoon after some of the morning
people have cleared out. Rattlesnakes! I recommend hiking boots to keep your
ankles fang-free. Bring water, sun hat, and sunscreen.

OTHER NEARBY PARANORMAL LOCATIONS

The Arboretum: Los Angeles County Arboretum and Botanic Garden, Arcadia · arboretum.org · 301 North Baldwin Avenue, Arcadia, CA 91007.
The centerpiece of this park is Elias Jackson "Lucky" Baldwin's Queen Anne cottage, built in 1886 as a honeymoon gift for his fourth wife, sixteen-year-old Lillie
Bennett. She left and Baldwin turned the home into a living memorial for his
third wife, whom he'd never gotten over (part of the reason that Lillie left him).
Baldwin was believed to be a victim of the Griffith Park curse, which eventually
led to his downward financial spiral and his death. He is said to stroll around
the park mourning his lost love and fortune. This is a spectacular venue that
was unfortunately closed for renovations when I was visiting. The Arboretum
and grounds remain open. Some of you may see the island home and think
it looks quite familiar—that's because it was used as Mr. Roarke's home on
Fantasy Island. The gift shop on this property has incredible offerings—
especially the interesting live plants.

The Drum Barracks, Wilmington · (310) 548-7509 **· drumbarracks.org ·**
1052 Banning Boulevard, Wilmington, CA 90744. This is the last remaining
Civil War–era military facility in Los Angeles County. The barracks served
as Union Army headquarters in the Southwest (Southern California and the
Arizona Territory) from 1861 to 1871. Visitors and employees are rumored
to have seen and heard rattling chains, wagon wheels, horses, smoke, soldiers, and apparitions of a woman wearing a hoop skirt. There have also been
moans and cries heard in the hospital area. Museum open to the public;
$5 suggested entry fee.

Griffith Park, Los Angeles · N34.129392°, W118.305285° **· laparks.org
/dos/parks/griffithpk/griffith.htm.** This park—all 4,310 acres of it—has been
cursed from its founding. It's a location chosen by many filming companies
(for example, *Batman* and *Star Trek*). In 1933 there was a fire that I've been
told killed as few as twenty-nine, but others have written that it was more like

three hundred. This was also Native American land, where tribal members lived out their lives and passed on the same grounds. The Mineral Wells area of the park seems to be best known for its paranormal activity. Ask the rangers— every one of them I spoke to off-record had some kind of paranormal story. The Griffith Park Observatory is also the location of the last scene of James Dean's *Rebel Without a Cause*. **The Greek Theatre (greektheatrela.com), The Autry** museum **(theautry.org)**, and the **Los Angeles Zoo and Botanical Gardens (lazoo.org)** are also here.

Hollywood Bowl, Hollywood · hollywoodbowl.com · 2301 North Highland Avenue, Hollywood, CA 90068. This is a lovely venue! When I lived up the hill from here all I had to do was make a Long Island iced tea, lie in my deck hammock, close my eyes, and listen. The venue brings in really top-shelf entertainers, and its amazing state-of-the-art outdoor sound system and huge trademark shell bandstand tucked into the side of Hollywood's beautiful mountains really completes the picture. Built during good times in 1922, it was little more than a stage with benches then. Now, it's an incredible venue—and you're lucky to get seats. You can bring your own picnic basket or have dinner delivered right to your seat. When I used to drive by going home in the wee hours, I'd see shadows darting about near the venue. The hills and canyons in and around this area were home to California's early Native Americans. This area has a wonderful spiritual feel. While in the museum one day, I was smacked on the shoulder by a friendly unseen hand that felt as if it was saying, "Good to see you!"

Pasadena Playhouse, Pasadena · pasadenaplayhouse.org · 39 South El Molino Avenue, Pasadena, CA 91101. Gilmor Brown, the charismatic founder of the playhouse, has been haunting the theater and adjacent office building since his death in 1960, and employees believe him to be the helpful ghost haunting the building. Ghosthunting-friendly, contact Laura Barr at (626) 921-1151 to book your investigation.

Santa Barbara, Ventura, and San Luis Obispo Counties

Rancho Camulos, Piru · (805) 521-1501 · **ranchocamulos.org ·** 5164 East Telegraph Road, Piru, CA 93040. The original Ramona's marriage place. A fabulous historic location to see how California's early pioneers lived. Reasonable fees for daytime tour. Private investigation by appointment only.

Glen Tavern Inn, Santa Paula • (805) 933-5550 • **glentavern.com** • 134 North Mill Street, Santa Paula, CA 93060 • Reasonable rates; friendly to ghosthunters and teams. This early-California hotel is in a pleasant location—a great way to explore Santa Paula and both the natural hiking areas near the dam, and to see for yourself where several famous movies were filmed. Reasonable rates for overnight stays, and you can record EVPs to your heart's content. Great restaurant and bar.

Mission Santa Barbara Park/Jail Ruins, Santa Barbara • Los Olivos and Laguna Streets, Santa Barbara, CA 93105 • No posted hours, dodgy location; free.

James Dean Memorial Junction, Cholame • Junction of California Highways 41 and 46, Cholame, CA • **jamesdeanmemorialjunction.com/history.html** • Dangerous at any hour.

OTHER NEARBY PARANORMAL LOCATIONS

Blackwell's Corner General Store, Lost Hills • (661) 797-2905 • 17191 Highway 46, Lost Hills, CA 93249-9740 • **en.wikipedia.org/wiki/Blackwells _Corner,_California.** The last stop James Dean made before his fateful crash. Pull up a chair to the counter and order a meal from the counter where James Dean ate his last meal. Interesting deaths have taken place around the property (see James Dean Memorial Junction chapter)—a must-stop! It's also the last place to get petrol for quite a while—and has an amazing array of almonds of all flavors made locally.

Cemetery Memorial Park, Ventura • Between Main and Poli Streets, with a crossroad of Aliso Lane, Ventura • **restorestmarys.org** • **tinyurl.com/cemeterypark.** Ventura decided in the 1960s to remove and dump the tombstones and carpet their city cemetery with grass and call it a park, and so it is today. Nearly 3,000 people from all walks of life and race are still buried under the city park. The seven-acre cemetery park has some freaky energy. There is also a rumor that a teen hung himself from one of the trees in the park.

Saugus Train Station, Heritage Junction, Santa Clarita • (661) 254-1275 • **scvhs.org** • 24101 Newhall Avenue, Newhall, CA 91321. A great investigation place where you can see several historical buildings moved, including the train station. This grouping of buildings is a fantastic place to investigate during the day or evenings during night events through **paranormalpractice .com** or the organization's holiday events. All the buildings were saved from different locations—so random histories of all the buildings make for an interesting array of sightings and experiences. Check out Paranormal Practice's page for captured evidence of the location. Free, but donations encouraged. Ghosthunting-friendly; call the office to schedule your group's investigation.

MOBILE APP

Paranormal iPhone App · ghostopedia.com. Find a haunting wherever you are! I've created a GPS-centric app that takes your location into consideration when suggesting a place where paranormal activity has been reported. Paranormal teams are featured, and they can rate the sites—plus, subscribers can rate their ratings. Historical locations are also pointed out. No matter what state you're in, you'll be able to plot a trip. Lots of paranormal information about equipment and digivids on how to use them. Available in 2013 on iPhone and on other platforms in 2014.

PARANORMAL GROUPS IN THE AREA OPEN TO THE PUBLIC

The San Diego Ghost Hunters · sandiegoghosthunters.com · facebook .com/sandiegoghosthunters. Maritza Skandunas leads this dynamic paranormal team. The group sometimes has public events; check for updates.

San Diego Ghosts and Paranormal Meetup Group · meetup.com /san-diego-ghosts. Great discussion; open to public, members, discussion, training investigations, events. A Meetup group you can join and meet other like-minded people.

3am Paranormal Meetup Group, Lakewood, CA · meetup.com/3-am -paranormal-meetup-group. Great discussion, training, investigations and events.

RADIO/INTERNET SHOWS

Coast to Coast Radio · coasttocoastam.com. A historic late-night/early-morning show with the latest in the paranormal, technologies, conspiracy, and other fantastical happenings. Reruns from Art Bell's days as host and current hosts George Noory, George Knapp, Ian Punnett, and John B. Wells. You often hear the unbelievable here first before hearing it in the mainstream media.

Kala Ambrose's *Explore Your Spirit with Kala* **·** **exploreyourspirit.com.** A fabulous Internet radio show to help you be all you can be spiritually and paranormally—live and archived shows with the top names in the industry in candid interviews with Kala. An excellent resource!

The Ghost Host with Sophia Temperilli **·** **liveparanormal.com** **·** **facebook .com/events/441518589194583.** This is a great show hosted by teen Sophia Temperilli and her dad, Gian, Saturdays at noon. Guests are great people involved in everything paranormal. Highly recommended for kids interested in the paranormal and their parents.

The Paranormal View **·** Geoffrey Gould cohosts this Los Angeles–based Saturday show (5–7 p.m. PST; 8–10 p.m. EST) that airs on **para-x.com** with Henry Foister and author Kat Klockow (and fill-in cohost "Ceiling Cat" Barbara Duncan). The show is a friendly, laid-back round-table discussion with paranormal investigators, researchers, and author guests covering various topics including but not limited to ghosts, haunted locations, cryptozoology, UFOs, etc. *The Paranormal View*'s online presence can be found at **geoffgould.net/2011pnv .htm** and **facebook.com/pages/The-Paranormal-View/175481362503293.**

paranormaltvnetwork.com **·** Online channel with many paranormal shows.

West of The Rockies **with Frank Argueta (The Engineer), Moheak Radio ·** **moheak.com/shows** **·** **facebook.com/westoftherockies.** Great late-night call-in show from Los Angeles about what's going on in the paranormal/ science/technology and conspiracy worlds.

RECOMMENDED BOOKS

Beautiful Stranger: The Ghost of Kate Morgan and the Hotel del Coronado by Christine Donovan (published by the Hotel del Coronado) is a great resource for the original documents involved with the case. Donovan is also the hotel's historian and has a great deal of knowledge regarding Kate Morgan's death.

The Death of James Dean by Warren N. Beath. Drawing on the inquest manuscript and other previously unpublished material, Warren Beath cuts through the conflicting reports and rumors to reconstruct of Dean's final hours. This book was instrumental in my writing the chapter on the James Dean crash site. If you're going out there, make sure you read this first!

The Everything Ghost Hunting Book. Tips, tools, and techniques for exploring the supernatural world (shadow people, cold spots, orbs, equipment, theory, etc.) by Melissa Martin Ellis. A high-tech journey into the supernatural world, including motion sensors, highly sensitive digital cameras, so-called ghost telephones, as well as the supernatural phenomena themselves, including poltergeists, electronic-voice phenomena (EVP), possession, and photo anomalies. Anyone getting serious about paranormal investigation needs this book! This is the one book that needs to be on every ghosthunter's shelf.

Heaven Can You Hear Me? by Gian Temperilli with the late Peter James. A fabulous resource about the *Queen Mary's* well-known psychic medium and the theories and stories regarding paranormal activity. **authorsden.com /visit/viewwork.asp?id=32048.**

PSIENCE: How New Discoveries in Quantum Physics and New Science May Explain the Existence of Paranormal Phenomena by Marie D. Jones (**mariedjones.com**). A great book that looks at the *why* behind paranormal phenomena.

San Diego Specters by John J. Lamb. Lots of local San Diego haunted treasures and the intriguing stories behind them. Fantastic research. A former homicide detective, Lamb rationally shares the information he's collected from haunted San Diego locations. **johnjlamb.net/books.shtml.**

Richard Senate's books: *Ghosts of the California Missions, Ghosts of the Haunted Coast, Ghosts of the Ojai, California's Most Haunted Valley,* and *Phantomology* are written from his thirty-three years as a paranormal investigator with his wife, Debbie Senate, who is a medium. See **ghost-stalker .com** and **phantombookshop.com** for a look at Richard's prolific list of paranormal books. Check the first website for conference dates near you. Senate also teaches ghosthunting classes in Ventura County and leads amazing tours: contact him at **hainthunter@aol.com.**

Authors and paranormal investigators Rob and Anne Wlodarski of G-Host Publishing wrote and published *Queen Mary Ghosts, Haunted Catalina II, the Haunted Whaley House II, California Ghosts, Bottles of Boos, Fullerton Ghosts, Haunted Alcatraz, Ghosts of Old Town San Diego*

State Historic Park, and numerous other books about history and hauntings throughout the United States. **ghostpublishingco.com/ipro.htm.**

Internet Resources

Kala Ambrose · exploreyourspirit.com/aboutkala.html. World-renowned psychic medium, author of *Ghosthunting North Carolina, Spirits of New Orleans, The Awakened Aura: Experiencing the Evolution of Your Energy Body, 9 Life Altering Lessons: Secrets of the Mystery Schools Unveiled*), intuitive, auracle, wisdom teacher, and voice of the highly acclaimed *Explore Your Spirit with Kala* show **(exploreyourspirit.com)**. Kala's blogs and workshops will help you develop the intuition needed to better sense the spirits around you. Fantastic interviews with lots of people in the paranormal.

Mark and Debby Constantino · spirits-speak.com. Great site for learning how to capture EVPs; also check their site for conference dates near you. If you have an opportunity to go on an investigation with them at a conference, make sure you go; seeing them pick up EVPs live is quite an experience.

Paranormal Practice · paranormalpractice.com. Bridget and Larry Odien and Linda Casebolt make up this great paranormal group that has captured some really awesome EVPs—check it out. This is also the group that created the EVP Field Processor—you've seen it on all the reality shows.

Classes

Here is a list of organizations that host classes regarding the paranormal, intuition, and speaking with Spirit. Some of them also have courses on spirit photography.

Harmony Grove, Escondido · (760) 745-9176 · **harmonygrovespiritualist .org ·**2975 Washington Circle, Escondido, CA 92029. This Spiritualist camp is more than a century old and has weekend institutes where you can stay at one of its many cabins and take classes about mediumship and healing. This camp is much like New York's Lily Dale Spiritualist community. There is also an annual Halloween party open to all who wish to attend. If you rent a cabin during an institute, make sure you do so through the director of education and not the front office—both will take a reservation, and two people may end up with one cabin. Check out the labyrinth, meditation garden, and metaphysical bookstore, where you can usually find dowsing rods and pendulums for your ghosthunting work and books on mediumship. You can also participate in an old-fashioned séance/circle or healing and just hang out with some great people.

NSAC · nsac.org. Find out where your local Spiritualist camp or organization is—there is usually a metaphysical/paranormal/physical mediumship class going on somewhere near you.

Spiritualist Church of the Comforter, Santa Barbara · (805) 965-4474 · **churchofthecomforter.nsac-churches.org ·** 1028 Garden Street, Santa Barbara, CA 93101. The original charter for this church was in Summerland in 1891, but the church was destroyed when the building on the main street was demolished in 1951 in the name of progress (the highway was built through it). This is a great group of people; I stopped and met the entire board of directors (they just happened to be having a meeting) while I was researching for this book. If you're looking for somewhere to hone your psychic/intuitive abilities, check them out—they have classes.

MORE LOCAL ORGANIZATIONS THAT MAY OFFER PARANORMAL AND MEDIUMSHIP COURSES

Association of Independent Readers and Rootworkers · See **readers androotworkers.org/index.php?title=List_of_Spiritualist_Organizations** for a directory of Spiritualist associations, camps, and churches.

San Diego's Psychic Gym · meetup.com/the-psychic-gym. A Meetup group that has guest speakers and demonstrations on everything metaphysical.

Check your local **meetup.com** listings for paranormal and ghosthunting groups.

About the Author

Author Sally Richards with Roadside Paranormal's Security Analyst, Bulova.

SALLY RICHARDS had a near-death experience (NDE) when she drowned at the age of eight in Hawaii. Growing up in the fiftieth state, she learned a healthy respect for the dead ancestors who fiercely protected the sacred sites on the islands. Although she was able to see the dead before this time, her mediumship abilities seemed to become clearer after her drowning incident. Richards continued finding herself first on the scene of several murders, as the victims drew her to the locations and begged her to find justice. Years later, she experienced her second NDE when she was hit by lightning during a severe pre–Hurricane Katrina storm. Her abilities seemed to reach an even higher level after this, and she then set out to learn about what was beyond the veil between life and death. After spending years at century-old Spiritualist camps across the country, taking classes from the senior members in the hierarchies, she trained as a medium and shifted those skills toward her work as a paranormal investigator, searching the globe for haunted locations, amazing stories, and unquestionable evidence.